THE LIMIT OF THE USEFUL

THE LIMIT OF THE USEFUL

GEORGES BATAILLE

edited and translated by
Cory Austin Knudson and Tomas Elliott

The MIT Press
Cambridge, Massachusetts
London, England

Originally published as "L'économie à la mesure de l'univers," "La Limite de l'utile," "Notes pour 'L'économie à la mesure de l'univers,'" and "Notes pour 'La Limite de l'utile'" © Editions Gallimard, Paris, 1976

This book was set in Century Schoolbook Pro by New Best-set Typesetters Ltd. Printed and bound in the United States of America.

Library of Congress Cataloging-in-Publication Data

Names: Bataille, Georges, 1897–1962, author. | Knudson, Cory Austin, editor. | Elliott, Tomas, editor.
Title: The limit of the useful / Georges Bataille ; edited and translated by Cory Austin Knudson and Tomas Elliott.
Description: Cambridge, Massachusetts : The MIT Press, [2023] | Originally published as "L'économie à la mesure de l'univers," "La Limite de l'utile," "Notes pour L'économie à la mesure de l'univers," and "Notes pour La Limite de l'utile," Editions Gallimard, Paris, 1976. | Includes bibliographical references.
Identifiers: LCCN 2022000765 (print) | LCCN 2022000766 (ebook) | ISBN 9780262047333 | ISBN 9780262371353 (ebook) | ISBN 9780262371360 (pdf)
Subjects: LCSH: Bataille, Georges, 1897–1962. | Bataille, Georges, 1897–1962. Part maudite. | Economics.
Classification: LCC B2430.B33952 E5 2023 (print) | LCC B2430.B33952 (ebook) | DDC 194—dc23/eng/20220815
LC record available at https://lccn.loc.gov/2022000765
LC ebook record available at https://lccn.loc.gov/2022000766

10 9 8 7 6 5 4 3 2 1

CONTENTS

INTRODUCTION

Cory Austin Knudson and Tomas Elliott

THE TALE OF A DESPAIR

By the end of the 1930s, Georges Bataille had been many things. He had been a dissident surrealist, numismatist, antifascist activist, the founder of a secret society, and the editor of several journals. These ranged from the now-legendary *Documents* to the short-lived *Contre-Attaque*. As an author, he had become notorious as the writer behind the scandalizing and pseudonymously published pornographic fiction *Story of the Eye*. He participated in or organized scholarly convocations for which the lists of participants read like a who's who of the French interwar intelligentsia. Chief among these were Alexandre Kojève's seminars on *The Phenomenology of Spirit*,[1] as well as Bataille's own College of Sociology, whose attendees included Roger Caillois, Michel Leiris, Hans Mayer, Jean Paulhan, Jean Wahl, Raymond Queneau, and Georges Duthuit. By the end of the 1930s, however, there was one thing Bataille was not. He was not the author of a scholarly monograph.

He had attempted two such endeavors over the course of the decade. In one, he planned to investigate the structure and rise of fascism in France. His 1933 essay "The Psychological Structure of Fascism" was the basis for this work. The other was projected to center on the work of Lev Shestov,[2] the mentor who so consequentially introduced Bataille to the thought of Friedrich Nietzsche in 1922 or 1923, when he was fresh from his medievalist studies at the École des Chartes and still nursing pretensions of becoming a priest. Neither book would come to fruition. In 1939 Bataille would make still another attempt—this time, on a book centering entirely on the elaboration of his own ideas. But again, he would fall short of his objective.

When *Inner Experience* appeared in 1943—the first book to bear the name of Georges Bataille on the cover—he included a preface in which he describes the work as "the tale of a despair." This tale, as one might guess, has a lot to do with the clear difficulty Bataille had with writing a book that adequately expressed his anti-philosophical philosophy. In fact, given what we know now, the tale has specifically to do with that third book he attempted to write in the 1930s—the book that, in *Inner Experience*, Batalle goes so far as to claim encapsulated his most profound philosophical reflections. In this nascent masterwork, he says,

> I actually went to the end of problems whose novelty and scope exalted me. Entered into unexpected regions, I saw what eyes have never seen. Nothing more intoxicating: laughter and reason, horror and light became penetrable. . . . There was nothing that I did not know, that was not accessible to my fever. Like some marvelous madwoman, death

opened ceaselessly or closed the doors of the possible. In this labyrinth, I could lose myself at will, give myself over to ravishment, but I could discern the paths at will, pick a precise passage with intellectual steps. The analysis of laughter had opened before me a field of correspondences between the data of a *communal* and *decisive* emotional knowledge and those of discursive knowledge. *Losing themselves in one another*, the contents of various forms of expenditure (laughter, heroism, ecstasy, sacrifice, poetry, eroticism or others) defined among themselves a law of *communication* ordering the play of the isolation and the loss of beings. The possibility of uniting *at a precise point* two kinds of knowledge hitherto strangers to one another or otherwise crudely confused gave this ontology its unhoped-for consistency: the entire movement of thought lost itself, but all at once found itself again, in a point at which the unanimous crowd laughs. Therein I experienced a feeling of triumph: perhaps illegitimate, premature? . . . It does not seem so to me. I rapidly felt what came upon me as a weight. What rattled my nerves was to have achieved my task: my ignorance turned to insignificant points, more enigmas to solve! Everything crumbled! I awoke before a new enigma, and I knew all at once that this one was insoluble: this enigma was even so bitter, it left me in an impotence so crushing that I experienced it as God, if he exists, would have experienced it.

Three-quarters finished, I abandoned the work wherein the resolved enigma could be found.[3]

This mysterious preliminary manuscript to *Inner Experience*—supposedly abandoned in despair by its author at the very point where it allowed him to "achieve [his] task"—is *The Limit of the Useful.*

Bataille, of course, is given to exaggeration. Presented here for the first time in English, *The Limit of the Useful* was never truly "abandoned" and it does not articulate some esoteric and supreme enigma that would confound even the mind of God. ("If he exists," as its author hedges.) What it does do is present some of Bataille's most extensive and original reflections on, for example, the history and structure of sacrifice, the fraught interplay between glory and greed in military conquest, and the role of speculation in the machinery of capitalism. Remarkably, it is also his most structurally consistent work even as it is his least complete. And we do indeed find herein a detailed elaboration of his theory of laughter—a topic that Bataille refers to frequently throughout his works but never lays out as systematically as he does here. Most importantly, this text offers a profound exploration of what in the preface to *Inner Experience* Bataille would call the "law of *communication* ordering the play of the isolation and the loss of beings." This is the key that "opened ceaselessly or closed the doors of the possible," the Ariadne's thread that led him through the "labyrinth," the winnow that gave his abandoned ontology its "unhoped-for consistency."

For those familiar with Bataille, reading *The Limit of the Useful* is rather like embarking on an archaeological dig where one progressively uncovers the foundations of his later work. In what Bataille himself admits toward the end of the manuscript are somewhat "obscure ideas about the stars," for example, we see the beginnings of his serious consideration of the galactic mechanics of expenditure. Admittedly, this notion had formed the gravitational center of Bataille's thought since his early surrealist work *The Solar Anus* (1931), but in *The Limit of the Useful*, we see him turning to astrophysics rather than mystic ecstasy to ground his notions of interplanetary excess. This new approach would prove pivotal to his move from a restricted to a general economy in his magnum opus, *The Accursed Share* (1949), in which he would insist on the need to "recognize in the economy—*in the production and use of wealth*—a particular aspect of terrestrial activity regarded as a cosmic phenomenon."[4]

So too with earthly expenditure. In the meticulously wrought sections of *The Limit of the Useful*'s third chapter, Bataille sketches a history of the degradation of the communal experience of sumptuous loss into increasingly individualized and suppressed forms of personal enjoyment that he, following Max Weber, associates with the efflorescence of modern capitalism out of Puritan-tilled soil.[5] Echoes of this narrative are clear in the fourth chapter of *The Accursed Share*, but, perhaps surprisingly, the earlier version is much more far-reaching. By the late 1940s, Bataille had retooled this section of his argument into a critique of the calcified Stalinism that, rather than opposing capitalism, had actually joined it in reducing "the multitude . . . to the somnolence of production, [to the] mechanical existence . . . of *things*."[6] In *The Limit of the Useful*, by contrast, Bataille offers an immanent critique of capitalism itself that is unparalleled in his body of work. This critique does not denounce the rabid instrumentalization of human life in the degenerated workers' state of the USSR, but it does offer a prescient theorization of how the mechanics of capitalist accumulation encompass both the speculative will of stock market gambling and the sober drive toward maximizing profits through production.

However, the idea that *The Limit of the Useful* can be seen as preliminary to *The Accursed Share* is something of a controversial opinion among some Bataille scholars. Michel Surya claims that "through its long analysis of the effects of death in societies and its history, [*The Limit of the Useful*] is closer to *Sovereignty* than to *The Accursed Share*."[7] In her introduction to the 2016 French Lignes edition of *The Limit of the Useful* (published without the hundred pages of notes, drafts, tables, and plans that are present in Gallimard's *Œuvres complètes*), Mathilde Girard similarly claims the following:

> The subtitle of *The Limit of the Useful*: "Fragments of an abandoned version of *The Accursed Share*," proposed by the editors of the *Œuvres complètes*, too quickly associates the one text to the other. The first part indeed contains the essentials of what will be *The Accursed Share*, but the second (beginning from Chapter IV, "The Gift of the Self") is too close to *Sovereignty*, which will be published later, and also too close to *Guilty* and *Inner Experience*, which Bataille was working on at the same period.[8]

Girard is close to the mark, but for a crucial reason that she neglects to draw out: namely, that what we have here is a deeply transitional work. It is *The Limit of the Useful* that most clearly shows Bataille attempting (and stumbling, perhaps even failing) to force himself into a new, more sober mode of presenting his ideas than his previous, densely metaphorical works had allowed—apart from that 1933 anomaly "The Notion of Expenditure,"[9] of which *The Limit of the Useful* is partly a continuation. It is in this sense completely understandable that Bataille attempted to write *The Limit of the Useful* over the same period that he wrote *Inner Experience* and *Guilty*, for it is in those texts that Bataille truly gives free rein to his most deranged compositional impulses. Surya's comments on *Guilty*—that "most characteristic of Bataille's books"—may be taken as descriptive of both these works:

> Intentionally disordered, with no more of a beginning than an end, uncompleted by nature, mingling, blending diary and thought, triviality and elevation, eroticism and the sacred, reality and fiction, biography and philosophy, beginning on one date and ending on another without either being justified, made of thematic annexes as if the object was to integrate a sort of residuality of the text.[10]

Given such a description, it is not difficult to see in *Inner Experience* and *Guilty* all the mad indulgence that Bataille attempts to deny himself in *The Limit of the Useful*.

He sticks with the attempt, however. In his biography of Bataille, Stuart Kendall situates this work at the start of Bataille's near decade-long effort to reconcile his anti-systemic commitments with the need to express his ideas in coherent, expository prose. That he began grappling with this problem in 1939 and *The Accursed Share* would not appear for another ten years is evidence both of how difficult he found this process and how committed he was to it. As Kendall writes, "Bataille's obsessive persistence with regard to the ebullient ideas presented in [*The Limit of the Useful*] is as obvious as his reluctance to speak in the tone of cold calculation demanded by those ideas."[11]

The fruit of his efforts emerged in 1949 under the subtitle of *Consumption*, it being only the first volume of a proposed series to bear the title *The Accursed Share*. The incomplete works that were to have formed volumes II and III, titled *The History of Eroticism* and *Sovereignty* respectively, would be published posthumously in 1976, though Bataille had mined each for stand-alone essays that appeared in various journals during the last decade of his life. Notwithstanding how unsatisfied Bataille himself was with his drafts for the later volumes, the arc that can be traced from *Consumption* to *Sovereignty* seems largely in keeping with the trajectory of *The Limit of the Useful*. Between them we can recognize the movement from staid science and discursive reasoning to poetic delirium and lurid meditations on the frightful ecstasy of sacrificial bloodshed. That both Surya and Girard associate the latter half of *The Limit of the Useful* with *Sovereignty* does not, therefore, dissociate *The Limit of the Useful* from *The Accursed Share*. Rather, it may in fact more intimately tie the former to the latter; or, at least, the latter in its more complete envisioning.

It might seem counterintuitive to propose that a fragmentary, partial text may present a "more complete envisioning" of Bataille's originally expansive plan for *The Accursed Share*. But it is worth recognizing, in this regard, that the very idea of completion was something of an anathema to Bataille's mode of thinking. For Bataille consistently positions himself as a partisan of the incomplete, the fractured, the aleatory, and his works bear witness to this stance. His object was the presentation of that superabundant share of thought and being that inevitably escapes the systematizations of philosophers. *The Limit of the Useful* represented an incredible undertaking for Bataille because it was the first time that he attempted to attain this object via discursive reasoning itself. In this, he attempted to be even truer to his promise in *Inner Experience* to "[form] a project to escape from project"[12] than he managed in *Inner Experience* itself.

But whereas it is easy to praise the later, published text for dramatizing its own incompleteness, readers may be more inclined to criticize the unpublished one for the same reason. When it comes to *The Limit of the Useful*, it cannot be denied that we are faced with a work that did not succeed in what it set out to do. So, while it would be paradoxical to demand from Bataille a "complete" work, we still must recognize that *The Limit of the Useful* was deliberately left by the wayside; it is the remnant of Bataille's "despair." In its pages, we can only glimpse the blueprints and foundations of the vast edifice he meant to build, but we nevertheless see Bataille pushing his thought in new directions and toward new limits. We can feel that "unhoped-for consistency" in how each chapter, in its own way, methodically works through a variation of that dialectical complementarity between isolation and loss that Bataille himself identifies at the core of his most profound reflections. More often than not, however, we feel it more as a weight than a triumph, as moments of revelation bring yet more enigmas to solve. Ultimately, we can only join Bataille in bearing witness to the moment when "everything crumbled!"

CONSTRUCTING THE INCOMPLETE OPUS: 1938–1944

Everything did crumble, almost from the moment when Bataille began work on *The Limit of the Useful.* First and most significantly, on November 7, 1938, at a quarter past eight in the morning, Bataille's mistress and long-time co-conspirator, Colette Peignot, died of tuberculosis in the bed she shared with Bataille at their home in Saint-Germain-en-Laye. While the death of "Laure," as she had been known, did not come as a surprise, it was nonetheless devastating for Bataille. Though it is important not to insist too heavily on an autobiographical reading, the sense of loss he felt seems keenly communicated in the parts of his manuscript where he explores the effect that death has not just on the person who dies but on the person who survives them: "when someone dies, their reality is snatched away, but the same is true for someone who looks on that dead person. A living being who sees his fellow die can no longer exist except *outside himself.*" Indeed, this very sense of being on the "outside" seems to correlate with the fact that the period after Laure's death was one of increasing alienation for Bataille. Elsewhere in *The Limit of the Useful*, he would write of how isolation is necessary for forming a "reflective consciousness" that might see "the foundation of things—that without which nothing would be." Aside from how the solitary condition in which he suddenly found himself may have helped him enter the state of mind necessary to ground his idiosyncratic philosophy in something approaching sober discourse, one might wonder whether Bataille's extreme proximity to death—even for one who wrote about little else—might have inclined him toward what was an unprecedented impulse to systematize his thought, to leave his mark.

At the center of the philosophical system he developed was a vision of the universe as engaged in an unceasing, dialectical oscillation between the concentration and dispersal of energy. Within that dialectic, dispersal inevitably wins out over concentration, animating the universe and everything in it—from the movements of the planets down to the economic and political machinations of human societies, and even into the microscopic interactions of atoms and molecules. By 1947, this grand notion would evolve into what Christian Limousin has termed "Bataille's Theorem": that "the amount of energy produced is *always* greater than the amount required to produce it."[13] The project that spanned this period developed themes explored throughout his earlier essays. It was likely intended to make good on the promise appended by the publisher to the 1933 publication of "The Notion of Expenditure" in *La Critique sociale*, which announced this as the preview to a larger, more methodical work. In the spirit of that incendiary essay, Bataille called his new (or, depending on how you look at it, quite old) project *The Limit of the Useful.* Around 1941, he began referring to it as *The Accursed Share, or The Limit of the Useful*, marking the first time that Bataille called one of his works by what would later become his most famous title.

If *The Limit of the Useful* is transitional in its content, then it is also transitional in its style. It marks Bataille's fraught and not fully realized passage from his esoteric and metaphorical writing of the 1930s to the more rigorously theoretical and even scientific orientation of many of his works after World War II. That this transition occurred during a period of personal and historical rupture is no accident. As early as 1937, Bataille had written Alexandre Kojève expressing a feeling of having become "negligible," of having had "exceptional difficulty" in making himself "'recognized' (in the way that other people are 'recognized')"—so much so that he'd developed a feeling of "irrevocable insignificance."[14]

Despite his accomplishments, the fact was that Bataille, at forty, felt he was overdue for a monograph. This sense could only have been intensified by the crumbling of several personal and intellectual relationships at the end of the 1930s. Shortly after laying Laure to rest, the College of Sociology also entered its terminal decline. Bataille had founded this organization in 1937 with Michel Leiris and Roger Caillois, but that formidable trifecta did not last through a second season. For Caillois, disagreements over the College's mystic bent led to a rupture with Bataille, while Leiris grew increasingly skeptical over the nature and purpose of the whole enterprise, and he eventually washed his hands of it. Bataille had to deliver the concluding remarks to the second lecture circuit by himself, on July 4, 1939. He opened his speech as follows: "It had been understood that there would be three of us speaking this evening, Caillois, Leiris, and myself, but I am alone. It is not without sadness that I acknowledge this."[15] *Acéphale* also became a one-man show by the spring of 1939, with Bataille alone writing the entirety of what would be the journal's final issue, which he dedicated to the mental breakdown and death of Friedrich

Nietzsche. Bataille dissolved the secret society of which the journal was the public face later that year.

Determined to push through, Bataille nonetheless made plans for an autumn resumption of the College of Sociology—only for those plans to be definitively scuppered by the invasion by the Wehrmacht on September 3. He remained in Paris during the initial days of the Nazi advance. On the inauspicious date of September 5, he started a diary composed of profound and often disturbing reflections on his experiences, ideas, and the war that would later provide material for the first two volumes of his *Summa Atheologica*. It was also during this heady time that Bataille worked on *The Limit of the Useful*, laying out several tables for its overall organization and mining his 1938 essay "Celestial Bodies" for chapter I.[16] Unfortunately, however, this optimistic pattern had already become familiar by this point in Bataille's career, with so many of his grand proposals having previously come to naught. "Over and over again," Stuart Kendall writes, "Bataille will conceive or announce an enormous project and complete only a part of it or, conversely, he will complete a small essay or fiction only to claim that the completed piece is in fact a fragment of a much larger whole, which itself will remain unfinished."[17]

Bataille may have been somewhat unsure about how successful—and indeed how true to his own vision—his voyage into a more or less traditional mode of philosophical expression would turn out to be. The preface to *Inner Experience* disingenuously makes *The Limit of the Useful* out to be some kind of mystic tome, a Trismegistian emerald tablet on which the formula for the philosopher's stone is inscribed. By contrast, it is, on the whole, a work of rather modest reasoning and in any case a far cry from nearly everything he had ever written. Notably absent, for example, is any extensive exploration of erotic themes. Indeed, both this shift and his overall reticence in talking about *The Limit of the Useful* may be bound up in Bataille's sense of a need for a vast overhaul of his life and work around this period, apparently spurred by the death of Laure the previous year. On October 29, 1939, barely a week away from the anniversary of her death, Bataille wrote:

> Walking through the streets, I discover a truth that won't leave me alone: this kind of painful contradiction of my whole life is associated for me with the death of Laure and with the bare sadness of autumn. It is also the only means of "crucifying" myself. On September 28th [1939], I wrote: "I perceive that, in order to renounce my erotic habits, it will be necessary for me to invent a new way of crucifying myself. This way should be as intoxicating as alcohol." What I sensed in the moment could make me afraid.[18]

Bataille contemplating how to "renounce" his "erotic habits" is strange enough—Kendall argues that it heralds a "reversal at the center of Bataille's experience," though he also notes that the actual character of that reversal remains unclear.[19] For Bataille here seems possessed of a secret he can't even reveal to himself, one whose mere contemplation could make him tremble—so much so that he can't even bring himself to write about it in his own diary. In this connection one might be inclined to believe the unverified story told by Acéphale member Patrick Waldberg that, at what would be the final meeting of the secret society earlier that same October, Bataille asked his fellow communicants to kill him. Either this request was not actually made, or the members refused. In any event, on October 20 Bataille announced the dissolution of Acéphale. Laure, then the College of Sociology, then the journal *Acéphale*, and finally the society Acéphale—Bataille's personal, intellectual, and religious communities (and it is difficult to extricate any one of them from any other)—had withered by the autumn of 1939, with the last evaporating into air as defensive preparations were beginning in Paris.

Then the storm broke. On May 10, 1940 the Nazis advanced, swiftly defeating the French army and moving on Paris. Sixteen days after the start of the invasion, Bataille fled Paris with his partner Denise Rollin-Le Gentil for the pair's shared birthplace of Auvergne, an experience that Bataille transcribes in the "Exodus" chapter of *Guilty*. In Auvergne, Bataille would attempt once more to cobble together some sort of community, inviting his daughter to live with them, along with André Masson and his wife, Rose. But the relationship between Bataille and Rollin grew tumultuous and Bataille's thoughts turned morbid once more. During this period his diaries include many reflections, if not on suicide, then at least a general and disturbingly earnest desire to be dead.[20] There is still no discussion of his work on *The Limit of the Useful*.

By the end of August, Bataille was back in Paris, shortly to be joined by Rollin, and thereafter he split his time between Rollin's apartment on the Rue de Lille and his own on the Rue Saint-Honoré. It was at the former residence where Bataille, finally, was able to gather a stable intellectual community once more. Over the course of 1941 he organized a reading and discussion group under the somewhat tongue-in-cheek title of the Socratic College. This group included Maurice Blanchot—whose momentous acquaintance Bataille had made the year before—Raymond Queneau, Pierre Prevost, Michel Leiris, and others. The meetings centered on readings of the manuscript for *Inner Experience* and elaborating its central categories of experience and communication, which signifies that by this point Bataille had started to definitively turn his attention away from *The Limit of the Useful.* And indeed, the following year, *Inner Experience* would be published by Gallimard, with the prefatory note cited above in which he claims to have abandoned his previous manuscript "three-quarters finished."

Biographers who mention *The Limit of the Useful* at all tend to gloss over it in a sentence or two, undoubtedly as a consequence of the paucity of documentary information about the work's composition or what Bataille thought of it. Many go further, taking at face value Bataille's claim that he abandoned the manuscript. Consequently, most characterize it as an abortive experiment quickly forgotten. But such a view is belied in the first place by Bataille's clear if largely silent commitment to the work, evidenced not only in the at times meticulously tight argumentation but also in the bare fact that he clearly spent such a substantial amount of time planning and writing it. The dossier of notes, sketches, plans, and drafts that comprise the final section of this volume is as long as the extant portions of the actual work itself, and it clearly shows the range that Bataille planned to cover in *The Limit of the Useful.* Even those sections that Bataille did not end up realizing nevertheless hint at what far-off vistas he meant to explore: one can only guess what he might have written in chapter III's planned subsection on "The State, Reason, and Science," for example, or in the whole section enigmatically dedicated to "Transparency" that is sketched out in table of contents C.

More importantly, though, the dominant, dismissive view is undermined by the fact that, despite what he wrote in the preface to *Inner Experience*, Bataille never truly abandoned *The Limit of the Useful*. He was in fact still working on the text in 1943 and 1944, drawing up tables of proposed chapters and writing rough drafts of some sections. In the process, he seems to have grown more acutely aware of the paradoxical nature of discursively articulating a stable, coherent philosophy oriented around the kind of irrecuperable loss occasioned by immediate experience. In this regard, he writes the following note on the "Beginning of the second part of *The Accursed Share*" (the title that Bataille, by 1943, had started using in reference to what before had been called *The Limit of the Useful*):

> [An] author normally disguises the incomplete nature of his work. Like a house, a book is built on a plan: once the plan has been executed, the edifice remains in its rhetorical isolation. The lie of a book is that it looks finished, dressed up in the literary artifice of the author. In truth, it is nothing but a construction site.
>
> This method has its advantages. A reader, like a book, gives an impression of calm authority. . . . The author himself yields before the fiction of a finished work just as he yields to a necessary subject matter.

> It would be impossible to relieve the significant tension that is attached to the anxiety of finishing without causing some harm.
>
> . . . To write a work by carrying out the intended plan seems strange to me: that supposes that the results can be acquired independently from the execution, that thought stands immobile during all the time of execution.
>
> . . . Carrying out the work becomes a time of anxiety for me. I never stop changing. I have been [*dragging?*] this work out for years. I intend to continue it in a different way from how it began. Up until now, I have tried to express something known: I have had to begin what came before again. From now on, I will try to translate an unfinished movement, such as it is.

This note was likely written in 1943. The paradox it expresses of writing a work that describes an unfinished movement as if it were or could be the product of thought rendered immobile prefigures the very dilemma that Bataille reprises years later in the introduction to *The Accursed Share*:

> As I considered the object of my study, I could not personally resist the effervescence in which I discovered the unavoidable purpose, the value of the cold and calculated operation. My research aimed at the acquisition of a knowledge; it demanded coldness and calculation, but the knowledge acquired was that of an error, an error implied in the coldness that is inherent in all calculation. In other words, my work

> tended first of all to *increase* the sum of human resources, but its findings showed me that this accumulation was only a delay, a shrinking back from the inevitable term, where the accumulated wealth has value only in the instant. Writing this book in which I was saying that energy finally can only be wasted, I myself was using my energy, my time, working; my research answered in a fundamental way the desire to add to the amount of wealth acquired for mankind. Should I say that under these conditions I sometimes could only respond to the truth of my book and could not go on writing it?[21]

The very persistence of Bataille's grappling with this dilemma leaves small wonder as to why the work took so long to complete—and why he spoke so little of it during the anxiety-ridden, dragged-out process of its piecemeal construction. To discursively limn the experience of communication whereby beings shatter the isolation in which they enclose themselves by way of an encounter with unassimilable excess, a book must be simultaneously planned and spontaneous, closed and open; it must "stand in isolation" and yet "never stop changing." It must itself be the residue of an unfinished movement—which, in a manner of speaking, it is.

"MY ROLE . . . IS THAT OF A BRAKE": AMBROSINO AND BATAILLE

Bataille would gather his strength to complete his recalcitrant project one final time—and he would enlist the help of a friend in the effort.

In 1945, Gallimard published the final volume of the *Summa Atheologica*, entitled *On Nietzsche*, in which Bataille admits that "in my manner of proceeding there is an aspect of play, of unbearable disorder." He then immediately reaffirms his commitment to finding a more coherent manner of expressing his ideas: "I will show," he says, "precisely when I come out of this vagueness, this incoherence, that I can proceed otherwise."[22] It is not by accident that this book was dedicated to Bataille's close friend, Georges Ambrosino, with whom the author had begun talks on a joint project. Given the evidence offered in an extensive cache of correspondence between Bataille and Ambrosino recently compiled by Claudine Frank, it is clear that this collaboration was, precisely, an overhaul of *The Limit of the Useful*—that long-deferred book wherein the gnomic philosopher would finally find a way to "proceed otherwise."[23]

Bataille and Ambrosino met in 1933 at the meetings of the Democratic Communist Circle, an anti-Stalinist, Marxist political discussion group associated with Boris Souvarine's journal, *La Critique sociale* (where "The Notion of Expenditure," along with its prefatory note promising more extensive elaboration of its themes, was published). "Zino," as his friends called him, was then a young student of nuclear physics, whose interests also led him toward surrealism and radical politics. It was a particularly happy twist of fate that while participating in Souvarine's group he would be joined by those whom he described at the time as "some old surrealists . . . Leiris, Queneau, and Bataille."[24] Ambrosino quickly became a partisan of Bataille in the often fractious disagreements that arose within the Circle. After it dissolved in 1934, Ambrosino joined Bataille in forming the radical antifascist group Contre-Attaque and also contributed to its eponymous, short-lived journal.

Claudine Frank has cast doubt on the notion, put forth by Christian Limousin, Sylvia Patron, and most recently Cédric Mong-Hy, that Ambrosino encouraged Bataille to become more interested in science, which Limousin, Patron, and Mong-Hy variously argue culminated in both the unprecedented style and theoretical orientation of *The Accursed Share*. "Nothing is less certain," she says, citing a lack of documentary evidence.[25] She is not wrong about the lack of explicit documentation; however, what we do have are the records of Bataille's loans from the Bibliothèque Nationale, which clearly show a major spike in Bataille's interest in quantum mechanics, atomic energy, biology, zoology, evolution, and astrophysics between 1934 and 1935. It may indeed be that "Zino" exerted no influence on this score; but it seems more likely that he did. As for Ambrosino, during this period he continued his studies in physics at Strasbourg and then Grenoble. He obtained his agrégation in physics in 1938. After a brief stint in the military, he taught at secondary schools in Nantes, Lyon, and Paris until the war, whereupon he joined the Resistance as an intelligence officer under the celebrated Henri Frenay. Meanwhile, he joined in just about every endeavor that Bataille undertook, from the College of Sociology, to Acéphale, to their eventual, fitful collaboration on the work that would become *The Accursed Share*. Ambrosino was a signatory of the founding document of the College of Sociology, and his name appeared as a director of Acéphale's journal. It was in fact Ambrosino who served as Bataille's first lieutenant in Acéphale, and he was tasked with conducting new members (dubbed "larvae" by Bataille) to the sacred grove where they would be initiated into the group's mysteries.

So by the summer of 1945, Bataille and Ambrosino were close enough personally and intellectually to hit the ground running with a co-authored volume. At first, the plan for the work was still broadly laid out along the lines of Bataille's original conception of *The Limit of the Useful*, with sections on ancient Mexico, capitalism, and the military orbiting a general theory that Ambrosino appears to have understood as follows:

> The sphere of objects is transcendent. Communication is a rupture of this sphere in which for a moment immanence reveals itself (the absorption of food, sacrifice, laughter, eroticism . . .). This operation is dangerous (for an adult). It accompanies expenditure. There can be no communication without expenditure, nor expenditure without communication.[26]

We see here the "law of communication" that Bataille identified at the core of the manuscript begun in 1939 persisting into 1945, through all the personal calamities and historical upheaval endured between those years.

Over the course of the summer of 1945, Bataille and Ambrosino would work together on this manuscript at Bataille's home in Vezelay. It is during this period of collaboration that Ambrosino began to temper his friend's overambitious project, zeroing in specifically on the implications of its primary thesis in relation to basic biological and ecological operations. Ambrosino pulls Bataille back down to earth, introducing him to Vladimir Vernadsky's concept of the biosphere in August and thus providing the project with a distinctly earth-bound theoretical basis—the rudiments of "general economy"—that would persist throughout its composition. Bataille was particularly interested in the limits to available growth and consequent wastage of energy implied in the conception of a bounded terrestrial sphere inundated with solar energy. He composed an article over the course of that autumn that reoriented his thinking about the planetary mechanics of expenditure to focus more specifically on the terrestrial globe rather than the movements of distant stars. This article would be published in July 1946 by the London-based review *La France libre*, under the title "Economy at the Scale of the Universe: Brief, Preliminary Notes toward an Essay on 'General Economy' to Appear Under the Title: *The Accursed Share*." This heading would mark Bataille's first explicit announcement both of his crucial category of general economy and *The Accursed Share* itself.

While this article was undergoing review, Bataille sent it to Ambrosino, asking that he tell him "as quickly as possible what [he thought] of it and *precisely with a view to some small, eventual corrections*." He also noted, "It is a shame that we did not write it collaboratively."[27] Ambrosino duly returned a set of notes and corrections "that I *suggest* to you, no more." "My role is thankless," he added, "it is that of a brake. I will try to exaggerate as little as possible, trusting myself to you, however, to restore ardor and joy to things."[28] This kind of exchange would become characteristic of their collaboration, with Bataille surging forth and Ambrosino paring back: a seemingly productive back-and-forth that reminds one of the complementarity between spring and winter of which Bataille writes in the lurid fifth chapter of *The Limit of the Useful*.

The scientist would also compile notes and summaries on, among a range of subjects, the relation between energy and economics (compiled under the heading "Energy Plus value, etc.") and on the basic definition, constitution, and operations of an organism. The fruit of their exchanges is evidenced most prominently in the text, composed between 1946 and 1947, that the editors of the *Œuvres complètes* appended in the notes to "Economy at the Scale of the Universe" under the title "Preliminary Notes to the Writing of *The Accursed Share*." An appropriately anonymous draft, this brief text appears to be a residue of the period of closest collaboration between Bataille and Ambrosino, as the pair carefully worked their way toward what would become the theoretical introduction to *The Accursed Share*. It is also, chronologically, the final document included in this volume.

It is after these "Preliminary Notes" that the collaboration between the errant philosopher and the radical scientist would begin to fall apart. Sometime in 1947 a progressive estrangement began to set in, evidently as a result of editorial conflicts over pieces Bataille had commissioned from Ambrosino for *Critique* in addition to increasing differences of opinion over the direction of *The Accursed Share*. Ambrosino's wife, Esther, also proposed that her husband's increasingly close friendship with the analytic philosopher Éric Weil led him to becoming less and less interested in "all Bataille's ideas."[29] Bataille himself suggested that the pair break off their collaboration in a letter sent at the end of 1947, which Ambrosino initially resisted. By July 1948, however, Bataille made clear that he felt abandoned by his partner and bound to move forward with the project without him. In 1949 *The Accursed Share* was published under Bataille's name alone, though the author did include a prominent (if somewhat enigmatic) acknowledgment of his erstwhile collaborator in the introduction:

> I must thank my friend Georges Ambrosino, research director of the X-Ray Laboratory, without whom I could not have constructed this book. Science is never the work of one man; it requires an exchange of views, a joint effort. This book is also in large part the work of Ambrosino. I personally regret that the atomic research in which he participates has removed him, for a time, from research in "general economy." I must express the hope that he will resume in particular the study he has begun with me of the movements of energy on the surface of the globe.[30]

Alas, Ambrosino would not return. He would, shortly after *The Accursed Share*'s publication, write an article for *Combat* that was markedly critical of some of Bataille's analyses. Then, in January 1951, a frosty exchange during a philosophical discussion seems to have put the two on the outs. Bataille would extend an olive branch in 1956, and thereafter he would regularly send Ambrosino copies of his newly published or reissued books with warm inscriptions invoking the friendship they once shared. It is unclear if Ambrosino ever replied. Bataille tried reconciling again two years before his death, but his former lieutenant, intellectual partner, and dear friend seems to have definitively moved on.

FROM EARTH TO SUN TO SACRIFICE: THE SHAPE AND STRUCTURE OF *THE LIMIT OF THE USEFUL*

The main body of *The Limit of the Useful* is divided into seven chapters that are primarily organized around the theme of unproductive expenditure. Bataille ranges across various subjects, but there is a unity to the project's overall shape, and it covers many of the areas of inquiry that were prominent in early-twentieth-century continental thought. Bataille begins with hard science in chapter I, exploring the difference between the physical dynamics of the universe and life on earth. He then moves quickly to sociology and anthropology in chapter II, treating such topics as the gift and festival economies, as well as capitalism's roots in the spirit of American Protestantism. This economic account is further developed in chapter III, as Bataille brings Marx's critique of political economy up to date for his current era of what he calls "mature capitalism," which is characterized by share trading and stock market exchange. Thus, in these three opening chapters (which are the most fully developed in the work, along with chapter VII), Bataille offers a comprehensive and interdisciplinary survey of recent developments in the hard and social sciences. He builds, for example, on new discoveries in cosmology and theoretical physics by thinkers like Albert Einstein, Edwin Hubble, and Sir Arthur Stanley Eddington (whom Bataille cites in the opening pages of *The Limit of the Useful*). He develops his work on the foundational sociologies of Émile Durkheim and Max Weber, as well as the nascent structural anthropology of Marcel Mauss.[31] And he updates the Marxist critique of political economy, which he filters through Alexandre

Kojève's influential interpretation of Hegel, which was so prominent in French intellectual life at the time. It is only then, after these more systematic (if still ebullient) explorations of (meta-)physics, sociology, and economics, that Bataille allows himself more poetic license, pursuing some esoteric lines of inquiry in chapters on the gift of the self, the seasons, war, and sacrifice.

Overall, therefore, in *The Limit of the Useful*, we see Bataille working at the forefront of multiple strands of thought, striving to unite them in his overarching vision of excess. The revised version of his 1938 essay "Celestial Bodies," which makes up the opening pages of chapter I, announces Bataille's entry into the serious study of science. Fittingly, though, that scientific orientation broaches almost immediately into his familiar surrealistic territory. Bataille begins by imagining a reader "inclined to self-reflection but who will accept nothing not already grounded in science." He claims, however, that such a reader would have to grapple with a rather remarkable notion: that even as he (here and throughout the work, it is almost always "he") is reading about the cold, hard, unshakable logic of scientific facts, he is also spinning out of control, rooted on a planet that is, at every moment, hurtling through space at an unthinkable speed. Science itself, in other words, is the basis for a surrealist dream: "Our books inform us that this globe moves at a dizzyingly rapid pace: the earth, gravitating around the center of the galaxy, travels a thousand times faster than a bullet." If a person were to grapple with the true reality and meaning of science, in other words, they would suffer from the sickness that is referenced in the epigraph to the book, which Bataille takes from Søren Kierkegaard: "the madness of the man aware at every moment that the earth is spinning."

Thankfully, most of us are spared this madness, for we remain blissfully unaware of the earth turning beneath our feet. According to Bataille, though, the problem with this ignorance, be it conscious or unconscious, is that it has formed the basis for many of our erroneous ontological and epistemological assumptions. Bataille refers to this as the "fundamental error of the immobile ground." He argues that in the history of so-called rational thought, which encompasses both science and philosophy, human beings have tended to use "the ground as a foundation for real things." Ironically, we have searched for stability, permanence, and eternal truths, when in fact the physical reality of our planet makes a mockery of that search. The ground on which we build our lives is far from stable; it is, rather, just one small drop in a dizzying expanse of movement, more a "whirlwind of exploding matter" than a cold and permanent foundation. The idea that we, in contrast to the rest of the universe, should claim to exist on *terra firma* is either a laughable example of human arrogance or a sad indictment of our myopia. "In the midst of a universe spinning in splendor," Bataille writes, "our *immobile* world seems deprived." If, by contrast, we were to consider the "movement of the whole" (if, as Bataille will put it in *The Accursed Share*, we were to look not at the "restricted economy" of the earth but at the "general economy" of the universe), then we would find at that movement's core an urge toward what Bataille will refer to variously as "sumptuous expenditure" or "glorious loss." We would find, in other words, a universe that is not "subjected to any *useful employment*," the employment that is most valued within the confines of an earthly (or more properly, modern, Western) capitalist economy.

The greatest symbol of that universe and its movement is the sun. The sun (along with every other star) gives up its power and its resources absolutely. It radiates light and heat in a glorious sacrifice of itself. The sun contrasts, therefore, with a planet like Earth, which is a cold celestial body, absorbing or storing more energy than it gives out. As Bataille puts it, "The 'intimate movement' of the earth runs counter to the movement of a star. The star is radiant, and our soil is cold. The star *lavishes* its power: our soil divides itself up into particles greedy for power."

Fittingly, for Bataille, this glorious power of the sun can be glimpsed simultaneously through the lens of astrophysics and of religious mysticism. The "ever-present authority of religion," in fact, recognized the significance of the sun long before modern science. Bataille, for his part, views these two epistemologies as equally valid. In the language of science, he writes:

> the radiation of the sun is the ceaseless projection of a part of its substance into space in the form of heat and light. . . . Like the sun, every star gives itself over to immeasurable loss . . . the atom of a radiant body—at least in a star of an elevated temperature—is *under the direct control* of that star's mass and its "intimate movement": there is no isolable state that it could belong to.

A few pages later, Bataille says much the same thing in the language of religion:

> The sun is the symbol of glory. The sun shines: glory is represented as luminous and shining like the sun. For primitive man, light symbolizes divinity. Its splendor and brilliance are not useful, but they endow it with a sense of freedom. Even if we consider life today, if we recall the services we perform, if we make accounts of usefulness, we are still ultimately enraptured by those *things that shine*.

That these two visions of the sun—the spiritual and the scientific—should overlap is significant. As Bataille puts it, "the fact that the path of science . . . should lead to a spiritual revelation is, of course, not without consequence for man." For Bataille, it throws much of the purported stability of scientific reason into doubt. It shows that in our urge to separate ourselves from the glorious economy of the universe, we have tended to base our scientific principles and our supposedly rationalist, post-Enlightenment society on what is just a small part of the whole; we have focused on our cold, utilitarian, terrestrial system, rather than on the warm, generous, celestial one that encompasses it.

This central notion that the sun's brilliance runs counter to the utilitarian ontologies and social structures that predominate on Earth—or, at least, that predominated on Earth as it was conceived in twentieth-century Europe—also lies behind Bataille's interest in the sacrificial rites of Mesoamerica. Toward the end of the first chapter, Bataille writes that the Aztecs knew how to "acknowledge the glory of the universe" through the sacrifice of human life. By spending life lavishly, just like the sun, they sought to give "the gift of the self." Bataille writes:

> The peoples of ancient Mexico used to fuse man with the glory of the universe: the sun was produced by a sacrificial frenzy—by dying in a brazier, a god in human form gave birth to the splendor of daylight. In this way, the Aztec people saw what "civilized people" might see but in fact see only rarely: the unity of sacrifice and light, the equivalence between intoxicating gifts of the self and no less intoxicating glories.

The "god in human form" that Bataille mentions here is Nanauatzin, who cast himself into a fire to give birth to the sun. This story was reenacted in the rites of the Aztecs, wherein a human subject would be sacrificed to ensure that the sun would continue to offer up its life-giving resources of light and heat.

It is not without reason that Bataille says in *The Limit of the Useful* that this Aztec story "encapsulates this entire book." Its significance is also seen in chapter II, in which Bataille explores the structure of Aztec society in more detail, arguing that its logic ran counter to that of "modern" society. In the course of this analysis, Bataille lays the foundation for what would become the primary insight of *The Accursed Share*: that the aim of "acquisition is the wasted share that it makes possible." What he means by this is that the seemingly primary drive toward gain and growth is actually secondary to a more overwhelming urge to waste, spend, and consume. This desire to waste, to spend the surplus that makes up the "*part maudite*" or "accursed share" of his later work's title, is what lies behind the "glorious" or "useless" expenditure involved in sacrifice (the waste of human life). Indeed, while acts like sacrifice did have a certain usefulness in the eyes of the Aztecs—literally, within their mythological landscape, bloodletting was required to keep the sun shining and the fields growing—the significance of those acts, for Bataille, is that their aim is expenditure itself, rather than expenditure in the service of production or gain. For Bataille, sumptuous expenditure in service of "glory was the one true goal of the Mexican people"; the waste of life was central, rather than ancillary, to the social structure. Put simply: one ate in order to kill rather than killed in order to eat.

In perhaps overly schematic and general terms, Bataille argues that this principle underwrote all of Aztec society, most notably the relationship between the people and their sovereign. According to Bataille, the sovereign "embodied the glory of the community. The sovereign is always the image of the people: the masses he unites expect him to faithfully express their communal will. The will of all the people was that he express prodigality." For this reason, it was the sovereign's duty to expend all the riches he accumulated through the creation of "art, festivals, and wars. He was obliged to spend them lavishly."

Bataille sees this same impulse in other pre-modern societies, primarily in the institution of potlatch. Practiced among the indigenous peoples of the American Pacific Northwest and Canadian coast, potlatch refers to the act through which a person, typically the sovereign, acquires glory by giving, rather than gaining. In Bataille's analysis, potlatch and its various analogues express a fundamental "subordination of production to expenditure," which runs counter to the economics of accumulation and utilitarian efficiency elaborated in classical economics. "In contrast to a commercial transaction," Bataille wrote in a section of his manuscript that he later crossed out, "a potlatch reveals the very image of the human heart, in all its turmoil and generosity, if also in its aggressiveness."

Perhaps surprisingly, Bataille also sees this ethos of generosity encapsulated in the Catholic church of the Middle Ages, which he argues was "not by definition opposed to glory." Specifically, Bataille identifies a logic of useless expenditure in the "glorious edifices" of pre-Reformation Christianity, namely churches and cathedrals, whose "*useless* beauty proclaimed the principle of festivals aloud." According to Bataille, insofar as Catholicism encouraged people to dedicate their labor and lives to the creation of monuments that were—from the perspective of utility—completely superfluous, it preserved some of "the truth of religion from the earliest times." Indeed, Catholicism even preserved, albeit in a sublimated form, some of the remnants of human sacrifice as part of its central ritual, in which it encouraged believers to repeatedly consume the body and blood of the crucified Christ. In both its buildings and its "fabulous ceremonies," therefore, Catholicism continued to make sacrifice—the gift of the self—its central focus, obsessively bearing "witness to Christ, to the gift that he made for all mankind through his death."

It is unsurprising, in this regard, that Bataille should view the Reformation as a dividing line in European (and subsequently global) history. "Beginning from the Reformation onwards," he argues toward the end of chapter II, "a moral hostility toward all waste and a utilitarian society developed under the direction of the grand bourgeoisie." As mentioned, Bataille here repeats Max Weber's account of the development of capitalism from the spirit of Protestantism, noting that the Reformation introduced a fundamentally different economics of salvation into Christianity, one that hung on the theological opposition between grace and works. Catholicism had insisted that it was through the gift of God's grace that a human being might be saved. In the words of Ephesians 2:8–9: "For by grace are ye saved through faith; and that not of yourselves: it is the gift of god." Protestantism, by contrast, emphasized the importance of works for the promise of salvation, which led to a new worldview. According to Bataille, from that moment on, "for the man of God, being useful and charitable [was] enough." In the Protestant ethic, in other words, though charity continued to prevail, it became inducted into an economy of self-interest, where doing good deeds, "being useful," was ultimately thought to lead to a reward: entry into heaven. Put in the terms of French sociology, therefore, we might say that the Reformation transformed a gift economy (one focused on expenditure) into an economy of interest and gain (one focused on production). As a result, salvation became less a gift from God than a return on Christian investment, and wealth began to lose its status as a sign of the power to spend lavishly; it became, instead, "a means of production: *capital*," whose "only God is growth." This led ineluctably, in Bataille's narrative, to the rise of Protestant America, which introduced the world to the modern businessman, who "doesn't make money either for the enjoyments it buys or to live resplendently . . . the money he makes exists to be invested; it must be used for nothing but growth; it has no value or meaning except for the endless enrichment it makes possible."

Those familiar with *The Accursed Share* will recognize the contours of this Weberian history. What is interesting about Bataille's treatment of it in chapter III of *The Limit of the Useful*, though, is his detailed excavation of its relevance to the finance capitalism of his day and, to a significant extent, our own day as well. He explores that relevance in much more detail than he does in *The Accursed Share* and argues, perhaps surprisingly, that "mature capitalism" still harbors some traces of the glorious acts of earlier social formations. Bataille's account centers primarily on a dialectic he establishes between what he calls the "project" (*projet*) and the "game" or "gamble" (*jeu*). The project (which retains, for Bataille, some of the Latin connotations of "throwing forth, *projecting* toward the future") is generally what "predominates in capitalist activity." Projects involve very little risk and are "calculated" (also an important term for Bataille). As a result, Bataille argues, the project was the basic enterprise of the "honest Calvinist," who subordinated the present to the future, carefully investing his time and energy into extracting an anticipated return. In this sense, the Calvinist was the precursor to the "modern industrialist," also characterized by his willingness to reinvest gains in search of future growth:

> The Calvinist industrialist diverted his riches from their glorious usage and put them toward the growth of the forces of production, but his austerity stopped him in his tracks. The modern industrialist, having understood the consequences of the Calvinist attitude, ends up dedicating the excess fruit of his riches to his own personal well-being. But he is held

> back by the fictional idea of useful activity and by his status as a man of project.

Against this post-Calvinist "man of project," Bataille opposes the embodiment of finance capital: the "speculator," who is heedless of the future and prepared to risk everything on the vagaries of the stock market. "Speculators are more likely than industrialists or capitalists to be beings of vain glory, driven to making extravagant personal expenditures." Bataille argues that the speculator is defined by his willingness to engage in a "gamble" or a "wager," both of which we use to translate the French word *jeu*. In French, though, as well as being a "stake" or a "bet," a *jeu* is more commonly a "game," and Bataille seems to observe a kind of playful exuberance in the activities of the speculator, linking him to the glorious extravagances of earlier individuals (in the notes that accompany *The Limit of the Useful*, Bataille writes that speculators are "heirs, to a certain extent, to the spirit of potlatch"). Moreover, this is further reinforced by Bataille's use of the verbal phrase *mettre en jeu*, which we translate by "to put at stake" or "gamble," but which was also used by Kojève to translate the central operation in Hegel's dialectic of the master and the slave. For Hegel, via Kojève, the master was the person who put his entire life *at stake* (*mise en jeu*), who risked everything for recognition as an independent subject; similarly, for Bataille, the speculator is the one who is prepared to risk it all, purely for what he calls the "thrill of losing."

A further lexical field also animates the meanings at play in this context. In mechanical engineering, *jeu* can refer to the looseness or freedom of movement between, say, the cogs of a machine or a wheel and its axle, and the speculator is therefore the person who finds space for glorious expenditure within the overarching mechanism of capitalism itself. But this is not simply because of the speculator's ingenuity; rather, Bataille argues, capitalism "accommodates itself" to the speculator. In fact, he remarks in his notes, it "makes use of a spirit that runs counter to it. Capital uses the wagers to drain the surplus of available resources, making money flow as quickly as possible and with all the fluidity it requires." Though speculators preserve something of the glory of potlatch, therefore, capital, "lacking its own existence . . . can hijack glory."

In the transition from chapter III to chapter IV, *The Limit of the Useful* shifts. At the start of chapter IV, Bataille writes: "From this point on I will no longer discuss those movements whose traces can only be glimpsed in the operations of the economy but rather those stronger movements that are active today and that still connect man with death." This takes the form of an analysis of—or perhaps a delirious obsession with—war. This obsession, which is also dominant in chapter VI, was undoubtedly fueled by Bataille's reaction to the horrors of World War I and those of World War II that were unfolding around him. In both chapters, he takes on the perhaps impossible task of trying to explain why it is that human beings have—in all places and times but most acutely in recent history—been willing to indulge in the extravagant waste of human life that constitutes warfare. In forming a response, he takes his lead from Nietzsche, arguing that war is a continuation of "the gift of the self," recapitulating the sacrificial rites of early religions. "Just like religions," Bataille argues, "wars demand the gift of the self, the total dedication of one's life." While politicians may rationalize wars as necessary for certain gains (power, influence, wealth, territory), the soldier on the battlefield can only be motivated, according to Bataille, by glory. "The one true mark of services rendered in blood is that they are repaid solely in glory." Bataille extends this analysis in chapter VI in brutally visceral terms, arguing provocatively that the descriptions of life at the front in World War I recall "the language of mysticism," the language of religion. But, Bataille claims, the plight of the soldier is much more fraught than that of the servant of God; the "horror" that the soldier faces "*is right there* in abundance," whereas the faithful believer can only "fabricate" that horror through ritual. In terms that again recall Hegel's account of the staking of human life, Bataille states that combat—the war of human being against human being for no other purpose than "recognition" or "glory"—is the most essential human endeavor. Warfare, like sacrifice, is what separates man from base utility; again, it shows him eating to kill rather than killing to eat.

The gruesome meditations of chapters IV and VI are separated by the most poetic and least scientific section of the book. Chapter V, entitled "Winter and Spring," is a macrocosmic meditation on both the irreversible trajectory of a single individual's life and the cyclical ebb and flow of the seasons. This is the section, mentioned above, in which Bataille reflects on what happens when we witness our fellow human beings die. Though that experience rips through our reality, Bataille claims that it also has the important effect of binding us together with others, knitting the fabric of communal experience in a way that laws or social structures never could. Though he crossed it out in the manuscript, Bataille wrote that "people have the power to measure their existence through death: the life of every community must not only be beautiful but also great, because each time a living being dies, their presence must be felt by the helpless fellows they leave behind."

Such human deaths also play out against the backdrop of the much more expansive drama of degeneration and rebirth throughout the world. These extremes mark two agonistic poles in the poetry of death, between which human beings must choose. The first extreme is associated with winter, the time of year when the earth "moves away from the sun," and "withered life violently decomposes." The other extreme is associated with spring, in which, counterintuitively, Bataille sees another kind of death, the symbol of which is the glorious expenditure of the flower that "shines forth and spends its wealth lavishly." The death of the flower, which is the necessary culmination of its blossoming, does not "put an end to its triumph." Rather, it is its greatest achievement. In these two poles of winter and spring, Bataille sees two models of existence. Both of them are characterized by death, which is inevitable, but it is up to man to decide between the glorious and the catastrophic, between the death of the exuberant flower of spring or that of the frostbitten earth of winter: "Man is not wretched because he dies—to die is to live gloriously—but because he longs to escape his fate. The fear of death is the principle of greed. Man can only choose between dying richly or dying poorly, between the garlanded death of May and the somber death of November."

If readers find this interlude on the seasons and the chapters on war that surround it speculative, then they should know that Bataille did too. Seemingly anticipating their confusion, Bataille introduces the final chapter of *The Limit of the Useful* with an apology: "To those who have followed me up to this point," he says, "I owe a long explanation." He recognizes the strangeness of his investigations into the "bloody fantasies of sacrifice" and notes that his remarks "cannot be justified solely through obscure ideas about the stars." Almost in response, it seems, he embarks on what must be recognized as one of his most careful and capacious examinations of sacrifice—a concept so central to his philosophy. As in the opening chapter, his account combines science with speculation, tracing the theory of sacrifice down to the level of molecules and cells, before then expanding it outward to the level of individuals in society. He writes:

> It seems that, in the world of cells, communion prevails over the poorly established isolation of individual cells. The opposite is true in the world of stable organic unities and solid substances in which human thought has taken shape: for the most part activities can be traced to the clearly distinct foci (whether of people or forces) which cause them. But just as the *separation* of elements is already marked in a world where *communication* is limitless, so too does this world that is divided up into separate individuals find itself ceaselessly stirred up by efforts to maintain such separations due to fears about having to *communicate*: each of us must surrender ceaselessly to the loss of self—be it partial or total—which is involved in *communication* with others.

Bataille's reasoning is often difficult to follow in these passages, but his point seems to be that at various micro- and macroscopic scales, isolated individuals (cells, organic unities, human beings) are required to sacrifice themselves or part of themselves ("surrender ceaselessly to the loss of self—be it partial or total") in order to *communicate* with others.

One way of interpreting this is to say that Bataille argues for viewing sacrifice as a normal part of, rather than an exception to, the typical interactions of matter and the everyday experiences of human beings. This would help make sense of the otherwise rather strange parallel that he draws, later in this chapter, between the dynamics of sacrifice and laughter. Laughter, Bataille notes, is a common part of human experience. "Of all the most intense forms of connection," he argues, "none are more common than the laughs that we share together." In his notes, even, Bataille claims that laughter is, by its very nature, communal; it is "contagious" or, as we more commonly put it today, infectious. At the same time, however, laughter is also characterized by its violence; it erupts from us, often without warning, shaking us out of our cold, rational way of being (Bataille does not call us "repressed," though we might use such a term today). "Laughter is a major form of communication in which everything is *violently* called into question," he writes (emphasis added). And this violence is also what links laughter to the indulgent sacrifices of Aztec society. Taking the admittedly rudimentary example of a person who bursts out laughing when they see "their fellow fall over," Bataille claims that "the person who accidentally falls over is the substitute for a sacrificial victim;

the communal joy of laughter is the substitute for sacred communication."

Bataille does not develop this line of thought much further, and the manuscript breaks off just when he declares that he will "plow headlong . . . into the enigma of sacrifice," almost as if his repeated claims to explain that enigma cannot help but end in the "anguished silence" which he then goes on to describe. Nevertheless, this final provocation of the overlap between laughter and sacrifice would continue to dominate Bataille's thinking, as evidenced by the quote from *Inner Experience* with which this introduction began, where Bataille declares that his "analysis of laughter had opened before me a field of correspondences between the data of a *communal* and *decisive* emotional knowledge."

In this regard, it is also unsurprising to find that Bataille's nascent theory of laughter and sacrifice forms a prominent part of the one hundred or so pages of notes, sketches, tables, and drafts that complement the manuscript of *The Limit of the Useful*. Indeed, in these notes, we even encounter a diagram of the transition from "anguish to ecstasy," which Bataille saw as central to the experience of both laughter and sacrifice. This is supplemented, moreover, by detailed schematizations of the "parallel" between "laughter-sacrifice" and "comedy-tragedy." Interestingly, while these are only unfinished notes, they often provide some of the clearest insights into the thought processes that lie behind the discursive expositions of *The Limit of the Useful* and *The Accursed Share*. In them, we see Bataille's thought laid bare, offering hints at what, as mentioned, he would later claim as the "unhoped-for consistency" of his earlier work.

A NOTE ON THE TEXT

It is, in fact, the discovery of "unhoped-for consistency" that has characterized our experience of translating *The Limit of the Useful*, as well as the plethora of notes that accompany it. Although, like so much of his work, Bataille viewed this project as little more than a fragmentary introduction, it undoubtedly coalesces into a coherent, if unfinished, philosophical work. For that reason, the editors of the *Œuvres complètes* deserve considerable credit for having shaped its many archival strands into a textual whole. Translation is, after all, never the work of one individual—like science, as Bataille puts it in *The Accursed Share*, "it requires an exchange of views, a joint effort." The effort of compilation evidenced in the *Œuvres complètes* alone is a work of translation: of rendering legible, of giving voice. We are greatly indebted to that effort, and we hope that our efforts to chart a translation through Bataille's often-dizzying prose will allow an English-speaking audience to appreciate some of its nuances. We have made much of the incomplete nature of this work, but at its heart, *The Limit of the Useful* represents an immense, joint enterprise of reconstruction shared between many individuals across several periods of time, and the product of this effort may, eventually, gain renewed attention and respect from future scholars and readers of Bataille.

In trying to make the process of reading *The Limit of the Useful* as easy as possible for Anglophone audiences, we have taken a few key decisions in the way we have organized the material in this book. The first concerns the relationship between *The Limit of the Useful* and *The Accursed*

Share. In French, both of these works appear alongside one another in volume 7 of the *Œuvres complètes*. Since both texts were printed together, the editors of the *Œuvres complètes* made the logical decision not to duplicate material in *The Limit of the Useful* that also appeared in *The Accursed Share*. Instead, they encouraged readers to turn back from the former to the latter where relevant. The problem with reproducing this intertextual approach is first that the reader of the present volume may not have *The Accursed Share* at hand, and second, it gives the impression that *The Limit of the Useful* is more fragmented than it actually is. In this translation, therefore, we have restored the shared passages, using the classic English translation of *The Accursed Share* by Robert Hurley. These are presented in square brackets with a footnote citing both the English translation and the relevant French passage in the *Œuvres complètes*.

A related editorial difficulty has stemmed from the fact that Bataille composed several drafts of *The Limit of the Useful*, so the text exists in multiple manuscripts. Following the editors of the *Œuvres complètes*, we have recorded any significant manuscript variations in the footnotes, and an outline of the manuscripts used to establish the text is presented toward the end of this book. This is followed by an extensive "Dossier of Bataille's Notes and Outlines for *The Limit of the Useful*," which again was compiled by the Gallimard editors and provides extensive insight into Bataille's thought process as he developed his manuscript.

The final textual matter to be aware of is the structure of the notes in this edition. These are of three kinds. The first are Bataille's own footnotes that he made while drafting his manuscript. In this edition, these appear in text, at the bottom of the relevant page, so as to preserve something of the experience of reading the manuscript. Second, there are the extensive editorial notes provided by the Gallimard editors. These have been translated and presented as endnotes labeled "Gallimard eds. note." Where mention is made in these notes of other works in the Bataille corpus, we have endeavored to provide references to both the relevant passage in the *Œuvres complètes* and a published English translation. The abbreviation *OC* followed by the relevant volume and page number is used throughout. Third, there are our own notes, in which we provide more detail on our translation choices or try to illuminate something that might otherwise be obscure to English readers. Where possible, we have also tried to track down the references that Bataille makes in his manuscript to other philosophers and thinkers, but this has not always been possible. Where Bataille quotes from other sources, we have tended to provide our own translations of the French text unless a clear and easily accessible English version of the material exists. In general, we have tried as much as possible to keep the many notes, appendices, plans, and manuscript fragments together in the order they are presented in the Gallimard edition.

Alongside editorial issues, translating Bataille's prose has posed issues of its own. Part of the reason for this, of course, is that Bataille took pains to frustrate the logical forms of expression that he associated with discursive reason. All of Bataille's books are performative in this sense, effecting at the level of language and composition the very derangement of the senses that they so often describe. Bataille himself often takes on the performance, such as when he stops the thread of argument in the first chapter in order to momentarily "remain dazzled by the splendor of the heavens," before narrating how his thought manages, as if by some substantial effort, to "[retake] its course." "My task," he continues in this vein, "is to take that part of life, fallen from the sky into me, and enter it into the sequence of earthly considerations. [*Crossed out*: Though I long to lose myself in the night, in the plain light of day my activities are those of a mole. At times my sense of this fall oppresses me.]" The very composition of the work seems to become, from the start, emblematic of the dialectical movement that threads throughout the volume, whereby the cold "sequence of earthly considerations" is made to account for the unintelligible, fulgurating glory of the sun. More often than not, language can only bear witness to its own breakdown in the face of such dazzlement. The impossible task of describing the indescribable defies the best efforts of Bataille himself, and it has frequently proved the same for us in translation. To the greatest extent possible, we have taken care not to smooth out passages in which Bataille clearly intends to frustrate efforts to make sense of that which resists sense as such and thereby to illustrate the feebleness of words in the face of his object of inquiry. Deliberate inconsistencies and conspicuous gaps in logic or syntactic sense are therefore preserved.

For Bataille, existence does not conform to the strictures of rationality; the notion that it does, or should, is the original sin of every idealist and, to borrow the phrasing he uses in "Celestial Bodies," "the crowning achievement of anthropocentrism." A language consummate with the Heraclitean movement of being must itself be mobile, playful, even self-immolating—not only at the level of composition but also at the more granular level of the individual word. By using a single word to designate myriad interweaving and abrading ideas, Bataille textually reproduces the theorem whereby all systems (language included) contain the impetus toward their own excess. Discourse, which labors to render meaning through time, gives over into a lack of any distinct meaning and, finally, into a recognition of the death of meaning itself: immediacy, nonknowledge, inner experience. We have noted, where appropriate, terms that present particularly potent nodes of such self-destructive multiplicity.

On the other side of the coin, however, we are confronted with the more mundane difficulties presented by unfinished drafts, notes, and sketches, which make up the majority of this volume. There are illegible and, on occasion, apparently misspelled words. There are references to passages that are either lost or existed only in the mind of Bataille. Pages are missing, and arguments are at times presented only in the form of bullet points or are otherwise underdeveloped. In the dossier of drafts and notes included at the end of *The Limit of the Useful*, for example, Bataille presents an extensive excursus on his theory of knowledge. In elaborating this theory, he initially seems to place emphasis on the distinction between two different types of knowledge: *savoir* and *connaissance*. In extremely broad strokes, these may, as readers of Foucault might recall, be defined as knowledge in general on the one hand, and specific forms of knowledge on the other. In this vein, Bataille argues that "all knowledge [*savoir*] is the implementation of the sum of forms of knowledge [*connaissances*] accumulated up to now," which is a broadly empiricist claim that one might reasonably expect Bataille to make. However, in subsequent passages, this distinction begins to break down, with Bataille appearing to use the terms more or less interchangeably. In this same section, he additionally notes how his own definition of "objective" knowledge might be misleading, and he muses over whether to change the term to "realist." Throughout this section and others like it, what we see is not so much Bataille performatively demonstrating the insufficiency of discursive reasoning as his struggle to piece his way through the vicissitudes of his own ideas. As his candid note suggests, he may well have changed his mind halfway through writing his notes on knowledge, or the very act of schematizing them may have led him to recognize how deeply complicated his object of inquiry truly was. It is also possible that he simply reached for whatever term was convenient at the time with the intent of smoothing out the draft later. But one could speculate in this direction endlessly. In any case, we have endeavored to retain rather than correct the incomplete and uneven quality of much of this material. At times, however, we have altered overly baroque or unnecessarily recursive formulations in order to retain meaning when a more direct translation might have obscured it.

"Direct" translation is, of course, itself a contradiction in terms. Translation is both an intimate and a violent form of interpretation, no matter how modestly one tries to approach it. It is an attempt to allow a text to present itself while, at the same time, wresting it from itself. One must inevitably acknowledge the impossibility of keeping the act and the product of translation free of one's own biases, idiosyncrasies, and all the various forms of historical residue that are inseparably bound up with producing, or reproducing, a text. We acknowledge this impossibility, while also acknowledging that translating Bataille multiplies this problem *ad absurdum*. For this laughing mystic's ultimate joke hinges on the simultaneous imperative and impossibility of transcribing experience, of rendering legible an intimate encounter with something (or someone) irreducibly other, which by definition defies definition. Like laughter redoubled purely out of the fact of its own absurdity, much of what Bataille wants to explain is, precisely, inexplicable. Following him to the end of his inquiry, we see that the very rupture by which communication establishes itself between two beings—an author and a reader, say—reveals that there is *nothing* to communicate. For the one who takes Bataille to heart or is otherwise infected with his contagion, revelation necessarily terminates in laughter, philosophy in poetry, work in play, and sense in nonsense. We thus may be tempted to follow the later Bataille who (with a laugh no doubt) wondered whether he should have even continued writing a book of which the message, had he followed it to the letter, would have enjoined him to silence. Or we may be more inclined to follow the Bataille of *The Limit of the Useful*, who in the thick of his work says, somewhat more poetically, "I am nothing when placed alongside the book that I write: if it communicates what has set me aflame, I will have given my life to write it." If nothing else we hope that, in the end, this translation manages to communicate what set him, and through him, us, aflame.

THE LIMIT OF THE USEFUL

CHAPTER I
THE GALAXY, THE SUN, AND MAN

The madness of the man aware
at every moment that the earth is spinning.
—Søren Kierkegaard

I. THE CONDITIONS OF HUMAN LIFE ISOLATED FROM THE UNIVERSE

We often say that the facts of science are abstract and meaningless.[1] But such easy platitudes do not hold. I am picturing someone inclined to self-reflection but who will accept nothing not already grounded in science (all the while considering science itself dispassionately, as one should). Science would doubtless seem to him a trap: he would have no qualms about telling intellectuals of his horror that they might turn out to be worthless. But what he learns about the world in books would not seem meaningless to him. He would read the following in the course of his studies.[2]

1. THE GALAXY AND ITS MOVEMENT

At some lost point in unintelligible space, we come and go upon the surface of a transitory globe inhabited by plants and beasts. Our books inform us that this globe moves at a dizzyingly rapid pace: the earth, gravitating around the center of the galaxy, travels a thousand times faster than a bullet.

This globe on which we live cannot be separated from its flight: it depends for its very existence on this movement that gives life to it (as much as on the mass from which it is formed). The sun carries the earth, amidst the swarm of planets, on a journey so vast that, with the sun traveling at a speed of 300,000 meters per second, it takes 250 million years for it to complete its circuit.

But this journey on which we are carried is not just immense and rapid. If the sun and the stars turned stably around a center, this universe in which we live would be nothing more than a swirl of planets (the scale alone would be different); as far as it seems, though, this is not the case: the whirlwind of stars looks like a flower unfurling itself. If, in a realm beyond the limits of the sky, we should come across one of the giant worlds that is organized like ours, it would not have a closed structure like Saturn encircled by rings: it would look like a whirling explosion.

Science tells us that the galaxy* within which the earth whirls is composed of myriad stars. Light (traveling at its rate of three hundred thousand kilometers per second) takes a hundred thousand years to cross it. We would not even know the form of this group of stars in which we commingle

*This name belongs specifically to the whirlwind of stars of which the solar system is a part. The Milky Way is the aspect by which we perceive its unfolding in space.

if we had not discovered other worlds like ours. Situated far beyond our galaxy's most distant stars, these swirls revealed by long-exposure photographs resemble discs with swelling centers. Some of these appear to us in profile and recall Saturn with its rings (the central sphere, however, is flattened, and very small compared to the rest). But viewed head on, their luminous limbs coil out, like the hair of the Medusa, in spirals (hence where they get their names: "spirals" and "spiral nebulae"). Their central core and coils are composed of clusters of multiple stars, as distant from one another as are the stars in our night sky. These nebulae recall the rotating Catherine wheels of our nocturnal festivals; they look like an explosion brought to life by a rapid spinning movement. It may be that this explosion-like appearance is misleading, but according to Eddington*[3] these nebulae would not be stable: the length of time that the "explosion" lasted would correspond to the vastness of its extent: the world would be a whirlwind of exploding matter.

2. THE FUNDAMENTAL ERROR OF THE IMMOBILE GROUND

Without any doubt, these images are a long way from the original science that inspired them. We must recognize, moreover, that their data are unstable and will be modified someday by the perpetual changes of science. The image makes sense, however, if I contrast it with the common idea of the ground as a foundation for real things: the beauty of this idea provokes laughter, given our apparent situation. In the midst of a universe spinning in splendor, our *immobile*

---

*In *The Rotation of the Galaxy* (Oxford, 1930).

world seems deprived. The freedom that men attribute to themselves ebbs away, like the freedom of a vassal under the power of a suzerain. Amidst the heavenly firmament, a puny kingdom has bestowed independence upon itself. The true weight and unreal stasis of the earth have detached themselves from the movement that carries everything else away. As I write, I recognize the truth of this world that bears me, but my weighty existence cannot escape its laws: thus, as of yet, this truth is only something that can be seen from an external perspective. How could I ever drink in the intoxicating universe? I must *look*: and *looking* requires me to be entombed at a point within the world. My human condition ties each and every sensible truth that I recognize around me to the error of a fixed earth, to the illusion of an immutable foundation.

3. THE GIFT OF THE SUN AND THE DIVISION OF THE EARTH'S SURFACE INTO GREEDY PARTICLES

Keeping with this scientific approach, I now come to consider the galaxies with their innumerable stars (or the star systems that are linked by a "movement of the whole"). To their central stars solar systems add the whirl of planets: these planets are also spinning themselves, and sometimes that spinning is doubled by rings or satellites. Each celestial body in the system is animated by its own "intimate movement" that goes beyond the movement that links it to the rest of the group: its own activity particular to the mass that comprises it.

The central star—the sun—shines: the radiation of the sun is the ceaseless projection of a part of its substance into space in the form of heat and light (energy expended in this way comes from an internal destruction of its substance). Like the sun, every star gives itself over to immeasurable loss: by contrast, the radiation of a planet is negligible . . .

Celestial bodies are composed of atoms, but the atom of a radiant body—at least in a star of an elevated temperature—is *under the direct control* of that star's mass and its "intimate movement": there is no isolable state that it could belong to. The atom of the earthly ground, by contrast, is free from this central power: it belongs to powers that are very small and, to a certain extent, autonomous. The surface of the earth is formed of molecules; every molecule is composed of a certain number of atoms; often the molecules themselves coalesce, forming groups of a colloidal or crystalline nature. These colloids can join together to form the autonomous individual that is a living being: this is how plants, animals, and men escape from the general movement of the world; each one becomes a little island, a world unto itself. Moreover, animals can join together. Men assemble into small groups, and the small groups into larger groups, then into states. At the height of these *compositions*, one finds oneself maximally distant from "nature." I could say, in this regard, that the "intimate movement" of the earth runs counter to the movement of a star. The star is radiant, and our soil is cold. The star *lavishes* its power: our soil *divides itself up* into particles that are greedy for power. There is no limit to the greed of these particles. For example //

. . . .

[4][. . .] The "intimate movement" of the earth runs counter to that of the sun. The sun shines, and our soil is cold. The sun

seems to possess the *unity* of fire, the sun madly *lavishes* its power: our soil *divides* into particles *greedy* for power. The greed of these particles knows no bounds: they absorb the energy of the sun and the energy of the earth in its free state. The strongest seize the energy stored up by the weakest. Men harvest whatever power is available to them: they absorb, use, and accumulate resources of all kinds—solar, mineral, animal, vegetable. In the end, the strongest seize the labor of the weakest.

II. THE UNIVERSE ENCOUNTERED BY PRIMITIVE MAN

1. PRIMITIVE CONSCIOUSNESS

Without science, I could not have said what I just said; science has given me the authority to discourse at length.[5] The rest of this book develops from these premises: it demonstrates that in human life there exists both an economic greed (inherent to the divided elements of the earth) and a nostalgia for a glory that has only ever really belonged to the heavens. In truth, each path leads to much the same thing. But the fact that the path of science, skirting dogma through the detour I have chosen, should lead to a spiritual revelation is, of course, not without consequence for man.

In principle, it is religion, the ever-present authority of religion, that sets the terms of the debate. This authority traces itself back to a primitive belief that still lingers even in the most civilized of men. A rigorous separation is normally the rule in this regard: in the same person, the civilized part shuns the primitive part; this lack of knowledge on the part of science makes man a stranger to himself. In contrast to this, I have tried to show the alignment between primitive beliefs and established data. At a certain point in the course of its development, science rediscovers the primitive without contradicting it; this is the price man pays if he is not to turn his back upon himself.

In the common and uncultivated consciousness, the sun is the symbol of glory. The sun shines: glory is represented as luminous and shining like the sun. For primitive man, light symbolizes divinity. Its splendor and brilliance are not useful, but they endow it with a sense of freedom. Even if we consider life today, if we recall the services we perform, if we make accounts of usefulness, we are still ultimately enraptured by those *things that shine*. The measliest bourgeois dreams of equaling the sun (though he never says as much).

Although we have not known about them until now, nebulae are greater than the sun in terms of magnificence. The clichés that we use to talk about them make them seem like huge spiders made of light: but they open themselves up, lose themselves—whereas the spider crouches to cling on in the darkness (the depths of space hold untold layers of irony with regard to our dusty expectations). The gentleness of the starry night and the shredded grandeur of nebulae both have the purifying beauty of a sacrifice. I have been fooled by the diffuse vastness of the Milky Way, the sleepy stillness that it seems to drape across the vault of heaven. I perceive it as a louse perceives a head of hair: without understanding its full extent or purpose. If I could get far away, leave the earth, and stand in outer space, following the course of the Milky Way from its central axle as it turned like the rim of a wheel, I would see it *in all its glory*, unfurling its monstrous arms of light in immense coils: for us, the Milky Way is nothing but the representation of the galactic nebulae, analogous to all those that we now know stretch out across unfathomable distances with their measureless limbs.

2. HUMANITY'S BELIEF IN A FALL

For an instant I remain dazzled by the splendor of the heavens: but my thoughts immediately retake their course.[6] Even in writing sentences, in carrying out my work, I am quickly transported back into the realm of ordinary labor. My task is to take that part of life, fallen from the sky into me, and enter it into the sequence of earthly considerations. [*Crossed out*: Though I long to lose myself in the night, in the plain light of day my activities are those of a mole. At times my sense of this fall oppresses me.

It is a cliché to say of man that he is a "fallen god who recalls the heavens": this, nonetheless, is the least outlandish of all descriptions.] My life takes place at the heart of an immense universe. I experience this with a feeling of anguished grandeur; but scarcely have I felt my grandeur than a sense of comic absurdity knocks me back down to size. Nothing seems further from the clear divinity of night than this world that is measured in labor, where those who don't labor are left cold and hungry. The myriad stars in the sky toil not; they are not subjected to any *employment*: but the earth demands a pound of each man's flesh; it forces him to exhaust himself in labors that never end.

The belief in a fall is common to all ages and expresses itself almost everywhere in myths of disillusionment. Genesis bitterly translated this belief, informing us that the ground was cursed in the wake of our sin. God raged at his creation, declaring: "In the sweat of thy brow shalt thou eat bread, till thou return unto the ground, for out of it wast thou taken."[7] The wretchedness of man is more degrading than cruel: what could be more *humiliating* than a weary greed, fixated on insignificant things, spoken in words sometimes bitter, sometimes ironic, but always dull? Our perfidious existence recalls the feudal lords who slowly detached themselves from their weak suzerains. Yet our ignorance of the earth and the starlit sky of which we are a part extends far deeper than that. The vassal gives up control of his affairs: man in principle knows nothing of the universe that carries him along (just as a louse knows nothing of the movements of the child's tangled hair that it infests).

[*Crossed out*: Personally, I myself remember, I know I am a passenger and am shocked that no one else cares, but fundamentally this does not change how things are.

The misunderstanding grows if the principle of *utility* prevails over others.

The greed of the "great, nameless multitudes" is less arbitrary than the greed of earlier men. It has no knowledge of the compensations afforded to the "small, nameless few," compensations that great lords or kings previously offered in a small way. The multitude adopt a utilitarian morality for themselves. Even with respect to the most widely held values, they persist in asking the ultimate question: "What use does it serve?" They are satisfied with vague responses, but peace cannot hold without introducing a few confusions: between technology and disinterested culture, between pleasure and necessary rest. Anything without a use is held to be base, devoid of value: yet whatever serves a use is nothing but a means to an end. Utility is linked to acquisition, to the piling up of products or the means of production: it is opposed to nonproductive expenditure. Insofar as man adopts a utilitarian morality, we can say that the heavens close in around him: he understands nothing of poetry or glory; the sun in his eyes is nothing but a source of calories.[8]]

3. GLORY REGAINED IN THE GIFT OF THE SELF

The fall of modern man is different from that in the Bible. Modern man's fall does not have the character of anguish; indeed, it is the expression of reason. In a manner completely contrary to this, the fall of primitive man came from outside, as if it fell from heaven; it was less a state of being than a refusal to succumb to that state. Primitive man was not a stranger in the universe. He looked on all the troubles he faced as a spectacle, a festival to which he had been invited. He perceived their glory and felt compelled to respond by covering himself in glory as well. The sacrifices of ancient Mexico, which put this into the cruelest possible relief . . . //

....

[9]// black hat: when in front of the statue of a god, the remains of a fearful age, the petit bourgeois will cover the divine head with his hat. The more primitive men of the past, whom wise men sneer at nowadays, did not conduct themselves like we do, as strangers in the universe. They felt a sense of anguish in the face of its unfathomable nature, but they viewed its spectacles as a festival to which they were invited. For them, the fall was less a state of being than a refusal to succumb to that state. Because not only did they know how to recognize the glory of the universe, but they felt that the

best way they could recognize it was to conduct themselves gloriously. People nowadays give much more to glory than they would believe, but they misunderstand more than they understand about those gifts. The peoples of ancient Mexico used to unite man with the glory of the universe: the sun was the fruit of a sacrificial frenzy—by dying in a brazier, a god in human form gave birth to the splendor of day. In this way, the Aztec people saw what "civilized people" might see but in fact see only rarely: the unity of sacrifice and light, the equivalence between intoxicating gifts of the self and glories no less intoxicating.

The Franciscan friar Bernardino de Sahagún,[10] whose notes date from the middle of the sixteenth century, reported what the early Mexicans told him as follows:

> It is said that before day existed, the gods met in a place called *Teotihuacan* . . . and that they said to one another: "Whose task will it be to illuminate the world?" To which a god named Tecuciztecatl responded: "I am the one who will illuminate it." The gods // [11][then spoke again and said: "Who else among you?" They looked at one another then, wondering who this would be, and none dared accept the charge; all were afraid and made excuses. One of the gods who usually went unnoticed did not say anything but only listened to what the other gods were saying. The others spoke to him, saying, "Let it be you, *bubosito*." And he gladly accepted, replying: "I receive your order gratefully; so be it." And the two that were chosen began immediately to do penance, which lasted four days. Then a fire was

lit in a hearth made in a rock. . . . The god named Tecuciztecatl only offered costly things. Instead of branches he offered rich feathers called *quetzalli*; instead of grass balls he offered gold ones; instead of maguey spines he offered spines made with precious stones; and instead of bloodied spines he offered spines of red coral. And the copal he offered was of a very high quality. The *buboso,* whose name was Nanauatzin, offered nine green water rushes bound in threes, instead of ordinary branches. He offered balls of grass and maguey spines bloodied with his own blood, and instead of copal he offered the scabs of his *bubos.* A tower was made for each of these two gods, in the form of a hill. On these hills they did penance for four nights. . . . After the four nights of penance were completed, the branches and all the other objects they had used were thrown down there. The following night, a little before midnight, when they were to do their office, Tecuciztecatl was given his adornments. These consisted of a headdress of *aztacomitl* feathers and a sleeveless jacket. As for Nanauatzin, the *buboso,* they tied a paper headdress, called *amatzontli,* on his hair and gave him a paper stole and a paper rag for pants to wear. When midnight had come, all the gods gathered round the hearth, which was called *teotexcalli,* where the fire had burned for four days.

They separated into two lines on the two sides of the fire. The two chosen ones took their places near the hearth, with their faces to the fire, in the middle of the two lines of gods. The latter were all standing

> and they spoke to Tecuciztecatl, saying: "Go on, Tecuciztecatl. Cast yourself into the fire!" Hearing this, he started to throw himself into the flames, but the fire was burning high and very hot, and he stopped in fear and drew back. A second time he gathered his strength and turned to throw himself into the fire, but when he got near he stopped and did not dare go further; four times he tried, but could not. Now, it had been ordered that no one could try more than four times, so when the four attempts had been made the gods addressed Nanauatzin, saying: "Go on, Nanauatzin. It is your turn to try!" As soon as these words were said, he shut his eyes and, taking courage, went forward and threw himself into the fire. He began at once to crackle and sizzle like something being roasted. Seeing that he had thrown himself into the fire and was burning, Tecuciztecatl also cast himself into the flames and burned. It is said that an eagle went into the fire at the same time and burned, and this is why the eagle has scorched-looking and blackened feathers. An ocelot followed thereafter but did not burn, only being singed, and this is why the ocelot remains spotted black and white. (Bernardino de Sahagún, *Histoire des choses de la Nouvelle Espagne*, trans. Jourdanet and Siméon, 1880, book VII, ch. 2)

A short while later, having fallen on their knees, the gods saw Nanauatzin, "who had become the sun," rising in the East. "He looked very red, appearing to sway from side to side, and none of them could keep their eyes on him, because he blinded them with his light. He shone brightly with his rays that reached in all directions." The moon in turn rose up over the horizon. Because he had hesitated, Tecuciztecatl shone less brightly. Then the gods had to die; the wind, Quetzalcoatl, killed them all: The wind tore out their hearts and used them to animate the newborn stars.]

[12]// Then the moon also rose above the horizon: Tecuciztecatl hesitation had dampened its splendor. All the gods, rebellious or not, then had to die: the wind killed them all, so that their sacrifice might stir the newborn stars *into movement*. Others will say that these tales bear witness to a belief in the magical value of actions and mistake the laws of the universe for those of human life. However, magical acts aim at the glory of the sun, which cannot be entirely enclosed within the sphere of utility; the analogy between a sacrificial immolation and solar radiance is the response of a man to the manifest splendor of the universe. Men whose greediness prevents them from partaking in the intoxication of worlds nonetheless regain access to this intoxication through sacrifice. I have chosen the myth of Nanauatzin, whose sacrifice is similar to so many other cosmogonic rituals. It transforms the solar hearth into a glory that human life aspires to but that it only reaches in death: Nanauatzin, the little syphilitic god (the *buboso*), escapes the greed of the earth by giving himself to the flames; he jumps in a brazier, he is no less prodigal than the sun.

MEXICAN HUMAN SACRIFICES

This Aztec tale encapsulates this entire book. The "solar star" is at its center; like a mirror, "sacrificial death" reflects the intensity of its radiance; the "anguish" of Tecuciztecatl attests to the heavy sense we have of our mortality. But it is not just this tale that encapsulates my argument; rather, it is the whole Aztec empire. If a certain heaviness in our lives separates us from the universe, could it not for all that be introduced to a light movement that would release it from this great weight? In my eyes, this movement is what stirs us when we are thirsty for glory. The very excesses of glory and sacrifice that Mexico produced are more enlightening for us than the less gruesome approaches taken by others. A will to glory exists in we who wish we lived like suns, *lavishing our gifts and our life*.

The death of the *buboso* was connected to the bloody sacrifices of Mexico. Each year, the four days of fasting observed by the gods were, in a sense, observed by the Aztecs in honor of the sun: during these times of fasting, leprous captives, whose sickly skin resembled the *buboso*, would be sacrificed. There are no massacres more terrible than these; none have been recorded in greater detail than those carried out in Mexican temples.

....

[13]// the god that a victim embodied would be placed under the obsidian knife of the priest. They would tear out the heart with one violent blow so they could lift it toward the sun before it stopped beating. Most victims were prisoners, whence came the idea that war was necessary to revitalize the sun, that if there was no more war, the sun would burn out.

The most moving of these sacrifices was the one in which a flawlessly beautiful young man was "resurrected around Easter."[14][He was chosen from among the captives the previous year, and from that moment he lived like a great lord. "He went through the whole town very well dressed, with flowers in his hand and accompanied by certain personalities. He would bow graciously to all whom he met, and they all knew he was the image of Tezcatlipoca (one of the greatest gods) and prostrated themselves before him, worshipping him wherever they met him" (Sahagún, book II, ch. 5). Sometimes he could be seen in the temple on top of the pyramid of Quauchxicalco: "Up there he would play the flute at night or in the daytime, whichever time he wished to do it. After playing the flute, he too would turn incense toward the four parts of the world, and then return home, to his room" (appendix of book II). Every care was taken to ensure the elegance and princely distinction of his life. "If, due to the good treatment he grew stout, they would make him drink salt-water to keep slender" (book II, ch. 24). "Twenty days previous to the festival they gave this youth four maidens, well prepared and educated for this purpose. During those twenty days he had carnal intercourse with these maidens. The four girls they gave him as wives and who had been reared with special care for that purpose were given names of four goddesses. . . . Five days before he was to die they gave festivities for him, banquets held in cool and gay places, and many chieftains and prominent people accompanied him. On the day of the festival when he was to die they took him to an oratory, which they called Tlacuchcalco. Before reaching it, at a place called Tlapituoaian, the women stepped aside and left him. As he got to the place where he was to be killed, he mounted the steps by himself and on each one of these he broke one of the flutes which he had played during the year" (book II, ch. 5). "He was awaited at the top by the satraps or priests who were to kill him, and these now grabbed him and threw him onto the stone block, and, holding him by feet, hands and head, thrown on his back, the priest who had the stone knife buried it with a mighty thrust in the victim's breast and, after drawing it out, thrust one hand into the opening and tore out the heart, which he at once offered to the sun" (book II, ch. 24).

Respect was shown for the young man's body: It was carried down slowly to the temple courtyard. Ordinary victims were thrown down the steps to the bottom. The greatest violence was habitual. The dead person was flayed and the priest then clothed himself in this bloody skin. Men were thrown into a furnace and pulled out with a hook to be placed on the executioner's block still alive. More often than not the flesh consecrated by the immolation was eaten. The festivals followed one another without interruption and every year the divine service called for countless sacrifices: Twenty thousand is given as the number. One of the victims incarnating a god, he climbed to the sacrifice surrounded, like a god, by an attendance that would accompany him in death.

INTIMACY OF EXECUTIONERS AND VICTIMS

The Aztecs observed a singular conduct with those who were about to die. They treated these prisoners humanely, giving the food and drink they asked for. Concerning a warrior who brought back a captive, then offered him in sacrifice, it was said that he had "considered his capitve as his own flesh and blood, calling him son, while the latter called him father" (Sahagún, book II, ch. 21). The victims would dance and sing with those who brought them to die. Efforts were often made to relieve their anguish. A woman incarnating the "mother of the gods" was consoled by the healers and midwives who said to her: Don't be sad, fair friend; you will spend this night with the king, so you can rejoice." It was not made clear to her that she was to be killled, because death needed to be sudden and unexpected in her case. Ordinarily the condemned prisoners were well aware of their fate and were forced to stay up the final night, singing and dancing. Sometimes they were made to drink until drunk or, to drive away the idea of impending death, they were given a concubine.

This difficult wait for death was borne better by some victims than by others. Concerning the slaves who were to die during one of the November festivals, we are told that "they went to the homes of their masters to bid them goodbye. . . . They were singing in a very loud voice, so loud that it seemed to split their breast, and upon reaching the house of their masters they dipped both hands in the bowls of paint or of ink and put them on the lintels of the doors and the posts of the houses, leaving their imprint in colors; the same they did in the houses of their relatives. Some of them who were lion-hearted would eat as usual, others could not eat thinking of the death they soon would have to suffer" (book II, ch. 34). A slave who represented the goddess Illamatecutli was dressed entirely in white. "Previous to being killed, this woman had to dance, and the old men played the tune for this dance, and the singers sang the songs; and while she danced she cried, sighed and worried, knowing that her death was so close at hand" (book II, ch. 36).] In autumn, women were sacrificed in a temple named Coatlan. "When the unfortunate women ascended the steps, some sang, some cried out, and some shed tears" (book II, ch. 33).

4. WARS AND THE DEATH OF WARRIORS

What is most remarkable about these rites is that they are a comedy of the "gift of the self." While gods in myths might have offered themselves up, it was not the same for the victims who incarnated them: a prisoner cannot give himself up; he would have to be free to give such a gift. However, the sacrifices of captives cannot be separated from the conditions that made them possible: wars and the risk of certain death. The Mexicans would not shed blood except on the condition that they were risking death.

[15][They were conscious of this enchantment of war and sacrifice. The midwife would cut the umbilical cord of the newborn baby boy and say to him:

> I cut your navel in the middle of your body. Know and understand that the house in which you are born is not your dwelling. . . . It is your cradle, the place where you lay your head. . . . Your true land is elsewhere; you are promised for other places. You belong to the countryside where battles are fought; you were sent to go there; your function and your skill is warfare; your duty is to give the sun the blood of your enemies to drink and to supply the earth with the bodies of your enemies to eat. As for your native land, your legacy, and your happiness, you will find them in the house of the sun in the sky. . . . You will be fortunate to be found worthy of dying on the

battlefield, decorated with flowers. What I now cut from the middle of your stomach rightly belongs to Tlatecutli who is the earth and the sun. When war begins to seethe and the soldiers assemble, we shall put it in the hands of those who are valorous soldiers, so that they might give it to your father and mother, the earth and the sun. They will bury it in the middle of the field where the battles are fought: this will be the proof that you are offered and promised to the earth and the sun; this will be the sign that you profess this office of warfare, and your name will be written in the field of battle so that your name and your person will not be forgotten. This precious offering collected from your body is like the offering of a maguey spine, of reeds for smoking and *axocoyatl* branches. Through it your vow and sacrifice are confirmed. . . . (Sahagún, book VI, ch. 31)]

Wars and holocausts were bound together by a rigorous series of customs, authentic gifts of the self, and ritualistic parodies. As it was the last act in a drama set "in open country," one could have said that the soldier was not able to avoid the harmful effects of sacrifice. The individual who brought back a prisoner played just as much of a part in the sacred game as the priest. [16][A first bowl of the victim's blood, drained from the wound, was offered to the sun by the priests. A second bowl was collected by the sacrificer. The latter would go before the images of the gods and wet their lips with the warm blood. The body of the sacrificed was his by right; he would carry it home, setting aside the head, and the rest would be eaten at a banquet, cooked without salt or spices—but eaten by the invited guests, not by the sacrificer, who regarded his victim as a son, as a second self. At the dance that ended the feast, the warrior would hold the victim's head in his hand.

If the warrior had himself been overcome instead of returning a victor, his death on the field of battle would have had the same meaning as the ritual sacrifice of his prisoner: it would also have satisfied the hungry gods.

This was said in the prayer to Tezcatlipoca for the soldiers: "In truth, you are not wrong to want them to die in battle, for you did not send them into this world for any other purpose than to serve as food for the sun and the earth, with their blood and their flesh" (Sahagún, book VI, ch. 3).

Satiated with blood and flesh, the sun gave glory to the soul in his palace. There the war dead mingled with the immolated prisoners. The meaning of death in combat was brought out in the same prayer: "Make them bold and courageous; remove all weakness from their hearts so that they may not only receive death joyfully, but desire it and find charm and sweetness therein; so that they do not fear arrows or swords but rather consider them a pleasant thing, as if they were flowers and exquisite dishes of food" (Sahagún, book VII, ch. 20).][17]

CHAPTER II
UNPRODUCTIVE EXPENDITURE

I. GLORIOUS ACTS IN THE AZTEC ECONOMY

The Mexicans' abuse of death brings us to the brink of an abyss. It is an abyss that we doubtless never cease to approach, attracted by fear, but for now I want to turn away from it and focus only on *glory*, the one true goal of the Mexican people.

The Mexicans did not sink into the abyss they opened up. One might say that when Cortés arrived, Mexico let itself slip away, but that was just one day. Until the end, Mexico was drunk with glory. Not as we are nowadays: there, true tragedy and the feeling of irony were more completely mixed. For a Mexican, glory was not relegated to a sphere separate from daily life, as it is for us. It wasn't something tawdry or superficial. Many of us see superfluity in glory, even futility. A Mexican lived with glory as simply as one lives with legs (and paid just as little mind to it). They didn't discuss it; hence their deep sense of irony regarding human life (and even regarding the gods). Glory was the measure of all things: it ruled over every other possibility and gathered every other movement within itself. The tumult of festivals, like that of wars, held tangible power,[1] analogous to that of a beating heart. Man and all his actions—even his most humble—were measured at the scale of the universe. It was this concordance that drove the work in the fields and made it fruitful. Dances and sacrifices expressed the same meaning as harvests.

The Aztecs were wrong when, like other primitive peoples [*peuples naïfs*], they accorded a power similar to agricultural labor to their religious rites; nonetheless their lives, their harvests were basically aligned with the splendors of the heavens. There is nothing more logical than to assign splendid ends to economic activity: the reign of pure necessity is more profoundly hostile to life than horror is (man in particular is more degraded—and no less cruel—if he is motivated by wretched necessity rather than giving in to his passion for excess). Sacrifices welded the link between man and the universe. A belief that the rites would achieve something lay at their root, but to make sense of them it is necessary to invert their meaning: *the Mexican people could not make nature submit to them; rather, they lived in unison with nature*.

1. THE GENEROSITY OF THE SOVEREIGN

In their festivals and their wars, the Aztecs paired themselves with the universe, in a certain sense; they connected the turmoil of peoples with the heavens and the earth.

That turmoil gave life a rhythm to which agriculture and commerce must have contributed. The goal of economic activity was not merely to prolong an arduous life but to give everything in the service of glory. The figure of the sovereign embodied the glory of the community. The sovereign is always the image of the people: the masses he unites expect him to faithfully express their communal will. The will of all the people was that he express prodigality. //

....

[2][. . .] The will of the people was that he express prodigality. Sahagún writes:

> [3][The kings looked for opportunities to show their generosity and to achieve a reputation in that regard. This is why they would contribute large sums of money for war or for the *areitos* (dances preceding or following sacrifices). They would pledge very precious things in the games and, when one of the commoners, man or woman, ventured to greet them and speak a few words that pleased them, they would give food and drink, along with fabrics for wearing and sleeping. If someone else composed songs that were agreeable to them, they would give gifts that were in keeping with his merit and with the pleasure he had caused them. (Book VIII, ch. 29)]

....

The sovereign possessed great riches that it was his duty to expend *ad majorem gloriam populi sui*[4] in the service of *art*, *festivals*, and *wars*. He was obliged to spend them lavishly—and even lose them in *games*.[5]

People of all times and places have demanded generosity from their rulers. That is the key to all social activity, which would be meaningless otherwise. Reason wrongly sees this activity as conforming to the principles on which it is founded. Economic theories account for all changes in terms of the laws of conservation or equivalence. The operations that respond precisely to these laws are already rather obscure; they pose quite significant difficulties themselves. Why leave to one side, moreover, the movements of wealth that respond to the innate needs of the masses, which are expressed through the function of the royal body?

As a rule, rational thought views these movements in the light of the odious wreckage often left in their wake: it rightly denounces such abuses, but it forgets the old uses that people once ascribed to them. In this way, the true meaning of wealth escapes our understanding: we are tricked by the need to rationalize, that is, to give an account of everything.[6]

2. THE GIFT AS A FORM OF EXCHANGE

In ancient Mexico, generosity was one of the attributes of the sovereign, the "chief of men." But the sovereign was only the richest of all those who were expected to satisfy the expectations of the community. Nobles, merchants, and wealthy men were held similarly responsible, each according to their ability [*force*]. During festivals, all the riches that powerful [*puissant*] men had been able to amass had to be wasted. Warriors and "dealers" procured the victims (whose lot it was to be offered to the gods) either by capturing them in war or purchasing them. Temples had to be constructed, the number of valuable offerings had to be increased, priests and victims had to be finely decked out, and the price of the ritual festivities had to be paid. Some festivals linked to public worship were put on personally by the rich, particularly merchants.

[7][The Spanish chroniclers left precise information concerning the "merchants" of Mexico and the customs they followed, customs that must have astonished the Spaniards. These "merchants" led expeditions to unsafe territories. They often had to fight, and they often prepared the way for war, which explains the honor that attached to their profession. But the risk they assumed could not have been enough to make them the equals of the nobles. In the eyes of the Spaniards, business was demeaning, even if it led to adventure. The judgment of the Europeans derived from the principle of commerce based solely on interest. But the great rule of the "merchants" of Mexico did not exactly follow the rule of profit; their trading was conducted without bargaining and it maintained the glorious character of the trader. The Aztec "merchant" did not sell; he practiced the *gift-exchange*: he received riches as a *gift* from the "chief of men" (from the sovereign, whom the Spanish called the *king*); *he made a present* of these riches to the lords of the lands he visited. "In receiving these gifts, the great lords of that province hastened to give other presents in return . . . so that they might be offered to the king . . ." The sovereign gave cloaks, petticoats, and precious blouses. The "merchant" received as a gift for himself richly colored feathers of various shapes, cut stones of all sorts, shells, fans, shell paddles for stirring cocoa, wild-animal skin worked and ornamented with designs (Sahagún, book IX, ch. 5). As for the objects the "merchants" brought back from their travels, they did not consider them to be mere commodities. On their return, they did not have them carried into their house in the daylight. "They waited for nightfall and a favorable time. One of the days called *ce calli* (a house) was

regarded as propitious because they held that the objects of which they were the bearers, entering the house on that day, would enter as sacred things and, as such, would persevere there" (Sahagún, book IX, ch. 6).][8]

3. THE SUMPTUOUS EXPENDITURES OF MERCHANTS

In these practices, an object of exchange was not "debased" but retained a link with the world of glory. The *gift* one made of it was a sign of glory. The act of giving it was proof of one's wealth and good fortune. [9][The "merchant" was the man-who-gives, so much so that his first concern on returning from an expedition was with offering a banquet to which he invited his confreres, who went home laden with presents.

This was merely a feast celebrating return. But if "some merchant became rich and accounted himself rich, he would give a festival or a banquet for all the high-class merchants and for the lords, because it would have been considered base to die without having made some splendid expenditure that might add luster to his person by displaying the favor of the gods who had given him everything . . ." (Sahagún, book IX, ch. 10). The festival began with the ingestion of an intoxicant giving visions which the guests would describe to each other once the narcosis had dissipated. For two days the master of the house would distribute food, drinks, reeds for smoking and flowers.

More rarely, a "merchant" would give a banquet during a festival called *panquetzaliztli*. This was a type of sacred and ruinous ceremony. The "merchant" who celebrated it sacrificed slaves for the occasion. He had to invite people from all around and assemble presents worth a fortune, including cloaks "numbering eight hundred thousand," waistbands "of which there were gathered four hundred of the richest and a great many others of ordinary quality" (Sahagún, book IX, ch. 7). The most substantial gifts went to the captains and dignitaries; the men of lesser rank received less. The people danced countless *areitos*, into which entered splendidly dressed slaves, wearing necklaces, flower garlands, and rondaches decorated with flowers. They danced, taking turns smoking and smelling their fragrant reeds. Then they were placed on a platform, "so that the guests might see them better, and they were handed plates of food and drinks and attended to very graciously." When the time came for the sacrifice, the "merchant" who gave the festival dressed up like one of the slaves in order to go with them to the temple where the priests were waiting. These victims, armed for combat, had to defend themselves against the warriors who attacked them as they passed by. If one of the aggressors captured a slave, the "merchant" had to pay him the price of the slave.] The sovereign himself attended the solemn sacrifice, which was followed by the communal consumption[10] of flesh in the merchant's home.

These practices, "the gift exchange," in particular, are very far from our own; their precise meaning will only //

....

[11]// become clear if we compare them to the potlatch of the American northwest (if such a comparison did nothing to clarify them, we would only see them as misleading parts of a trivial reality). I will demonstrate below that a current of *glorious acts*[12] naturally animates the economy; the bourgeois economy is the only one that escapes from this.

This society of "men of profit" is the first one to have opposed itself to *glorious acts*. The bourgeoisie scoffs at *glory* when contrasted with *utility*. There are some glorious acts that serve material interests: the bourgeoisie tolerates these, even praising them while treating them with contempt. Nevertheless, the innermost desire of our blind bourgeoisie is to make us animal //

[13]I will demonstrate below how the economy is carried along by glorious acts. One could see this as a weakness. But while the greedy practices of large-scale industry and business escape this weakness, they are all the more hostile to man as a result. The bourgeois world disdains glorious acts and views them as inferior to useful ones. It does not permit glorious acts unless they are useful. In truth, the bourgeois makes man a servile and mechanical animal.

What I said about the "glorious acts" of Mexican merchants leads us to refute the utilitarian principles on which inhumane bourgeois civilization rests. Through an analysis of facts that have been little known before now, I will offer a new perspective on the history of economics. It will be easy for me to demonstrate that "useful acts" are valueless *in themselves*; it is only our "glorious acts" that determine *human* life and give it a price.

....

In the world where I write, awareness of the decline of bourgeois values is still uncertain. But the idea that these values have prompted tangible developments and have had an overwhelming impact is never questioned. A kind of juvenile hatred is expressed haphazardly, and asserts itself in an awkward way. The bourgeois economy has been put on trial from a number of different perspectives, but the attacks are always based on the unjust exploitation of labor. We never set much store by the fact that it destroyed the decadent institutions of the *ancien régime* without ever replacing them. My focus on Mexico and its customs introduces a new idea: one day every man must see that *useful acts* do not possess any *value* in themselves, that only *glorious acts* bring *light* into life, that they are the only acts that can *give it a price*. The bourgeoisie were forced to lower that price to grow their business. //

[II. THE PRINCIPLE OF EXPENDITURE OR NECESSARY LOSS][14]

....

[1. PRODUCTION FOR PRODUCTION'S SAKE]

....

PRODUCTION FOR PRODUCTION'S SAKE

Rational thought has the tendency to reduce human activity to the production and retention of goods. It recognizes that the goal of human life is to grow—which is to say, to grow and retain wealth. But it holds that consumption has a function equivalent to that of a carburetor in an engine: it views it as nothing more than a necessary element of production.

The remark of a Russian worker expresses these ideas with more ingenuity than is typical (and with less caution than is found in treatises penned by bourgeois professors): //[15]

....

[2. GLORIOUS EXPENDITURES]

[3. GLORY, THE "END" OF HUMAN ACTIVITY]

// that *the "end" of acquisition is the wasted share that it makes possible*. It would be pointless to linger over utilitarian explanations of loss. It is true that loss has the feeling of life, that it is often fertile when the closed systems of enrichment dry up. But this fertility that losses produce is not their "end." Such fertility is itself justified—it must find its "end"—in the new losses that it makes possible. The life of men is like the shining of stars: in truth, this shining is life's only end; *its glory* is life's final meaning.

III. ECONOMIC ACTIVITY IN GLORIOUS SOCIETIES

1. POTLATCH, THE ECONOMY OF VAIN GLORY

The subordination of production to expenditure emerges clearly from the ancient forms of exchange. Classical economics imagined primitive exchange as a form of barter. Why would it have ever believed that a form of acquisition, such as exchange, might originally have responded not to the need to acquire but to its opposite, the need to lose or shatter? This idea has only recently been dismantled.

I have shown how Mexican merchants engaged in gracious gift-giving. But such practices (even their custom of feasting) are not the most significant things. They must simply be related to them. The Native peoples of the northwest coast of America engage in a paradoxical system of exchanges that is still in use today: ethnographers call this system potlatch. They have found more or less clear traces of it in all societies.

Among the Tlingit, [16][the Haida, the Tsimshian, the Kwakiutl, potlatch is of prime importance in social life. The least advanced of these small tribes give potlatches in ceremonies marking a person's change of condition, at the time of initiations, marriages, funerals. In the more civilized tribes a potlatch is still given in the course of a festival. One can choose a festival in which to give it, but it can itself be the occasion of a festival.

Potlatch is, like commerce, a means of circulating wealth, but it excludes bargaining. More often than not it is the solemn giving of considerable riches, offered by a chief to his rival for the purpose of humiliating, challenging and obligating him. The recipient has to erase the humiliation and take up the challenge; he must satisfy the *obligation* that was contracted by accepting. He can only reply, a short time later, by means of a new potlatch, more generous than the first: he must pay back with interest.

Gift-giving is not the only form of potlatch: a rival is challenged by a solemn destruction of riches. In principle, the destruction is offered to the mythical ancestors of the donee; it is little different from a sacrifice. As recently as the nineteenth century a Tlingit chieftain would sometimes go before a rival and cut the throats of slaves in his presence. At the proper time, the destruction was repaid by the killing of a large number of slaves. The Chukchee of the Siberian Northeast have related institutions. They slaughter highly valuable dog teams, for it is necessary for them to startle, to stifle the rival group. The Indians of the Northwest Coast would set fire to their villages or break their canoes to pieces. They have emblazoned copper bars possessing a fictive value (depending on how famous or how old the coppers are): sometimes these bars are worth a fortune. They throw them into the sea or shatter them.]

It has been said on the subject of potlatch that the origin of exchange was not barter but lending at interest. To charge a surplus on something when it is returned is to yield interest, to practice usury. Wealth, in lands where potlatch occurs, is increased in a way that recalls credit inflation (all the wealth that all the lenders possess by dint of their contractual obligations with the borrowers could never be cashed in at once). However, this is merely a secondary consequence.

The meaning of potlatch is the glorious effect created by losses—from these losses come nobility, honor, and one's rank in the hierarchy. Glory is accorded to the one who gives the most. The gain that follows can, in the long run, be calculated as a kind of greed: [17][but this concern was not considered—or was at least put off—when the appeal of the custom was determined. Even today, the ideal would be potlatch given in such a way that it could not be returned. There are some ritual destructions to which there can be no response.]

2. THE FESTIVAL ECONOMY[18]

[They say that good fortune shelters man from need. But if wealth in every age catered for troubles in hard times, then insofar as it was, at one time, a means of amassing power, that power was *the power to lose*. In the past, it was popularly thought that wealth was something possessed by glorious beings, linked to the existence of sovereigns, *to loftiness, to being at the mercy of the overwhelming need for loss*.

In non-industrial civilizations, it is the task of the rich to cover the cost of festivals. The most powerful [*puissant*] person sets his wealth aside in preparation for a sudden squandering: the labor of the people creates wealth, and the wealthy accumulate it: the entire community spends it in an instant, gloriously, without satisfying any need other than excess.]

Potlatch is the youthful stage of wealth. In many societies, there are now only vague shadows of glory's implications and the rivalry it represented. Traces of the institution are evident in other places. Our customs like funerary rites and marriages, debts of gratitude, and private festivals in which vast fortunes try to outdo each other—these practices ensure that we continue to squander euphorically and hostilely, even despite our greed. Such outpourings come as naturally to man as a rooster's cry comes into its throat: [in contrast to a commercial transaction, a potlatch reveals the very image of the human heart, in all its turmoil and generosity, if also in its aggressiveness.]

Potlatch is nevertheless but an individual manifestation of movements that belong to common life. Leaving aside reactions for which there are personal motivations, in general the custom *obliged* the wealthy to *donate* the riches necessary for the festivals. Thus, rich Romans had to pay for the cost of spectacles and games. This cost was not the same as a tax: it was essentially one of the *glorious acts* to which their rank obliged them; it was linked to the possession of land.

The meaning of this morality in which honor obliges one is that of festivals. The word *wealth* has retained something of this glorious meaning. Though the acts are not appealing in their entirety, [gold, on the other hand, by its very nature, associates wealth with brilliance. But brilliance itself cannot exist solely to satisfy greed. Even if the possessor enjoys the gold for himself, its brilliance must shine for the masses. The festivals staged and celebrated by Caesar gave his power meaning: the radiant happiness of the emperor whipped the crowd to fervor.

Wealth's natural brilliance is diminished by the shortcomings of private festivals. Festivals that are hidden, held behind closed doors, are a means of turning away]; the people are powerless before them. When the excesses of pleasure are enjoyed in solitude, the humble are led to curse wealth. That curse can be so harmful as to impact splendor itself and destroy it. Although they used to be accessible to the poor masses (indeed, they would upset the social order, with the slave becoming the master, the master serving the slave), festivals would still bear the sense of wealth.[19] In the long run, however, they were subverted, and their brilliance became detestable. The poor groaned at having been attracted by wastefulness and circus games. Rightly so, since the rich make an *undoubted* mockery of them by perverting the splendor they possess for their own selfish uses.

IV. THE ROLE OF THE CHURCH AND THE REFORMATION

1. THE CHRISTIAN ECONOMY BEFORE THE REFORMATION

[20]// or not to give—and which remains linked to the *personal* salvation of the soul. Christianity, mistrustful of the glorious acts of men, opposed them to acts of charity—which are not merely useful actions, since the expenditure of the charitable man is unproductive for him. Charity is in fact so far removed from self-interest that the Old Testament equates it with sacrifice.

It is true that, prior to the Reformation, Christians were only poorly disposed toward the spirit of glory in a vague way. Unlike the bourgeoisie, Christians are not by definition opposed to glory. They say that God created man so that he might be glorified through him. Once paganism had been officially destroyed, the Christian world allowed itself to be saturated by its spirit—witness the many festivals it still observes today. The Church even tolerated a true kind of religion that was practiced by the nobility despite being diametrically opposed to the church, in which the morality of honor (that is, of personal glory) was substituted for that of the Gospels. It allowed the tradition of gallantry to continue to one side and, in contradistinction to asceticism, it allowed for the development of a true faith in the intoxicating power of love. The Church opposed the exuberant movements that disturbed and transformed it even less effectively. It covered the earth with glorious edifices in which people indulged in fabulous ceremonies. Charity was redirected from its primitive ends toward more sumptuous ones. Above every town, every village, the church or cathedral bore witness to Christ, to the gift that he made for all mankind through his death. Across plains and valleys, bells and towers inscribed men, houses, and roads with the sign of his sacrifice. *Useless* beauty proclaimed the principle of festivals aloud: "Wealth," declared the tower, "must escape from necessity in part; the purpose of wealth is magnificence; it must be given freely, prodigally, for the creation of works open to all." Those works, however, would be nothing without sacrifice. Magnificence would be hollow if it did not evoke the blood of torment: the gift of wealth would itself be shocking if it did not open onto the one true gift. This truth proclaimed by the tower is not that of the Gospel: it is the truth of religion in the earliest days. I view this world that surrounds me, bristling with bells and towers, as a challenge that the past lays every day before the present: this collection of churches and buildings, the ceremonies celebrated within them, the priests' cost of living (to say nothing of the wealth of museum collections, whose objects have been removed from their purpose), all represent the share of the gift. But before me I see nothing but the remnants of all this. The glorious gifts given to the Church before the Reformation formed a sum of territories equal to that of a nation: if one had united all the "goods of mortmain" in the hands of a single party, one would have had an empire made up of free gifts, themselves issuing from the supreme gift. Anguish (the fear of hell) contributed somewhat to this edifice of magnificence, but anguish is, in any case, the companion of glory.

2. THE DECLINE OF THE FESTIVAL ECONOMY

[21]// when the principles are no longer observed, it is possible to remember them and reverse them. Nothing was more contrary to the Gospel than the Church of the Renaissance. The poverty of the evangelists was scorned. The Church's wealth was immense but decentralized; no army could have defended it: it was held according to the wishes of princes. The Reformation denounced and obliterated the glorious economy over which the clerical hierarchy presided. The world entered a crisis of expansion and the Church, in danger, had to return to fortifying its principles. Half of Europe forgot about religious splendor: the entire North displayed parsimonious simplicity, and Rome itself opted for moderation. Caprice was then repurposed in service of reason: beginning from the Reformation onwards, both a moral hostility toward all kinds of waste and a utilitarian society developed under the direction of the grand bourgeoisie.

In a time of invention and global discovery, men started to measure the share offered up to glory. The Italian city aligned itself with the heavens through the meaning and splendor of its edifices. But its apparent wealth was neither Christian nor rational. Reason limits the needs that we have to satisfy. A decent home and healthy food are necessities. By contrast, glory and, in general, all excitation is harmful to the economy. Evangelical faith is hostile to earthly glories and accords glory to none but the dead. For the believer, nothing is farther from true glory than the ruinous splendors of this world. To come to know heavenly glory, one must, as far as possible, flee from the glory of man and denounce its snares. For the man of God, being useful and charitable is enough. His charity must return to the rigorous spirit of the Gospel, which goes one better than the Jewish tradition: let the left hand not know what the right hand doeth![22] The Reformation founded life on an accord between earthly, humble utility and posthumous glory, salvation, which one was never sure of attaining but toward which the path of utility led. Vainglorious expenditures—which the masses demanded of the rich—appeared to the Protestant to contrast absolutely with piety. He distanced himself from them to such an extent that a decidedly individualist outlook developed that led him to oppose popular intoxication above all else. It so happened that the devout rich accumulated for themselves the profits of industrial activity, without finding any other way to dispose of these profits except by growing their businesses. This consecration of gold for useful activity coincides with the development of capitalism. Wealth lost the meaning of glorious brilliance it had held until then. *Money was seen as a means of production*: *capital* is a means of production and, just as the Church devotes men to God, bourgeois society devotes money to capital—only, more effectively.

From the age of the Reformation onwards, new inventions and global discovery led to an increase in the sphere of acts of utility. But this did not enrich people except in a paradoxical fashion: it channeled riches into a living network of businesses that extended their reach a bit further every single day. The laborious transformation of nature into *products*, into saleable stuff, began the very day when we stopped spending human resources in service of glory. The old world of churches linking cities to the heavens died in giving birth to that which we now haunt, where factories tower over clouded hills.[23]

V. PROTESTANT AMERICA AND THE DEVELOPMENT OF CAPITALISM[24]

1. THE ORIGIN OF THE BUSINESSMAN IN PURITANISM

The fall of Mexico occurred the same year as the Diet of Worms—when the Reformation truly began. Life abandoned the great Aztec city: since then, the sacrificial pyramids have remained deserted, and weeds have overrun them. For his part, Luther began an open revolt against the paganism of Rome. No one—neither the Spanish nor Luther himself—desired the world that came about, but in that world, practical reason could not help but reduce man, little by little, to the scale of interest.[25] Never was there a world so covered in riches, but its riches were disguised as poverty (which remained); they were covered by a gray mantle of utility: never was there a world filled with such need. Neither Cortés nor Luther could have foreseen an outcome so far removed from their original concerns. In response to loans offered at interest—the basis of capitalism—Luther adopted the old moral opprobrium of the Ancients. Cortés took to conquering and pillaging: if he destroyed a world, it was naively, the way a child destroys a bird's nest. Nevertheless, both of them contributed to the birth of a value system that organizes all of our opinions today.

Not only through the analysis of texts and facts but also through the use of statistics, Max Weber has shown the role played by Protestants in the development of capitalism (*Die protestantische Ethik und der Geist des Kapitalismus*, vol. 1 of the *Religionssoziologie*). Nowadays, in the same region, we see Protestants drawn toward business, whereas Catholics are more willingly drawn toward liberal professions. The Lutheran Reformation was not the most important factor in orienting society this way. Only Calvinism intervened in an active way, through a doctrine opposing luxury rather than just a general sense of opposition to it. Out of everyone, it was the English or American Puritans who brought the new principles to maturity: they closed themselves off to all contemplation—which they thought to be useless—and devoted their lives to useful work. They regarded useful undertakings and the decorum of a productive life as the sole signs of a heavenly grace that they were never sure they would attain. Nothing is more opposed to the spirit of festivals than Puritan morality: the Puritans of England attempted to suppress the merrymaking of Christmas and the popular custom of the Maypole.[26] In America, where the morality of merchants never came into conflict with the preestablished ideas of noblemen (who despise commerce), the Puritans held sway over the dominant way of thinking—their influence went far beyond their sect. The "businessman," hungry for profit, dedicating every hour of his day to work, growing his businesses, was to the New World what the saint or the man of honor was to Old Europe.

2. THE USE OF WEALTH REDUCED TO THE INCREASE OF WEALTH[27]

North America was even more distinct from the old continent than is usually recognized. In Catholic Europe, human activity led ceaselessly to the construction, amid smaller homes, of edifices in which the mystery of sacrifice was perpetuated and the spirit of magnificence was maintained. Even in Protestant Europe, the primitive relationships among men and between men and the heavens still abided: in a physical sense, towns and cities still gravitated around their old churches. Throughout the old world, the aristocracy expressed their contempt for merchants: the merchants threw that contempt back at them, pretended to make light of it, but in secret they suffered from the prestige of those whom they denounced as their parasites.

In the old countries of Europe, money was essentially used in the service of capital, *but that was not its noblest use.* The old system of values retained a prestige that was somewhat ludicrous, somewhat old-fashioned, but nevertheless captivating. The Puritan craze for business did not cynically insinuate itself anywhere except in the Protestant lands of America. In these lands, there was no older form of expenditure that interfered with using money for its only valuable purpose: the development and proliferation of business.

The true businessman doesn't make money either for the enjoyments it buys or to live resplendently. He doesn't work for himself or his loved ones: the money he makes exists to be invested; it must be used for nothing but growth; it has no value or meaning except for the endless enrichment it makes possible.

3. THE PARABLE OF THE SOW[28]

The American Benjamin Franklin, writing in the middle of the eighteenth century, provides an unrestrained formulation of this idea. In commenting on the following passage, Max Weber said that it expressed *the spirit of capitalism*—with an almost classical purity.

[29][Franklin writes:

> Remember that time is money. He that can earn ten shillings a day by his labor, and goes abroad, or sits idle, one half of that day, though he spends but sixpence during his diversion or idleness, ought not to reckon *that* the only expense; he has really spent, or rather thrown away, five shillings besides. Remember, that money is of the prolific, generating nature. Money can beget money, and its offspring can beget more, and so on. Five shillings turned is six, turned again it is seven and threepence, and so on, till it becomes a hundred pounds. The more there is of it, the more it produces every turning, so that the profits rise quicker and quicker. He that kills a breeding sow, destroys all her offspring to the thousandth generation. He that murders a crown, destroys all that it might have produced, even scores of pounds.]

The bourgeois world is shaken by this horrifying waste, these horrifying festivals and sacrifices. The Puritans at least recognized the glory of God as the final end. If they condemned this mortal life to labor, it was because they considered it vain or accursed.[30] The businessman, for whom asceticism paved the way, was the first to link value to utility: he chose capital for his standard—wealth invested in private enterprise. Regardless of whether the Puritan morality was destined to endure or vanish, or if it was to abide in a merely ornamental form, a world of new values established itself, set into motion by the ceaseless turning of cogs and wheels. Morally, the majority of men gave themselves over to making judgements based on calculations about factories: the judgments of God, which attributed value to glorious ends, remained in place in a nominal sense but ceased to have any meaning. Prosperity through private enterprise *without glory* became the goal; *utility became the basis of moral value.*

The factory was the measure of man: it displaced everything, made a vanity of all else. The factory was by no means a Behemoth—there was nothing sacred or monstrous about it: it was first and foremost a rational reality, reducible to accounting: it developed, according to constant laws, along the path that leads from each person's *ability* [*forces*] to the *needs* [*besoins*] that they must satisfy. Up until that point, man had only encountered cultivable land, a land quite as variable as his ability and his needs. That land called for neither the accumulation of abilities (the consolidation and then indefinite extension of capital), nor the adaptation of needs. As long as the economy was agricultural, the partial waste of riches had no effect on an otherwise stable mode of production: they were not detrimental to subsequent harvests. By the same token, the products of the fields sated a demand that was difficult to exhaust: goods flowed easily.

The idea that excesses of production might create need (and thereby require a kind of commercial forecasting) was inconceivable in the time of "agricultural man": "agricultural man" lived a rudimentary, scrimping existence, but one that was not regulated by changing daily interest rates.

Industrialization forced men to enrich themselves: they had to save up large amounts of money in order to increase the means of production. Advanced peoples, on the whole, have had to put Franklin's maxims into practice. Everywhere, the need for greater industrial development challenged the need for magnificence or sacrifice. The language of Franklin articulates the fundamental antinomy: he who wastes "murders"; he kills the sow and kills its offspring up until the thousandth generation . . . Once upon a time, "glorious men" would needlessly kill a fertile sow simply to achieve harmony with capricious gods. In the eyes of the "businessman," the murderer of sows, "sacrificial man," is immoral. Business, industry, capital, and accumulation *are the opposite of sacrifice*: the bourgeoisie incarnates in its members this need to reject squander; through his self-effacement, the monotony of his existence, the bourgeois showcases his cunning will to escape from sacrifice.

4. THE DEPRESSION[31]

North America was the country of industrial growth *par excellence*. There, the anonymous, impersonal greed of industry could extend the labor of ant-like workers indefinitely. Nothing stopped this blind movement: businesses could endlessly seize and accumulate power. Of course, the factories delivered the products, but the payment was for their delivery. Factored into their price was the *profit* necessary for the investment of capital. By contrast with the glory of the gift, the goal of a delivery is gain or the accumulation of gain: it guarantees ceaseless growth, day in, day out. A capitalist enterprise grows, destroying anything that resists it. It must transform and assimilate everything it encounters: sooner or later, the totality of labor power available will be incorporated into its machinery. The factory understands that each source of labor power has its place—proletarians, middlemen, accountants, technicians—but it ignores men as much it can. No communal hearth links together the men who are cogs in its system: a business runs on icy greed; it deploys labor heartlessly; its only god is its own growth. In times of prosperity, workers gain nothing from profitable excesses. But, when those profits start to abate, the employer casts the wage-earner aside: lacking glorious ends—lacking, quite precisely, *human* ends—men can share no solidarity with one another; among men there exists nothing but a divisive greed for things. Charity only remedies this division through gritted teeth, being nothing but a comic trivialization of solidarity.

An industrial society is a crowd *composed of isolated individuals*. The very nature of life itself changes in every sense: in place of proud cities with the union of heaven and earth etched into their appearance, there are towns lying lifeless, buried under a suburban sprawl where the misery cuts deep. Those depressed by prosperity and those worked up by poverty come together. Everywhere men revolt, rediscovering the best of themselves in their flight from reality, their humiliating negation of it![32]

The furious development of a form of industry that served its own ends rather than the ends of mankind marked the dawning of a folly that was unavoidable. In formulating the principle of the modern world, Franklin refused to see that one cannot save endlessly or make money that has been saved reproduce itself endlessly—just as one cannot make sows reproduce endlessly into the thousands. I can see in my dreams farmers perishing beneath a horde of innumerable pigs: this is already the fate of the rich inhabitants of America, who have started to get hungry, to wither away amidst unlimited capital. The "parable of the sow" illustrates this strange error. The origin of the word *capital* is linked to the simplest form of mobile and productive wealth: the herd, composed of heads, of *capita* (the word *cheptel* [livestock] which today signifies this sort of wealth is for its part the vulgar derivative of the Latin *capitale*). In the past, the shepherd would remove from the herd the accursed share, which the dark powers of the festival demanded. The American businessman disposed of his wealth as if it were an inert and harmless *thing*: a sow which had to reproduce to the thousandth generation . . . that one could not kill without committing a crime. In our day, the businessman is the victim of these thousands of sows; he has been ruined, reduced to longing for death.[33]

CHAPTER III
THE WORLD OF PRIVATE EXPENDITURE

I. MATURE CAPITALISM

1. THE IMPERSONAL NATURE OF RAPACIOUS GREED IN MODERN CAPITALISM

In truth, the spirit of the old industrialists, the narrow-minded hostility of the Puritans, and the infinite will to produce were all symptoms of a system, rather than the cause of it.[1] Nowadays, there is no doubt that Protestantism plays a very small role (maybe no role at all) in the mechanisms that bind us. The workshops in which the Puritans would carry out their personal endeavors have been replaced by impersonal corporations. That said, the mechanism still works according to the same logic. I would have been wasting my time if my aim had been to identify causes; I simply wanted to show the *direction* of capital.

At one time, the spirit of capital was expressed in the Puritan workshop, which was built by the owner who devoted his fortune to it, setting aside his profits for the growth of the factory. The Puritan workshop is an example of the movement toward organization contained in capitalist activity, which develops from clearly separating productive ends from glorious ends. But the capitalism of our day comprises a set of enterprises lacking any conception of individuality or any moral nostalgia. It is still animated by the spirit of Puritanism but in a purely mechanical way. The structure of the economy no longer appears linked to the sullen hours of the Christian conscience but to the relations between businesses themselves.[2]

One part of a business's operations is primarily dedicated to producing the means of production; the other part is dedicated to making products for consumption. If all businesses were to stop expanding, the efforts of the first part to ensure circulation would be thwarted. As a result, the first group would no longer be able to either buy the products necessary for its own production or produce the means of production that it would normally make use of itself. Having reached its current state, the system would wither away entirely. It therefore cultivates—in the most impersonal and constraining of ways—a will for the endless development of industry. This will is common to every single business, by dint of the general relations between them. Under current conditions, the possessive bourgeoisie's aversion to offering up their capital for glorious consumption is a requirement; in no sense does it stem from their personal virtue.

But it is clear that a business's greed for growth is indirect. We cannot say of any one of them, or even of all of them together, that they are possessed of a desire to absorb power [*forces*]. The only vital necessity that drives them is the circulation of products. A mediating step is required for their greed to be satisfied: a new business, *not yet existing*, or the expansion of an old business (the choice between one or the other only depends in a very limited way on the will of those who expect this to happen). It is only through external growth, through the consumption of surplus products, that a business is able to develop. This sort of indirect greed (the object of which, by definition, does not yet exist) is the *speculative* will of capital. It is this *speculative* will of capital that bleeds the globe dry, that draws all men and all available power [*forces*] into its circle of exploitation.

2. PUTTING AVAILABLE RESOURCES INTO PROJECT

This will is the result of free capital, of the part of all capital that can be invested. Free capital is not a specific, delimited part of capital. In general, accrued profits are not directly invested into the growth of enterprises (whether in terms of their number or importance). New money feeds the game (the stock exchange). In one sense, free capital is this new money: theoretically available for investment in the stock market, it becomes subsumed into a changeable mass. It is not the numerical sum of recent profits that determines the importance of available capital—still less is it determined by the amount of material produced and made available to whosoever has a mind to grow their business. It is not even the resources of the workforce. Free capital is, to be sure, the basis for the speculative will, but it is ultimately the same thing as that will, since ultimately this will either set a limit for its significance or extend that limit. Free capital is greed speculating on the possible. The possible being anything related to the growth of enterprise.

Selling is only a secondary concern when it comes to speculation. The opportunity to sell is translated into an opportunity to build. The operations of the industries of consumption can increase if their immediate sales grow.

Nevertheless, the totality of exchange rates depends on the investment of free capital. In normal times, high prices are a reflection of people's happy perception of investment opportunities. Speculation as a whole makes greed into a project.[3] The movement of all industrial activity is based on this condition: that it is possible to form rational projects for development. This allows it to satisfy its desire. What was once a goal that a man (and an entrepreneur most of all) would strive for has become the goal of an impersonal system. Within this system, it is not easy to grasp how the will is articulated. But it has not changed much for all that. Like the first Calvinist industrialists, the system consecrates money to expanding the means of production. In fact, in the long run, money becomes so tied to growth that it becomes merely a function of growth itself—to the point that the sum increases as the opportunities for growth increase or, by contrast, reduces as these opportunities decrease.

In this case, growth does not cease simply because greed is not satisfied. The systems of human activity—and of organic activity in general—have their states of equilibrium, but capitalism knows nothing of these. It either grows or it perishes. As soon as it stops growing, capital collapses. Furthermore, if growth stops, then this also has other disconcerting effects. When greed is not satisfied, it is not that it becomes materially impossible to proceed with the operations necessary for life, such as providing the worker with the means of subsistence, for example, or generally continuing with production or entrepreneurship (in principle, this all remains doable—it would in fact be easy). What happens is that it becomes impossible to implement a project. Without any possible project, the machine stops: we note that the system—the initial effects of which could be seen in the behavior of the austere industrialist, then in Benjamin Franklin's model businessman—depends on replacing primitive actions with the effort of transforming life itself into a project. Primitive actions were part of the festival economy, in which surpluses produced by labor were put toward sumptuary works (once a rudimentary standard of living had been guaranteed). Prior to the capitalist era, the possibility of making things better did not really occur to people. The desire to make existence more bearable was surely one of the reasons why a part of the surplus was put toward charitable works. We never dreamed, as we tend to do now, of dedicating the overall supply of labor to improving the general standard of living.

3. THE MORAL INDIFFERENCE OF CAPITAL

Capitalism is clearly distinct from any concerns about improving the human condition. Luxury industries have played an important part in its rise. The only trait that matters is the accumulation of capital, the project of systematically developing the forces of production. The most profound moral apathy has reigned right from its beginnings and still reigns over the use of products. It has become a banal fact that an industry of a country at war will furnish an enemy country with the products necessary for armament. Insects will continue to follow their instincts, paying no heed to the occasionally disastrous results that follow. The same is true of a capitalist industry. On the whole, however, the development of productive activity can only meet the existing needs, and—as long as the total mass of production continues to grow—it can only meet the average level of need. It might seem that in times of plenty and times of hardship, capitalism's only goal is the improvement of the standard of living, but this point of view is deceptive. Modern industrial production raises the average standard of living without ameliorating the inequality between different classes and, overall, it only ameliorates social ills by chance.

4. RELATION BETWEEN THE GAMBLE AND THE PROJECT

Capitalism is no less indifferent to personal earnings than to what greedy speculators make behind its back. Capital basically has just one need: to be put into a project of development that responds to the possible. For a long time this was enough for honest Calvinists. The essential thing is that a certain number of people have their projects and realize them. Others gamble[4] on these projects. Previously, a person would have an idea for a certain kind of production, accumulate toward this end, and then he himself would gamble on his project. This whole operation could be undertaken by a single person, acting in a single enterprise. Nowadays, the project, the accumulation, and the gamble are all distinct operations. These three operations can call upon different people or groups. A man can conceive and put his project into action without accumulating anything, or without having to gamble the capital he controls on himself; he can accumulate without gambling; he can even gamble, to a certain extent, without ever having accumulated.

This is remarkable: since capitalism has the project as its central element, and since accumulation from the point of view of the project is nothing but a consequence of the project, the gamble necessarily sits between project and accumulation. Under capitalism, the gamble is a heterogeneous thing: it is the result of a comparative *lack* of power. Capitalism would bypass the gamble if it could: its system of assurances developed as a corollary to the mindset connected to capitalism. But capitalism cannot eliminate risk: an accumulated sum of money does not contribute to a business venture except insofar as it is put at stake [*mise en jeu*]; reciprocally, a project of capitalist activity is nothing but a fantasy until the moment when capital is gambled upon it.

But there exists a fundamental antinomy between the gamble and the project. The spirit of project, to which capital is bound, is the precise opposite of the gamble, which is proper to the festival. This is an exaggeration: I should state more accurately from this point on that these contraries (in one sense of the word) are complementary. In a burst of laughter, it is true that there is often no real project to the joke [*jeu*]—when it comes to poetry, hatred of project[5] only makes things worse (and is pointless)—but, in any case, the project remains inherent in the gamble, just as the gamble is inherent in the project. Gambling is another word for the pleasure we take in offering ourselves up to chance; engaging in a project describes the pains we take not to leave anything up to chance. But these pleasures and pains have their limits: the gambler studies his moves; and even the most rational man must take risks. The gambler's efforts to make plans are subordinate to his love of the game, to which he is inextricably bound, as if by a pact with the devil. The gamble in any business is the share of it that is given over to chance, which is minimized as much as possible. One cannot draw a decisive line and say: this is a gamble, that is a project. One can only say: in this particular activity, it is the gamble or the project that predominates.

The project predominates in capitalist activity. The gamble is restricted to the operations of the stock market. In a certain way, the stock market removes the fever of gambling from industrial activity. With these operations being separated, it is the gambler who takes responsibility for his sickness. The large-scale capitalists or industrialists, heirs to the Calvinist tradition, are entirely distinct from the speculators. The latter are necessary insofar as they set capital in motion, making the former rich, but they are heterogeneous to the system. Speculation adds the attraction of gambling to the movement by which capital is established, to the tendency by which money is dedicated to the development of the forces of production. This tendency has to carry on alongside gambling: speculation puts a share of any profits toward waste. Speculators are more likely than industrialists or capitalists to be beings of vain glory, driven to making extravagant personal expenditures. Capitalism accommodates itself to their wastefulness. In principle, large-scale capitalists or industrialists are quite happy to give just their flesh and blood to a project. Their life is in principle given over to the work of conceiving and putting projects into operation. More accurately, it is not they who conceive projects and put them into operation, but they who are conceived by their projects and put into operation by them. Insofar as they are functions of society, that is to say, the cause of impersonal operations, they are the exact opposite of great lords or ecclesiastical dignitaries. Their role is to dedicate wealth toward production, to withdraw it from any glorious usage. They escape from this role in part, but only as individuals. They can only make brilliant expenditures in a personal capacity, and yet, paradoxically, they are compelled to disguise this brilliance. Speculators are even further removed from the principle of bourgeois discretion: they are nothing but gamblers [*êtres de jeu*]. There is no clear distinction between gamblers on the one side and men of project on the other. But each of these categories finds expression in certain types of individuals, between whom there must exist a necessary antagonism. Insofar as he remains a faithful exponent of capitalism, the business owner despises the speculator.

5. THE HYBRID CHARACTER OF THE SPECULATOR

The pure speculator is nothing but a heterogeneous element within the system. He spares the stolid leaders of capitalism from having to exist as gamblers [*créatures de jeu*] within a world of projects. The speculator accepts this and takes his first step down a moral cul-de-sac: when it comes down to it, he is nothing, nor has he ever been anything, but a testament to impotence puffed up by arrogant subterfuge. As he is not even a genuine gambler, he has no more claim to splendor than he does to morality. Wealth, in his hands, is destined neither to burn nor to produce, and a gamble that lacks the look of one is nothing but the servitude of gambling: utilitarian language cannot give his life the honesty of utility but it draws him away from the splendor of gambling. The arrogance of having money, empty of any meaning but that of private enjoyment, is his only escape.

6. THE WORLD OF INDIVIDUAL LIBERTY AND PRIVATE ENJOYMENT

What is striking, even disconcerting about capital, is its multiplicity. Essentially, it is a cycle of impersonal greed that is dominated in its development by an indifference either to private interests or public interests. It is a machine condemned to grow *generally*. But its impersonal nature eventually causes it to develop its own set of interests, which work to the detriment of social development. The capitalist machine produces decomposition. It broke up medieval institutions, clearing as much space as possible for individual will.

However, in this sense, industrial capitalists—just like machines—have not been able to lead the system, fully and openly, to its ultimate conclusion. This is worth noting: the speculator, despite his heterogeneous character, was the only one who became a true and perfect individual. The industrialist is also an individual, freed from the old social categories, bringing his endeavors to term with no regard for the public interest. However, his factories are communal operations that are only isolated when they are managed in a particular way. There is such a strong sense that factories are fundamentally subordinate to the public interest that capitalists have been morally compelled to feign this subordination in life, to be so hypocritical as to suffer sometimes as a result (having no other option). The capitalist does not have the gambler's easy access to cynicism and can only rarely take the plunge into brazen individualism. The gambler takes that plunge necessarily, so much so that, while his presence in the system runs counter to its general flow, it is nevertheless him and not the industrialist who represents its culmination. The Calvinist industrialist diverted his riches from their glorious usage and put them toward the growth of the forces of production, but his austerity stopped him in his tracks. The modern industrialist, having understood the consequences of the Calvinist attitude, ends up dedicating the excess fruit of his riches to his own personal well-being. But he is held back by the fiction of useful activity and by his status as a man of project. He does not go so far as to state these principles publicly. The speculator, on the other hand, is free and, as he is forward-looking and active, it is he who defines the moral atmosphere of capitalism. In this way, he combines the accomplishment of capitalism's ends with those values that spring from his own attitude: individualism and private enjoyment. The spiritual principles of Calvinism having been erased, the industrialist is reduced to pretending to be a functionary socialist, while the great speculator becomes the symbol of this new set of values.

If we think about it, this substitution is natural. Calvinist principles served to introduce the world to project (to useful activity). Once this world of project had come into existence and religious values no longer made sense, it was only natural that the idea of project, which is nothing by itself, should have come to be governed by a new set of positive values. A movement of uncontrolled growth is unsupportable, and the improvement of the general standard of living is a hypocritical concession made to the general will. The fact that there is no end to this process means that the person who expresses the values of capitalism is not the one who rises to the fore; rather it is the one who profits from it, the person for whom there is no escape from the process, who is nothing more than an individual, engaged merely in private enjoyment. This is the man who is seemingly rich but is, in reality, the poorest of all: the modern entrepreneur.[6]

II. THE DEGRADATION OF EXPENDITURE

1. FROM CATHEDRALS TO FASHION-HOUSES

We often simplify things to understand them better: then, in order to show their complexity, we must take up the matter again.

Capitalism required man to renounce the squander of festivals. We tended to gather the energy that was created by festivals and other similar forms of expenditure and put it toward the development of production. In theory, accumulation could have ballooned indefinitely. But only in theory. The products of industry had to be consumed (if they weren't, subsequent accumulation would stop). Capitalism did not entail the suppression of nonproductive expenditures: it curbed their movement first of all (focusing primarily on social expenditures), then it gradually reduced them to consuming the products of capitalism. It is difficult to say if the proportion of nonproductive expenditures increased from the Middle Ages onward. There is only evidence that they were transformed and were no longer of central importance.

There is no doubt that, after the Middle Ages, nonproductive expenditures underwent degradation. The kinds that had no place within the general flow of production tended to burn out. By contrast, those that fed on the products of capitalist enterprises found themselves favored.

The exhausting construction of great, luxurious monuments did not cease entirely but the practice nearly died out. To understand the importance of this practice in the

Middle Ages, it would be necessary to imagine a structure in New York devoid of practical purpose: it would tower over the skyscrapers like a church over the houses of a little village; it would be lavishly decorated even on parts of it that could never be reached. A cathedral cannot be exploited for commercial purposes. Its only claim is to have a *meaning* (and doubtless that meaning disappeared along with the ability to express it, with the ability to build new cathedrals). Only barely recognizable kinds of expenditure survived. Man's glorious expenditure became bounded by the limits set by commercial exploitation. Nothing (or almost nothing) survived that couldn't be turned into a lucrative activity. Nowadays literature and spectacles are reducible to monetary calculations. After steel, film was the United States' second industry. Every now and then a voice explodes with a resounding crack—all the more strange and troubling because it knows that it is lost from the outset. On the whole, the movement of the festival—at once tragic, glorious, rollicking—has been altered. Where once it gave men's faces the power to seduce, now these faces are disfigured by the bloated bulk of wealth (wealth that's bored sick). Wealth has by no means disappeared: having first passed from the many to the few, it has ended up somewhere in the middle. The petit bourgeois have now placed the ugly stamp of their face on it. It would take a madman, someone of the lowest class to conjure up a glimmer of those long-lost splendors: the regular possession of wealth weighs one down, and no one escapes that kind of degradation. A vast gulf separates the cathedral from the fashion-house (the old ladies who frequent the major couturiers are, in our eyes, the sewers of morality, hateful combinations of emptiness and pointlessness, meanwhile, cathedrals nowadays are little more than a distant echo of the old festivals, having been stripped bare by Christian degradation).

The mode of individual expenditure, excluding true splendor, is limited by the scale of capitalist production. It is organized around mass-produced objects, around substituting luxuries for pale imitations. Superfluous objects are certainly at the center of this kind of expenditure, but such objects also promote well-being. Indeed, the individual cut off from society can make no claims to splendor (he cannot understand the meaning of the payments it requires). If he succumbs to the seductions of luxury, he does so without any delicacy: as soon as he touches it, he squirrels it away, he destroys its sense of brilliance. The poverty that he accrues by piling up endless riches, accompanied by his fatigue, eventually leaves him feeling a sense of comfort and boredom with his excesses.

2. TOBACCO

It is far from certain that the general amount of waste is decreasing; we could counter such a claim by pointing to the evidence of the prodigious consumption of tobacco. The use of tobacco is bizarre. It is so widespread, it plays such an important part in the equilibrium of life that, even in hard times, it is the object of seemingly serious concern. It has the same status as other "useful" expenditures.

There is no form of waste that is more banal or more consistently linked to whiling away time. The poorest of the poor smoke (though the cost of tobacco at the moment I am writing is considerable, how many smokers will still use their rations, trade them against provisions they lack, though the lack of them makes them even worse off). Of all the luxurious expenditures, tobacco is the only one that affects everybody's purse. In one sense, widespread smoking is scarcely less of a collective activity than the festival. Nevertheless, it's different. The festival gives itself to all equally, whereas tobacco is not evenly distributed between the rich and the poor (currently there are few smokers who do not suffer—only the privileged can limitlessly smoke). Furthermore, in contrast to festivals which are limited to a set time, tobacco is smoked at every hour, from the start to the end of the day. This constant usage prevents the whole enterprise of smoking from having any meaning. What strikes one about the smoking masses is how little they think about it. There is no practice that is less well understood. The festival of smoking lulls the mind into thinking that a true festival is taking place. There is, however, a hidden sorcery at work here, which makes people believe that if they smoke, they are aligned with the world (with the heavens, with clouds and light). It doesn't matter if the smoker knows it or not: tobacco liberates him briefly from the need to take action. He is alive (even if he remains concerned about the fact). As smoke drifts gently from his mouth, his life is given the freedom and idleness we see in the clouds.[7]

3. THE MOVEMENT FROM THE TRAGIC TO THE COMIC

The most difficult thing to grasp is that the degradation proceeds in two different and equal directions (though in both ways it is linked to expenditures becoming individual in character). On the one hand, tragic expenditure becomes comic (as in the case of fashion-houses—while it is true that fashion-houses are wretched at their core, it's their comic nature that makes them wretched); on the other hand, expenditure tends to reduce consciousness (this is the case with tobacco).

The comedy of expenditure is associated with the bourgeoisie; in the most general sense, the failure to recognize the necessity behind certain acts of squander is what characterizes men of our time.

The most well-established thing about bourgeois man is his comic nature. Tragedy puts great lords and princes on the stage; comedy, the bourgeois. It is not only tragedy but luxury that belongs essentially to the caste of lords. Luxury also belongs to the domain of tragedy. Harshness is its fundamental characteristic. It is linked to domination. It belongs only to those people who have the privilege of committing murder or sacrifice. The slightest softening removes luxury from its natural element (which is its nearness to death). It is hardly ever lacking in violent pride—it incites laughter (since it is an ass in a lion's skin).

Luxury, it is true, does not belong exclusively to the landed gentry. Flowers are the luxury of the fields, and animals have their excesses (though these are associated with strength). For men, luxury was expressed through festivals—where people are mixed up in common—before it was expressed through social rank. But luxury became, precisely, less and less a thing of the people (like it still was in the cathedrals). What we experience of it now is little more than the luxury of separation that comes from those kinds of expenditures that establish social rank.

Lordly expenditures were certainly used to establish social rank, but they did so without severing social bonds. As a matter of course, they did not take place separately from the people but in front of them and for them. Indeed, it was the rousing and truly wasteful character of the expenditures that they made in such conditions that set them apart from the bourgeoisie, who wanted to accumulate in order to produce. When the bourgeois had produced enough that he found himself to be scarcely less than a great lord with an excess to squander, he was himself drawn to luxury in turn: he became the first to reach the culminating point of the movement that gave wealth the value of private enjoyment. In its turn the bourgeoisie demonstrated its status as the ruling class through luxurious prodigalities, but in a way that was suppressed, effaced, affirming their separate character all the more clearly through the laughable pretense that they were playing the part of noblemen.

A coarse, down-to-earth bourgeois woman, ignorant of the pride that rare noblewomen undoubtedly took in their attractiveness, looks completely ridiculous in the toilette of luxury. All personal luxury is anachronistic. As far as possible, men erase anything brilliant from their appearance (the ugly choices they make with their neckties are significant, since the necktie is the only relic of ancient splendors). Pomp and magnificence are clearly loaded with the trappings of tragedy, except that they devolve into comedy. Masculine clothes nowadays can be comfortable, fitting, sturdy. Within these limits, the clothes leave room for sophistication. Since social rank excludes all sense of the tragic, people must become unobtrusive. Many women are weak enough to give into their regrets and overdress themselves. Even if they are beautiful, these parodies of noble "ladies" are asking for a slap.*

It is true that the luxury of houses is less difficult to bear. If someone's drab clothing staves off all brilliance in him, the magnificence of his house, no matter how imposing it is, detaches itself from him and takes on a value similar to that of a museum. More often than not it is little more than a leftover relic. This is not the magnificence of Monsieur N. but of a lord from the past (it's no problem if his name is unknown). This kind of magnificence is a stranger to the present times: all that Monsieur N. has been able to do is buy the right to dwell where magnificence lingers. He's a dead man that owns and profits from it.

Similar to the comedy of clothing, a comedy of houses and furniture has taken shape. Everything that apes

---

*It is true that in part the luxury of women is of a different nature than that of men. Coquetry [*many lines crossed out*]. Insofar as she is linked to the courtesan's need to seduce, she is the opposite of a luxury of separation. In this respect, we can get further confused: so many "ladies" are trollops . . .

The luxury of peasants is—or rather, was—equally different than that of lords—or of the bourgeois. The peasants knew luxury in their festival garments. In our day, they put on bourgeois-style clothes on Sundays. Luxury is effaced or comically stands out (the bourgeois ape the great lords and, in turn, peasants ape the bourgeois). The garments that the peasants of yesteryear wore on parade were in no sense connected with tragedy. They were festival vestments. It is the festival, rather than the precise way that lords live, that is the precondition of luxury. In the festival, luxury belongs to everyone. Outside the festival, it belongs to the master—the *Herr* who, according to Hegel, staked his life and thereby founded nature.

greatness while lacking power—everything inscribed in this bourgeois universe where the threat of death is so far removed—is comical, if not painful. The clothes are perhaps funnier than the objects. But the comical is often inconspicuous (the tragic element of former times was no less so). In general, it is necessary to detect the comic (to draw it out) with the help of some artifice: we have found several tricks for that. Nevertheless, in response we resort to various methods to shelter ourselves from it. This is how we use the past—by hiding bourgeois fatuity behind it. This is also why we give our clothes the color and shape of bags. Architecture overwrought with pretentious ornaments is happy to imitate the utilitarian elegance of a boat.

4. THE LOSS OF AWARENESS OF THE MEANING OF EXPENDITURE

On the whole, as they were individualized and divided up, nonproductive expenditures lost the glorious meaning that they used to have. They are now ridiculous, like ladies' dresses, or elusive, like smoking. Luxury is off kilter: let's try to understand the junk, the trifles, the habits of dress and furnishing practiced by the moneyed petit bourgeoisie—they're part of the interminable extension that large fashion-houses made to appear enlarged, as if through a magnifying glass. In one sense, comic expenditure is itself linked to the lack of awareness we have about the need for expenditure. If we knew about this need, we would spend gloriously, paying for it with our own person if necessary, instead of going about it in the stealthy, stilted manner of the bourgeois. It is most remarkable that nonproductive expenditure survives among us as an anachronism that must be destroyed. It is sometimes developed by the interests of production but only in service of petty or foolish ends. Now it is no more than a sign of egoistic imbecility. The naïve insistence with which people in the seventeenth century spoke about glory is almost incomprehensible to us. In the seventeenth century, in France at least, man still seemed a glorious thing, dedicated to glory, possessed of no other goal than glory. But this conception could not survive following the failure of the *ancien régime*. We live now under the empire of disgust that it created. And save for a few bastard survivors, it is true that the classical conceptions of glory deserved the fate to which we condemn them.

Ultimately, however, this necessary hostility is linked to the ignorance into which we have fallen. We no longer understand that we must resolutely waste the excess energy that we produce. In fact, in our blind state, this pile-up of excess wastes us more than we waste it. Individual existence undoubtedly links this absence of awareness with its most profound element: a sense of delicacy next to which the cliché of the "grand siècle" appears shallow. A delicacy that cares nothing for waste. It transforms the consumption of tobacco into something elegant—*elegance is smoked*: smoking is the least studied of all actions, the least assertive in itself, and still the most transparent.

III. UNEMPLOYMENT

1. THE IMPASSE OF INDIVIDUAL EXPENDITURES

As far as individuals are concerned, the value of this loss of awareness[8] is that it provides an elegant solution. In opposition to the collective will and the emphasis placed on expenditure (in opposition to the glorious principles of the seventeenth century), it adds a layer of discretion, a guarantee of authenticity, to those expenditures that survive despite everything.

The loss of awareness of one's feeling of obligation freed up individual expenditures (and similarly the advertisements that represent the interests of capital became free to develop those interests however they wanted). Loss of awareness was accompanied, moreover, by comic degradation; it led, above all else, to the disappearance of collective expenditures.

Yet individual expenditures cannot exhaust the surplus of energy on their own. Every individual expenditure is commercialized, which means that it is linked into the system of capitalist expansion. No individual expenditure—almost no waste—is possible if it does not itself produce a surplus of energy.

If I buy a costly tie, it is true that I take the excess available to me—what I've produced on my own account and exchanged in return for money—and put it toward *a pure loss*. In this economic transaction, a sum of energy at least equal to that which was required to make the tie is wasted by me, lost for me. But the manufacturer gains a sum of money. In this form and via a system of equivalences, the manufacturer in turn gets to dispose of the sum of energy produced by me. This sum is even slightly greater than the sum of energy required for making the tie: this difference constitutes the profit of the manufacturer. If I keep an account of the average of these differences, I can say that an appreciable portion of the profit will go toward the accumulation of capital. Thus, I will have wasted energy only on the condition of contributing to the growth of businesses in general. *In the capitalist system, every nonproductive expenditure increases the sum of the forces produced.*

Undoubtedly, growing businesses can just as easily manufacture luxury products and, as far as production is concerned, my purchase of a tie drives it in this direction. The need to compensate for any act of destruction with a share of accumulation, however small, in no way changes the quality of expenditure. The construction of a Greek temple or a Roman church was not subject to this compromise, as the people were aware of its value. The people wanted and supported this construction. By contrast, the purchase of a tie is frivolous. We tolerate such an aberration with the following explanation: "Overall, it contributes to prosperity." More precisely, capitalism replaces proud and assertive wastefulness with a sort of cowering weakness—which is allowed to exist insofar as it contributes to the productive forces. Under these conditions, it remains impossible to discover a way out of the system. Since capitalism involves using wealth to increase the means of producing more wealth, there is no conceivable escape. The expenditures of individuals are integral to its operation—from which there is no escape. The essential part of the wealth that is set aside in the beginning continues to be set aside no matter what forms of nonproductive expenditure exist or develop. No amount of prosperity changes this. The system forever generates a feeling of poverty—the moral practices and ways of life of poverty.

As expenditure can from this point on do nothing but increase savings (and, through savings, production), it so happens that, eventually, we produce too much. A time of bloated production arrives in which we can no longer get rid of what we produce.

2. OVERABUNDANCE

The surplus of energy cannot be endlessly absorbed through an equally endless increase in the expenditure of the sum of energy produced. Nonproductive expenditures diminish as soon as a superabundance of products appears. There is not real poverty—far from it—but everyone is gripped by the feeling of poverty. A crisis reveals the extent of this feeling, which constituted the soul of capitalism from the beginning. Businesses shut down, workers go unemployed, consumption is reduced again: men are no longer aware of the necessary movement toward profligacy: their hostility toward glory leaves them at a remove from gifts and childish contagion; the wealth reserved for calculation has long since lost the power to catch fire, to be squandered.

Men's unhappiness is leading to an increase—if that is even possible—in the difficulties that are peculiar to life on earth. Not only do we only live by destroying (animal life), but we are becoming more and more dependent on offering up our labor to a system of forces that is superior to us in terms of complexity, so that we can acquire the means necessary for our subsistence. This tentacular system is different from all others in that it does not expend except on the condition that it absorbs *more* than it loses. Animals and men absorb, but they expend proudly. Purely voracious, capital is amoral and devoid of glory: everything that it provides comes on the condition that it will be sold for profit. It absorbs as much power as it possibly can and can only expend it by taking on more than it expends. This supposes the existence of forces that are outside the system and that have not yet been (but may yet be) mastered—either in the form of unexplored hinterlands or realms of possibility not yet exploited (made possible by new inventions). As soon as the system ceases to absorb new forces, it ceases to yield its products. It takes earthly greed to a higher level, or rather, changes it into an aberration. The laws of greed and avarice are painful: no being on earth shall expend without first having acquired. But capitalism has turned this means into an end (namely, greed). Its task is to let men die honestly, rigorously; it could not give them usable products without renouncing its own end (its greedy end: relentlessly increasing the forces of production). Every being on earth, though compelled to greed and miserliness, is nonetheless a being of glory. As it is impersonal, not a being with its own existence, capital has been able to turn its back on glory.[9]

3. THE INEFFECTIVENESS OF PUBLIC WORKS

....

4. THE HOLOCAUST OF UNEMPLOYMENT

IV. INDIVIDUALISM

....

[10]THE INDIVIDUAL STRUGGLING AGAINST SOCIETY, HEIR TO ITS GLORIOUS ENDS

We cannot easily recognize, first of all, what compensation we have received in our day in return for the decadence of the glorious customs of old. It seems that the new "glorious acts" appeared in a hostile sphere that was entirely focused on glory. *Individualism* developed through a daily struggle with society: the old society wanted glory, based its rights on the need for glory; the individual, who was not recognized by these rights, ardently disputed their basis: fate calls on individualism to negate glory. It is not, however, glory that the individual fights, but the society that merely pays lip service to it and thinks that it has a monopoly over it. If the individual refuses to be mixed up in social glories, if he refuses to pay the price, he is not compelled to seek out a lowly destiny as a result. Entirely to the contrary, he is condemned, in isolation, to the wearisome desire to find a grandeur that no longer proceeds from social conventions. The anguish of solitude leaves him searching for renewed splendors—he can only hope that those splendors are less false, that they respond more effectively to his deep-seated nostalgia than the institutions of old once did.

[11]At the same time that the utilitarian principles of industry were laying waste to the economy of glory, the *individual* became glory's new raison d'être. The individual was not recognized within the old economy of glory. In that economy, each person was merely an *expression* of the organized whole *to which they belonged.* The bourgeois economy made the individual the sovereign value. The bourgeois economy developed in connection with the idea that society is a sum of individuals. It developed in contradiction with the old social forms that were entirely glorious and wasteful. Violently or servilely, over the centuries, it compelled itself to destroy feudal society. In opposition to that society, it established the freedom of the individual and equal rights independent of hereditary caste. In truth, all forms of prodigal life

ran contrary to its spirit, the prodigality of individuals as much as that of princes—but the individuals were weak, the princes strong. That society believed it could take account of the needs of the individual, bring them into line with its interests, make them accord with its norms. Nothing of the kind would have been possible with the princes. The bourgeoisie allied itself to political movements that proclaimed the liberty of individuals. In this way, it discovered some opportunities to struggle, as a result of "glorious acts," opportunities that it had not expressly desired but that were necessary for its growth. On the one hand, it accelerated the fall of the *ancien régime*, while on the other hand it offered men a release valve for their natural turmoil. It created a world that was commensurate with itself: it wanted a world exclusively concerned with production, and it even knew how to make use of glorious, feverish movements in service of this end. The drums of revolutionary terror beat so that men's energy could be more narrowly funneled into industry.

In order to be favorably aligned with the general development of "useful acts," the fight for the rights of the *individual* had to end up substituting the "glorious acts" of individuals for those of peoples, princes, or priests. In a world where the individual became the limit of everything, it was the isolated individual who had to assume the functions of offering the gift of the self, of sacrifice, of fusion with the world. He could do so through struggle or revolutionary war, but that was not without abdicating his true rights in the service of combat, which quickly calls for unity, for the formation of parties and armies. For individuals, politics often opened up a glorious field for activities that were animated but always playing a subordinate role: politics must almost always content itself with following a modest path. The individual who refuses to dedicate his life to a cause greater than himself—because *individual* life is expressed in him— //

V. THE STATE, REASON, AND SCIENCE

CHAPTER IV
THE GIFT OF LIFE

THE GIFT OF THE SELF

I have described expenditure from the point of view of the economy: from this perspective, expenditure puts at stake values that are things.[1] I believed it necessary to begin with this approach because, wherever possible, a new notion should be introduced where it will make the most impact. The downside is that I have had to discuss matters of which people nowadays are ignorant. From this point on I will no longer discuss those movements whose traces can only be glimpsed in the operations of the economy but rather those stronger, perpetually active movements that still connect man with death.

"Wars," wrote Nietzsche, "are the only stimulants of the imagination, now that the ecstasies and terrors of Christianity have lost their power. The Revolution in society will be perhaps a still greater event; that is why it will come.

But it will be less successful than one imagines . . ."* The forms of expenditure implicated in economic life are meaningless when placed alongside more vital forms like war and religion. The *gift of the self*[2] rouses the imagination more than the gift of wealth. Religious giving depends on certain conditions of madness that no longer exist: conditions under which the movement of life would lead, by its own accord, to the gift provided by the soldier and glorify him for it. Before our very eyes, national revolutions have managed to assign to war the meaning of revolution and to revolution the meaning of war: the essence of Nietzsche's phrase still holds true.

"DEVOTION" AND INTEREST IN WARS

Setting the religious life and the life of the warrior alongside one another is the quickest way of making the upheavals that we are living through intelligible: just like religion, wars demand the gift of the self, the total dedication of one's life.[3] War's supposed goal is often not as meaningful as the need to dedicate oneself up to the point of death. People are only enamored of war when they dream about the dangerous assault rather than the economic outcome of victory. Glory and combat bring about delirium; collecting a tribute as payment does not.

There is a need for delirium—in revolutions as much as in wars. Among those who want revolution, some are the

*§69 of book IV of *La Volonté de puissance*, ed. Wurzbach, trans. G. Bianquis (N.R.F., 1937), written around 1880.

cold partisans of a world governed by reason: for them, the chaotic events of a revolution are just a necessary means to an end. But most have deliberately chosen a dangerous cause: the images of riots and barricades stimulate them in the same way that "the terrors and ecstasies of Christianity" stimulate others. The fervor and anger of the crowds are no longer just the means to the ends they pursue; they are signs of glory.

An impoverished mass would never guess quite how many people are born with a longing to squander their lives. And clearly, these profligates play a decisive role. It is vain to suppose that the world might ultimately end up organizing itself according to the laws of a bourgeoisie that is anxious to preserve its rights. Life renews itself ceaselessly, and the force of its renewal is like a surge of spring. In the long run, rich old men have no hope of imposing their moderation on it: the power [*pouvoir*] belongs definitively to those who are hungry for glory and who prodigally spend their blood. The wisest can *manipulate* this (if, at least, they relinquish the fields of conquest to the overflow of youthful energy): but this is only important in a secondary sense. The rulers who think only about utility soon fall into ruin. They would also fail if they were to follow the bloody impulse—which must find lines of interest for its survival. But the decisive role belongs to those movements that do not go on calculating everything and count death for nothing. A natural prodigality introduces a *surplus* into the play of forces which gives power [*puissance*] to the one who puts glory above interest—only slightly, to be sure, but above it nonetheless.

To perceive the meaning of prodigal giving, we must follow the vicissitudes of a debate in which sacrifice has the final word.

On the surface, all human undertakings follow the law of the activity of capital: it is not enough to get back what one has put in; one must get back more. Looking at things dispassionately, there is no benefit to war except in victory: each soldier swept up by the conflict has a fifty-fifty chance: these odds would have to be lengthened to account for the risk of death or grave injury. The benefit of a revolution is even more debatable. In cases of failure, the revolutionaries escape death more rarely than soldiers. If the revolutionaries win, assuming they have not been killed in combat, they still risk falling prey to attacks from their companions. For a militant who signs up willingly, a happy ending is far from likely. It often seems that the final result—an improvement in the livelihood of all—is the pretext rather than the goal of revolutionary action.

THE LAW OF CONCOMITANCE BETWEEN EXPENDITURES AND GAINS IN GLORIOUS ACTS

I have not meant to suggest that some actions are more delirious than others. I am sketching, in general, the way that "honest reason" (which I do not like very much) makes judgements about any kind of action. I will say of this form of decision-making that it seems to me to be both rigorous and weak at the same time. In encouraging men in the ways of revolution and war, those who enjoyed them wrote a history about them that does not seem to have been boundlessly wrong. Perhaps history is a more sensible judge than reason.

To begin with, every war, every coup d'état endows itself with meaning. The people who engage in them rationalize them from the point of view of interest. A defined interest plays a role in the action, even if the final results are disappointing. When a man dies believing that he has saved those who come after him from war, it is because his belief made it easier for him to offer up the gift of his life. The suggestion of a *gain* must always be made to the person who is going to *lose* his life. That suggestion would not work without the desire to lose: if it is addressed to those who make calculations, the suggestion is powerless. But the desire to lose would also not work without the lure of gain. The greediness for life—it goes without saying—is the major obstacle to the inverse drive that compels one to lose oneself without reserve. But that greediness can be sated by a hope—it can be weakened by enthusiasm: the intoxication of losing oneself breaks through all resistance.

In a battle in which life is at stake, the desire for victory pushes those who make war to their deaths. The fear of losing one's life, the greediness for life, is always opposed to the compulsion of the gift of the self: but this fear is eased by the greed for conquest. During the fevered hours when this desire is being satisfied, death becomes almost easy.

Thus, the gift of the self and expenditure occur within a set of conditions that remain constant. A first law can be stated as: "the law of concomitance":

An expenditure is facilitated by a simultaneous satisfaction of greed: reciprocally, an expenditure facilitates a gain (a satisfaction of greed).

We must not confuse this law with that of an economic exchange in which a service is followed by an equivalent payment. This economic law is ruled by the principle that the exchanged objects have equivalent values, that those carrying out the exchange have equivalent identities—both when providing a service and when paying. If John delivers a horse to Peter, John (and no one else) receives from Peter (and from no one else) the sum of money representing the value of the horse. That sum must, if possible, match this value exactly. If not, the transaction is not a *true* exchange but a gift, a mistake, or an act of fraud. The "law of concomitance" between an expenditure and a satisfied greed does not have to follow these principles. Economic laws rule over things or over men who live under the dominion of things. The law of expenditure understands the movements of life for which there is no *objective* measure. These movements are not subject to any fixed limit. The kinds of compensation for expenditure which count the most cannot be calculated. He who dies while responding [to his enemies with] the cry of his party makes no calculations, but rather gives his life. The greed that he satisfies is no longer his: he dies. It is his will to satisfy his party, rather than himself, that removes his fear of death.

On the other hand, the gift facilitates profits. The voice of the people declares and repeats that it is impossible to conquer without risk, to acquire without shedding blood or sweat. But one can *invert* propositions of this type: one cannot risk without attempting to acquire . . . There is a surplus in aid of expenditure. The constant advantage gained from expenditure dominates social life and transforms the fate of everyone.

VARIOUS ARMED STRUGGLES GIVE THE GIFT OF THE SELF AND GENEROSITY THEIR POWER

The profound meaning of wars and revolutions shows through in the play of expenditure. A revolution, a war is sometimes the expenditure of force in aid of acquisition, sometimes the satisfaction of greed in aid of increased expenditure. Following a large-scale obliteration of men, the first French Revolution gave rise to the bourgeois world: it was led by a class that needed to enrich itself through production. By contrast, Roman conquests directly amassed wealth with an eye to the conqueror's expenditure. The interest in acquisition dominates when a class that is productive and "circumspect" about expenditure comes to power; the interest in expenditure dominates when profligates wage wars. It could conceivably be a regular movement that balanced itself out. Over time, excesses of frugality would be followed by excesses of squander. In no sense would any kind of violent interventions have to take place. There would simply be a kind of equilibrium. But power has too rarely fallen into the hands of men who are both wise and miserly: there is little reason for an equilibrium to exist.

There is no doubt that wars and revolutions are extreme forms of activity in every sense. It is well known that violent revolts are opposed to wastefulness and destroy those who are wasteful. However, this depends on certain conditions: a form of squander that is decadent or obsolete, a form of revolt that is youthful and centered around work.

Even if we move from a lavish world to some kind of state oriented around the spirit of utility, the movement is made with a sense of vitality: from the weak to the strong. Sometimes, it takes a long time to get going again. After a crisis, the decadent course of events must be reduced. Even then, power falls into violent hands, and this remains as a token of prodigality.

Discomfort sometimes intervenes, putting the brakes on everything, but there is no escaping a fundamental law. Be it a war or a revolution, armed struggle for power will always ultimately strive to place power in the hands of the profligate—the hands of those who risk their life. Struggle wrests the course of things from the primacy of acquisition, diverting it from the path of "honest reason," on which there is no prize for putting one's life at stake. The lure of power has always been that it offers an opportunity to "senselessly" waste human life. The unmoving masses have always condemned this waste, but their condemnation is powerless [*sans force*]. To a politician, the "great masses" are just a mob of lunatics. Like the rationality or the rights that the politician idolizes, the mass is, in its entirety, dead weight, and heavy. Strength [*force*] is, on the contrary, found in the free gift of the self.* That strength becomes twisted

*The greatest evil of the present time resides exactly in the confusion of force with mass. If we build our armed force with mass, its opposite, we are left with a weightiness. Because mass can but *does not want*, in principle, to be force. This is a rationalist type of error.

and corrupted if it seeks payment in gold; the one true mark of services rendered in blood is that they are repaid solely in glory.

It is the game of strength [*jeu de la force*] that makes human life brilliant and glorious. If directed toward conquest, it gives pride of place to the gift of the self. Even conquest is, in that case, gilded with a glorious halo of death: it is *sacred*, it is less the living than the dead who have made it so through the act of giving their lives. The dead have not only gained power [*force*] and wealth: their sacrifice has raised life in its entirety up to the height of death; it has transformed an irrational excess of expenditure into something exemplary.

CHAPTER V
WINTER AND SPRING

THE EXISTENCE OF SOCIETIES AT THE LEVEL OF DEATH

The physical change that results from death is much more striking than other natural changes: it throws us between heaven and earth. In a single instant, we measure the speed of the movement that bears us away. The tangible presence of this movement disorients us and snatches the person who looks on a dead man away from reality as much as death snatches away reality itself. The living being who sees his fellow die can no longer exist except *outside himself.*

At the moment of death, the solid reality that we thought we possessed disappears. It does not exist anymore except as a presence both weighty and fleeting, violent and inexorable. It is this presence of a reality that is different from the one in which we normally live that the personified gods of death embody. Or, more simply, it is what we evoke when we speak of death as an impersonal force. When we sense this devastating force, nothing can survive within us apart from feelings of great intensity. Our childish interest in tiny things, in the little amusements that fill up our pointless days no longer have any meaning: a great wind carries them away. At this moment all existence is severely judged and laid bare: the lowliest of men is condemned to greatness.

In that moment, each of us is driven out of the narrowness of our individual personhood and, to the greatest extent possible, we lose ourselves in the community of our fellows. That is why communal life must hold itself to *the same level as death*. In private, most lives are fated to be trivial. But a community cannot endure except at the same level of intensity as death. It will start to rot as soon as it does not have to face the grandeur of danger. It must take on everything that is "unappeased" and "unappeasable" in human destiny and cultivate a rabid thirst for glory. For one man in a thousand, the level of intensity of his life over the course of a day is never much more than zero: he goes about his business as if death didn't exist and contents himself with existing below his level. [*Crossed out*: But people have the power to measure their existence by death: the life of every community must not only be beautiful but also great, because each time a living being dies, their presence must be felt by the helpless fellows they leave behind.]

Every community looks after its corpses and, in an impersonal manner, must comfort the person upset by death: "I understand what you are going through." On the subject of the decisive violence of death, the community must say exactly what could never be said if it were not itself possessed of violent life.

This is why the soldier and the priest are the only ones who can speak about this in a suitable way. The first confronts death; the second is involved with the afterlife. Profane attitudes have become unacceptable in the presence of death. The unraveling of the self before a corpse calls forth a sacred world. I must lose myself in a vaster sphere, where there are forces that brave horror. None of this would be able to take place in a café or a bank: it is only in the violence of an army or in the night that falls upon an old church that such a weight can be borne.

HORROR AND GLORY; HIBERNAL DEATH AND VERNAL DEATH

Death is total expenditure: it strikes horror in those it leaves out in the cold. It finds expression in the sorrows of winter, the frost-covered earth. A human death is the lament of the dying earth. The planet has ceased to radiate its force: the desolation on its surface is a sign of exhaustion. As this surface moves away from the sun during winter, everything closes in on itself and all expenditure withers. Only spring restores the power of the sun: withered life violently decomposes; vegetation gets drunk on manure and light. For a time, the planet's poverty ceases: the blue of noon sings with immense life. By a mad germination every flower makes itself solar: like a sun drunk with flames, the flower does what the earth no longer has the strength to do—it shines forth and spends its wealth lavishly. It blossoms and gleams, however, only to die. Prodigal spring dies like greedy winter. But its dead do not put an end to its triumph.

Death, like all expenditure, differs according to the different forms of wealth. The death of a galaxy or a star is the condition of its brilliance. Greedy death is anguishing. Man is not wretched because he dies—to die is to live gloriously—but because he longs to escape his fate. The fear of death is the principle of greed. Man can only choose between dying richly or dying poorly, between the garlanded death of May and the somber death of November. Yet the question he has posed himself is: "To die, or not to die?" endlessly stringing himself along with vague immortalities. Thus, he has chosen a miserly death.

But he only made this choice so as to triumph even more. On the whole, the course of human existence, like the rhythm of the seasons, is an alternation between barrenness and excess. This alternation increases man's triumph over death. Death, considered in isolation, is inexorable destitution. Far from denying the horror of death, man accentuates it. The community as a whole gives itself up to death, to the inevitable horror of [grieving] members of the community: it mimics their depression and their misery. But the violent actions of life quickly take over again: the community only mimicked depression so as to better facilitate its excesses. The community takes over when death has placed its members in a *sacred* situation. Its function, therefore, is to make those who are stricken by death live through the entire cycle, proceeding from a sacred degeneration to a renewal. The community draws its power from the *number* who enrich it, because the renewal of man is like that of plants. The triumph of life desires innumerable spring flowers: it is a renewed rush of blooming flowers.

This is the crucial game in the lives of men: through all their twists and turns, men heed the commands of earthly cold and solar fire. It is this that only the profligates can do. Like death, the dismal barrenness of winter is common to all men, but the miser contents himself by limiting the evil as much as possible. The profligate throws himself into the game: he trembles and does not back down from horror; he wants to conquer it. He cannot renounce the glory of spring. He knows that one cannot reach the May sun without passing through the mists of November, that a heroic expenditure is the condition for all glory. The gods know no resurrection without being put to death. Would it be possible for expenditure to propel us to the giddy heights of festivals—which presuppose wealth and favorable conditions—if we had renounced it under adverse conditions? Awful sacrifices are necessary for joyous expenditures. Religious acts throughout history spur the transition from anguish to shining ecstasy, from earthly sacrifice to solar exuberance. They follow the rhythm of the seasons and never neglect winter, in the barrenness of which death must have his day.

To play out this drama that incarnates the play of the stars [*jeu des astres*], armed struggle must take shape alongside religious rites. That struggle is the result of wretched suffering: it is the realization of the law that wills the particles of earth to grow at the expense of the forces they encounter. But those who expand war do so by giving themselves up. They bear the brunt of the most harmful fate on Earth: they are riveted to the task of acquiring riches. But their fortune is tied up in the extreme difficulty of their enterprise: they do not acquire anything without suffering extensive losses. These losses are the cost of the glorious aims of the conquest. The plunder from the conquest serves no purpose. For conquerors, wealth is but a means of splendor, a means for renewed war, a means of ostentation. The sun of victory, which gleams through a shroud of bloody mist, is not the sign of greedy gain (if it were, the soldier would not be able to make sense of death). It presides over the glorious communion of arms, over the radiance of shredded flags by which the dead are made present once more.

CHAPTER VI
WAR

The life of an army is always active. And one cannot imagine "contemplative" soldiers. Most often, if the games of war are "contemplated," it is to denounce their extreme absurdity. This was done from 1914 to 1918. To live up to the values of battle—courage, the gift of the self—it is a bad idea to reflect on them. You must let yourself be swept up by them. But there is an exception.

No one has described the battlefield and its horrors more acutely than Jünger.[1] I want to show that there is an equivalence between *war*, *ritual sacrifice*, and *mystic life*: they involve the same play of "ecstasies" and "terrors" through which man links himself up with the games of the heavens. But more often than not, war is distorted: we cover up its glories and its horrors. This is why I cite Jünger, who does not avoid anything.

"The horror of this spectacle outstripped all predictions; peoples' strength evaporated in the presence of this sad, gray figure, sprawled out on the side of the road, around whom fat flies were already making their rounds. His face and all those that came after it reappeared again and again in many different poses: shredded bodies, cleaved skulls, pale phantoms that harrowed the memory . . . During the long nighttime marches in this agonizing desert, the heart felt as isolated and stranded as if it were far above the mortal reflections of a sea of ice. The inevitable ambush that surrounded us extinguished the flame of our zeal. How many times did someone's dying cries expire without an echo in the course of their slow agony! . . . Although we had spent many years wandering these abandoned wastelands, we would always return to them with our bodies trembling profoundly, as when one wakes after a fit of madness . . . Where were we? On some outcrop on the craterous surface of the moon? Cast off into the depths of hell? This land, surrounded by yellowish flames, where the infernal dance of death would rage, could not have been any place on earth." This is how Jünger described the front.

Jünger goes on: "The smell of rotting bodies is unendurable, heavy, sickly-sweet, repulsive, penetrating like a viscous paste. It would waft so intensely over the plains after great battles that starving men would forget to eat. We often saw groups of heroic fighters, isolated in the mists of battle, clinging to part of a trench or a line of ditches for days on end the way that shipwrecked people cling to sundered masts in a storm. In their midst, all-powerful Death had planted its flag. Fields littered with men, mowed down by their bullets, unfurled before peoples' eyes. The corpses of their comrades lay beside them, mingled with them, with the seal of death on their eyelids. Their harrowed faces recalled the frightful realism of old images of the crucifixion. The heroic fighters, almost collapsing with starvation, would stay crouched down, enveloped in a stench that became unbearable every time the storm of steel set the tragic dance of death in motion once more, launching rotting corpses into the air. What good would it have done to cover the tatters of their flesh with sand and quicklime? What good would it have done to hide them under tent canvases to shroud their black and bloated faces from sight? Their number was truly too great! Our pickaxes collided with human flesh at every strike. All the mysteries of the tomb revealed themselves, so atrocious that the most hellish nightmares seemed as nothing in comparison to them. Tufts of hair came flying off their heads like autumn leaves from trees. Their putrefied bodies took on that greenish hue of fish skin and shone, at night, from between the gaps in their ragged uniforms. Our feet, squashing them, would leave phosphorescent footprints. Others dried out like chalky mummies that were slowly falling away to dust. The skin of others sloughed off their bones in a reddish-brown jelly. During the heavy summer nights, these swollen corpses seemed to wake like phantoms and, from their wounds, eructations of gas escaped with a whistling sound. But the most horrible spectacle of all was the wriggling of the worms . . . Is it not true that we stayed on the road four days, among the corpses of our comrades? Were we not all, the living and the dead, covered with the same whirlwind of bluish flies? Is there anything more terrifying in all of Horror's kingdom? Among those who were sleeping forever, more than one had shared our nights of vigil, our canteen of wine, our scrap of bread! . . . When, after days such as these, the bent, ragged soldiers trooped off toward the rear for some rest in long, gray, silent columns, their march would freeze even the warmest heart. 'They look like they just stepped out the grave,' murmured one passerby to his daughter."

This is the language of mysticism. The great care taken over horror is neither a vice nor an effect of depression. It is the threshold to a church.

"Blood," writes Jünger, "gushes through the arteries in divine incandescence when a man advances on the battlefield fully aware of his valor . . . Whoever arrives at this highest point of his personality has respect for himself. Is there anything more sacred than a warrior? A God??? . . ."

He adds: "Courage is the total wager of one's own person. . . . If one . . . understands the true reason for combat, one cannot fail to honor heroism, to honor it everywhere and particularly in one's enemy. . . . The warrior defends his cause as bitterly as he can and we have shown this to be true on both sides of the barricade—we, warriors the world over . . . we have broken the stone vessel of the world . . . we have chiseled a new face onto the earth . . . *the vast swathes of sacrifice that we have agreed to form part of a single holocaust*[2] *that unites us all!*"

Only the horrible "slowdown" of the war of 1914 could have permitted this kind of "contemplation" of horror and oneself—as well as this mysticism. Mysticism, paradoxical contemplation, occurs when the contemplative person acts, when he contemplates action! The overly rapid rhythm of classical wars prevented anyone from probing their depths: people would travel across the kind of landscape Jünger describes at breakneck speed (instead of haunting it over four years). The feat of having overcome the impossible—and having communicated such mastery—is a moment of decision and of [*rupture?*].* But nothing can alter the natural law of things: *war does not want to have its hidden depths revealed*, and the lyricism of horror is poorly suited to it. The lightning war brings about well-known conditions: conditions wherein "the rest is silence."

If not for the acute crisis that has stricken us since 1914, Jünger's reactions would be unintelligible, out of place: to proclaim them would be unacceptable. The army acts without making proclamations. When it comes down to it, its showy aspects and the fanfare of its parades go alongside its modesty. The macabre horror and the grimace of Christ on the cross belong in a church, not a barracks. Soldiers want action, not ecstasy. Jünger's lyricism profited from the momentary impotence of a will entirely dedicated to decision. It fed itself on failure and sluggishness. But just as a slow-motion film breaks down the gallop of a horse and allows one to understand how it works, a slow war and the

*The passages of Ernst Jünger that I have cited are extracts from *La Guerre, notre Mêre*. The fact that after the most recent war, an edition of this book was able to sell out in some few weeks recalls the lucid judgment of Nietzsche: "Wars are the only stimulants to the imagination now that the terrors and ecstasies of Christianity have disappeared. . . ." In light of this fact and this judgment, the world in which we live is less obscure.

form of expression it inspired revealed the underlying game. We look for "terrors" and "ecstasies" in combat as much as we do in a church. The bugles deny it on parade, but that ostentatious denial is nothing but a hurried impulse and a systematic easing of the game. Jünger's testimony, weighty as it is, is more legible: "A remark on ecstasy: this state that is particular to saints, great poets, and great lovers is precisely analogous with true courage. In both cases, fervor raises one's energy to such a height that the blood boils through one's veins and foams as it flows through the heart. It is an intoxication that surpasses all intoxication, an unleashing of forces that sunders all ties."

Action and decision cause wars to move quickly and all horror to be forgotten. The conqueror must move fast: everything he does is in service to the final result. Terror or horror increase ecstasy: both diminish the chances of destroying the enemy. One must override and deny them sharply. The attitude of soldiers toward horror marks them out in opposition to the religious faithful. For the former, horror *is right there* in abundance; the latter must fabricate it. Whereas combat is never stationary, someone who performs a sacrifice lingers over the victim, shows him off, glorifies him, then consumes him as an intoxicating draught.

Compared to war, sacrifice is a paradox. War is explained by conquest. There are many explanations given for sacrifice, but while the means are always the same, the results can be different. All things considered, we see that sacrifice differs from war insofar as it seeks results in such a way as to not limit the amount of wealth that can be gained from undertaking actions—quite the contrary. In a certain sense, sacrifice is a free activity, a sort of mimicry. Man aligns himself with the rhythm of the universe. And because the only thing that matters is mimicking the universe, there is no reason to hurry through the places where the road gets narrow. Quite the opposite: we can increase our anguish. Since that is the road that must be taken, and there is no reason to hurry, the only thing to do is to push things to their limit, to linger until the sundering reverberates throughout life in its entirety. Religious life is a deepening of our convulsions and our conditions of life.

This deepening is made possible by gaining a certain amount of distance from reality, which is overly terrifying. Gaining a gradual distance at the very least. Soldiers killed to conquer. The sacrificial priest who put his fellow to death did not have this excuse. He simply had the desire to go deeper. Thus, he made himself the accomplice of the most horrible aspects of life, those aspects that we must overcome before acceding to glory. It is surprising that such a practice was at one time almost universal—but the fact is undeniable. In the most civilized cities of today, we still celebrate sacrifice. Symbolic sacrifices at least. We put a human God to death, we eat his flesh, we drink his blood. That subdued nature of this practice, which is basically reduced to nothing, is the clearest demonstration of its significance. At the same time, we perceive its universal nature—enduring through all time and yet unacknowledged—in such a way that we must flee from it even as we linger.

In principle, sacrifice demands human victims—better still, it demands kings or gods. Animals are often victims by substitution. A long time ago, people looked on human sacrifice as something horrible. It was almost entirely suppressed by the ancient world. But when a sacrificial myth has taken on a uniquely human meaning, it goes without saying that it is a matter relating to man—not only man but king and God as well. However, the inability to bear it has become more and more intense. Sacrifice is first and foremost symbolic, but this has not always been the case. The divine Christ, the supposed king of the Jews, was actually put to death. We must give an account of this execution. We must say why it took place. Should we say that Christ was put to death to be glorified? That is possible. But if that is the case, then priests deliberately took it upon themselves to execute him in order to glorify him. Symbolic sacrifice also commits one to doing the same thing. A priest today still sees himself as carrying out a true sacrifice. But he refuses to take responsibility for it. Or if he does take responsibility, it is to the extent that he makes himself out to be that which he longs not to be at all costs: a miserable sinner. Because it is the sins of the world that put Christ on the cross.

Reason comes into play in this way of seeing things. Because there is nothing more inconceivable to reason than the idea at the heart of this book: that loss is necessary not to gain some kind of result but for the glory of losing or losing oneself, and that loss is only glorious if it is, before anything else, horrible. Reason rightly thinks that the world would be lacking in laws if it were to submit to such a strange and necessary idea. In the eyes of reason, the world must possess some kind of fundamental justice. Death alone, even unprovoked, is undoubtedly enough to make one doubt this justice. In any case, justice is lacking to such an extent that people will willingly make their fellows suffer death. But the rational principle of the world is not necessarily compromised by the mistakes of its creatures. Maybe these mistakes, these sins, have been justly punished, with death being imposed on all creatures as a punishment. Then, since justice wanted to redeem itself, that punishment was sanctified by putting God-as-man to death as the final outcome of human sin: death itself, the punishment, was transformed into the path of salvation.

In seeking their fate's ultimate goal, men find obstacles wherever they apply themselves. Military life is clearly subject to the needs of real action. Religious life, by contrast, melts away [*perd*] insofar as there is no [*unquestionable?*] need for it. The "terrors" that flow from it must be located in conventions or rites whose fantasies or savageries are questionable. It loses in its wavering and lack of rigor what it gains in liberty. Those who enter its domain have the potential to tear it down under the weight of their fatigue. Normally, it's possible to avoid the exhausting and feverish aspects of religious life by trickery. Sacrifice brings into play the attractive qualities of a great power: it is the effect of a violent need to lose. And as such it threatens, first and foremost, he who carries out the sacrifice. Possessed by the need to lose, a priest incarnating a god could, like this god himself, become a victim in the act of sacrifice. But he rarely makes the same demands of himself as his myths make of gods. A holocaust consumes [*consume*] the god and puts him to death, but it does not consume the celebrant. A religious suicide would be the only thing that could measure up to the demands that are given free rein during a bloody sacrifice.

There are more examples of religious suicide than one can imagine. The English introduced police measures to prevent pious Hindus from throwing themselves under Jagannath's chariot. A French traveler who saw Morocco before its conquest recalled a scene at which he was present: a young dancer belonging to a fanatical sect, with the tip of his tightly clasped dagger pointing ahead, closed in on the bare breast of an old man; in a trance, he rested the tip on the man's heart and the tip slowly cut through. . . . The execution of kings, which seems to have been frequent in days past, can in a certain sense be understood as a practice approaching suicide. The King of — entered the tomb that he would be buried in himself, as was the custom. Even though the king might not have willingly taken part in the practice, if he who commands the destiny of his people is actually sacrificed by them, there is no longer any question of trickery or any substitution of victims.

But not much has ever been done along these lines, with people taking such firm decisions. As a rule, people try to escape.

Military holocausts are forms of intervention. They are real and possess a value of abundance. In truth, soldiers cannot tolerate either the trickery or the real actions of priests. They counter these tricks with the true gift that they make of themselves; they respond to weighty and murderous gestures with their principle of efficacious action to which they rigorously hold themselves. Nothing is more opposed to the military spirit than religious sacrifice. A mystic community of soldiers such as Islam is the only kind of religion in which there is no place for God to be sacrificed and where the myths do not involve the sacrificial death of a divinity. The army opposes its true and intentional sacrifices to the simulations of priests, as well as to their excesses. On the other hand, the faithful could say that military life, subordinated as it is to action, does not measure up to what they desire. The army is too permissive in its choice of members and only cares about the effective actions they take, rather than caring about their true lives. Soldiers die and sacrifice themselves easily and without "mystery," as in a sudden accident, without any preparation that would enrich their death with meaning. These silent deaths lack any sign of the [*illegible*] virtues that are required if our game is to be thrown forth [*projeté*] into the games of the universe: this task requires the detachment from action and the minute attention contained in religious rites.

Let us no longer imagine that we are Jünger's companion who "burst into piercing and prolonged laughter as his head was shattered by a bullet," but rather the Tibetan monk retiring into solitude in the shadow of towering mountains. The place he longed for is one "where corpses are cut into pieces to be abandoned to the wolves and vultures." He surrenders himself to a "comedy" of sacrifice. He does not die, but a long meditation makes him more acutely aware of his own body as "dead prey, fleshy, succulent-looking, enormous—filling the universe." Then, his vision shifting, he sees his own shining intelligence in the form of an "Angry Goddess" holding a skull and a knife: the Goddess cuts his head from his corpse. In her fury, this "Goddess" (that is actually himself) tears the skin, piles bones and flesh up before him, rolls it all together and "binding it with intestines and snakes for rope, she swings it around her head and dashes it down to earth with great strength, reducing it and all its contents to a pulpy mass of flesh and bone." Then the meditator "sees" savage hordes throwing themselves on this heap, devouring all of it down to the last morsel.

There is nothing real about this exercise. The body treated in this way remains intact. But the ascetic man possesses—undoubtedly—the ability to make what he sees in his inner contemplation as tangible as anything in the real world. And in the ecstasy of this terrifying vision, it is as if the old man really had been crushed: the limited life of the human being is lost to a much vaster reality, in the same way that a crashing wave loses itself as it falls back into the ocean that surrounds it.

I must try to find a way to connect the achievements of the Tibetan monk with something that we might all be able to achieve, given similar conditions. A dizziness and a light laugh, a power that stretches forth but loses itself painfully and transforms into a torturous violence—that is what grows in sudden silence, *like in the act of sacrifice.*

Because the condition for an excess of joy is, within oneself, to kill, to be morally cruel, to strike an *accord* with the *discordant* movement of everything that exists—to strike an accord with death. He who does so happily discovers inside himself, as part of a violent upheaval that is entirely interior to him, that nature does nothing by halves, that it does not kill by halves, that the life within it does not pulse by halves. An excessive feeling of victory lifts up the man who puts on the mask of a dead man: this feeling is not intoxication, since it is lucid, nor terror, since it is happy: at one and the same time it contains something of the mad laughter—which sickens—and of the cry that can no longer be contained.

CHAPTER VII
SACRIFICE

To those who have followed me up to this point, I owe a long explanation.[1] I give man an inhuman image, and I know that I make the air barely breathable. I justified the most somber Molochs[2] when I said that there was a meaning behind the bloody fantasies of sacrifice. Even if my words join choirs innumerable across time, even if they resound with the echo of divine festivals, I know they must appear hostile. No one is likely to say that I wish to initiate new cycles of holocausts: I am simply explaining the meaning of old customs. Savages used cruelty to respond to needs that we now satisfy in other ways. But I affirm that life demands the gift of the self and that such a gift brings with it mortal anguish. I am one of those who holds that men are destined for something more than the endless increase of production, one who incites them to sacred horror. And my call, which clashes with common sense, cannot be justified solely through obscure ideas about the stars.

And yet, I can reverse the positions! Even if I lack common sense, even if I have to explain myself, for my part I still question "tranquil, reasonable man." Even if I am crazy, in the line I am following I am nonetheless still in agreement with those who used to engage in sacrifice. Were I alone, I would first have to justify myself. But the fathers of "tranquil man" themselves conducted sacrifices. And I come to say of these executions of men and beasts—which really happened—that they are the enigma that man must solve if he wants to survive, if he wants to remain this thing that he is: a tranquil and reasonable person! *How can it be that in all places, without having consulted one another, men found themselves in agreement concerning this enigmatic activity, that they have all felt the need or sensed the obligation to ritually kill living beings?*

Before he answers, "tranquil man" can no longer do anything except listen to me. He must suffer beneath the weight of such an enigma—*as much as I do*. He must recognize—*with me*—that death, tragic terror, and sacred ecstasy are linked; and that, for lack of knowing how to how to respond, all men remain paralyzed by not knowing *what they are*.

We mustn't linger over answers that have already been given. The Ancients thought that the benevolence of the divine world had to be acquired through payments or presents: Christians received this point of view from them. An Oxford professor, Sir James Frazer,[3] proposed the idea that people might have seen immolations as a way of obtaining bountiful harvests.* French sociologists have seen that the rites of sacrifice knotted together social ties between men and provided a basis for the communal unity of groups. These explanations offer an account of the *effects* of sacrifice: they do not say what compelled men to religiously kill their fellows. It must be said that the last of these explanations[4] formulates the problem precisely: it is the key to all human existence.

We must ignore any subsidiary explanation that reduces the "why" of things to contingencies. It should be said of the question of sacrifice that it is the *final question*. Reciprocally, it is clear that every proposition that seeks to respond to the *final question* must at the same time resolve the problem of sacrifice. Any discourse on being, any metaphysics is meaningless if it does not take into account the games that life has been made to play with death.

We must link the problem of the religious execution of beings to the problem of their structure. It is time to go to the heart of the matter, without fearing what is difficult and repulsive. It makes sense to begin with the representations provided by "French sociology." French sociology, which attaches great importance to the study and interpretation

---

*This bias did not deprive *The Golden Bough* of sense: at the same time that it shows the richness, the extent, and the universality of sacrifices, this book has the merit of linking them to the rhythm of the seasons.

of sacrifice, has dedicated its work to the conception of the *social being*. That conception has typically tended to be shocking: but we can accept it if we accept that such a *being* is *composed*.[5] Clans, cities, states, in the same way as persons, are beings that possess a single consciousness. The idea of a "collective consciousness" does not sit easily with the principles that underlie the idea of consciousness as an indivisible moral entity. But these principles are not very defensible. Consciousness is undoubtedly nothing but a field of concentration—this field is poorly limited by a concentration that is never complete or closed: it does nothing but gather together what the many mirrors of life reflect. More precisely still, it appears as a multiplication of each *reflection* that is produced when this *reflection*, this game of mirrors, passes from one point to another, from this man here to that man there, just as from one cell to another. We never get to pause in this game: there is always movement, activity, passage. Beings (such as man has defined them in taking himself to be one) are never present like the pebble in the river but like the flux of its waters or, better yet, like the flow of electrical current. If there is some unity in a being's presence it is held in whirling eddies, in circuits that stabilize and tend to close in on themselves. I readily grasp what changes in myself when I *communicate* with others—if I speak, if I laugh, if I am lost in some stormy assembly. And the average man seizes it if he embraces the woman he loves. This change sticks to the flow of a current of life from one person to another, but these flows generally happen without forming stable circuits, as happens in the formation of a clan, a city, or a state. But there is no need to speak of being unless a form of subsistence is assured through time, as in the case of a social formation brought together by numerous individuals (almost in the same way as the animal brings together numerous cells).

I will develop these general considerations—derived from ideas made familiar by French sociology—in order to put the final question of being at stake. Sociologists link these considerations to an analysis of religious facts that they want to perceive from the outside: they do not know how to orchestrate the themes they introduce. However, if we follow the transformations of beings into different states, if we see the wholes that compose them form themselves and then fall apart, we discover at the same time the path followed by these religious acts for which the crucial moment is sacrifice.

And not only the path, but the need that drives it to pass through this point and not any other. Nothing is less surprising. If man's meditation on himself and the universe reaches its extreme limit, it rediscovers the blind and sure approach of those who were not led astray by the complexities of reflection. It is sated by the knowledge that a man recognizes himself in his distant ancestors.

It is necessary to insist on the fact that all beings we know of are composite. Strictly speaking, we are referring to simple bodies (electrons or other particles), but we can only say a few things about their nature: the phenomena to which they give rise sometimes express themselves as if they were the effect of clearly distinct corpuscles or molecules of energy, sometimes as if they were caused by continuous, undulating waves. What we can say of simple bodies appears still more obscure if we consider that they possess very little identity. The elements must reach a level of complexity that is significant enough so that we can say of one of them: it is this one rather than that other one which, despite being absolutely similar to it, is nevertheless not the same. There is undoubtedly nothing more to say about a particular electron than about a particular wave. Insects that are clearly single entities, wholly separate from one another, obey the general law of probability. If one were to place two similar flies into a cage divided in two by a movable partition, and if one fly was marked blue and the other was marked green, then (supposing that no other factors entered into the equation that might attract the flies toward a particular side) four distributions are equally possible when we slide the middle partition closed. One possibility is that both the flies are together on the left side; a second is that they are together on the right; a third is that the green is on the left, the blue on the right; a fourth is that the blue is on the left, the green on the right. Electrons do not obey the same law: under the same conditions, with equal probability, only *three* positions are possible: two electrons together on the left, or two on the right, or one on the left and the other on the right. This means that we should make no logical distinction between the following two cases: on one hand, electron A on the right with electron B on the left, and on the other hand, A on the left and B on the right. This absence of difference itself means that we cannot usefully distinguish A from B, no more than one can distinguish between two waves. Wave B, some seconds after the passage of wave A, lifts the same mass of water—is it wave B that conserves in a single point the identity of wave A or does this identity belong to the movement of the wave that follows it?

10-5-40[6]

A precise response to this question wouldn't make sense. But on its basis the possibility of a lasting confusion disappears. An organism, a solid fragment represents so many isolable elements once and for all: for their part, an electron or a wave are isolable but only for a specific amount of time—not once and for all but only once: for that specific time, not for any other. Separation and isolation are the rule for the latter of these two sides; the rule for the former is communion and fusion, wherein elements are not separated from one another except fleetingly. A law like that which governs the probability of the position of electrons has placed man on the path to his fundamental truth: the isolation that rigorous reflection manages to lock him into (when, affirming "*I think, therefore I am*," he links the *I* to thought like to his irreducible molecules) is not the law of nature as a whole but only a limited aspect of this nature.

Further still!

It seems that, in the world of cells, communion prevails over the unstable isolation of individual cells. The opposite is true in the world of stable organic unities and solid substances in which human thought has taken shape: for the most part activities can be traced to clearly distinct foci (whether of people or forces) which cause them. But just as the *separation* of elements is already marked in a world where *communication* is limitless, so too does this world that is divided up into separate individuals find itself ceaselessly stirred up by efforts to maintain such separations due to fears about having to *communicate*: each of us must surrender ceaselessly to the loss of self—be it partial or total—which is *communication* with others. A first opposition between two worlds (a world of light and of electric forces as opposed to a world of men and of solid substances) gets confused with a second opposition internal to each of them. But for us, who are inside the world of men and solid substances, the opposition before us is not abstract, but rather, we live it: it is the battle waged between life and death, prodigality and greed, conquest and the gift of the self.*

---

*In principle, considerations made on the basis of scientific facts, far from offering the mind any foundation whatsoever, serve above all to provide new spaces for it to move through like the Wandering Jew. Strictly speaking, if thought completes the circle, returning to the elements of its birth, it has a chance to escape quickly from the particularities that separate it from the bare reality of its object: if one makes use of a "scientific fact," it follows that thought, beginning from a denatured object, cannot in and of itself make naked contact with the object that it must grasp. It is only because thought is itself the denaturalization of every object that the operation takes on, however, a charged meaning. Thought can undoubtedly rediscover nudity, but thought is above all just the garment we use to cover each object. Its development and its return suppose that after having dressed something up, it lays it bare. If by chance a "scientific fact" lays something bare, tearing away the cloth that gave the object its misleading appearance, then we could make use of this for ends that are not proper to it but that we have faithfully pursued for a long time: with the aim of trying to destroy what separates man from the exterior world that is his truth, the thought of his object. The recourse to science, to that which uncovers, is nothing but a detour in this enterprise: it would not be of extreme importance if this detour, once taken, one day ceased to have any practical value—if the human sciences, always unstable, should one day come to remove the possibility offered in the course of their twists and turns.

Each of us seems trapped in narrow isolation. In each person's eyes, the only thing that matters is the self. When something affects someone from the outside, a man typically boils it down to the happy or sad impression he receives from it. The only radical limit to this innate solitude is death: it is the only serious refutation that illusion ever encounters because, if I die, the world stops being reducible to the reflection I have of it in my mind. Everything told me that I was the only thing that mattered. But death warns me that this is a lie: because I don't matter at all, it is the world alone that matters. I matter only insofar as I am in the world not as a stranger isolating himself and closing himself off but as a molecule of energy losing itself in light. I see therefore that, if I must live, it is on this tragic condition: that in losing this life, which belongs to me, I give myself up to what is ignorant of me, to that which is wholly outside myself. But, at the same time, I again feel the absurdity of a loss which, seen from the point of view of my inevitable solitude, looks like the annihilation of the entire universe.

In this way each man must simultaneously contemplate keeping himself locked up in isolation and escaping from this prison. On one side he sees the foundation of things—that without which nothing would be: a particular existence, egoistic and empty. On the other, he sees a world in which splendor emanates from particles that communicate and engender each other reciprocally like the flames in a hearth or the waves of the sea. In his heart of hearts, an unmoved consciousness lurks: outside, the blind movements and excesses of life rush past. By necessity, a man is torn between these irreconcilable poles because he cannot choose one direction or the other. He can renounce neither his isolated existence nor the exuberance of the world that mocks such isolated existence and sets out to destroy it. A daily conflict wages between the tiny enclosure and free space; and first and foremost, between other men and the self, between generosity and greed. But to go from within to without, one must go through the strait gate whose name is Anguish.

The sphere of isolation is like a prison that would protect you from the dangers outside while keeping you locked up inside. This prison wouldn't be entirely closed: a narrow conduit would be preserved, hidden in the wall. But this conduit wouldn't be a true escape: it would be almost impossible to use and would cruelly destroy any prisoner who tried to use it: outside, the armed sentinels would keep watch, ready to kill as the storm outside the walls raged on. One of the strangled ways in which the interior being communicates with the free space outside is doubtless only rarely through actual death, but communication is always a kind of sketch of death—either its image or its prelude. What will later on appear as the decisive victory of life appears first as a horrifying threat to this isolated being who, in the depths of his isolation, believed himself the necessary condition for all that is.

LIFE IN COMMUNICATION, NOT IN ISOLATION

On the inside, what am I? The activity uniting the numerous elements that compose me, their continuous communication with each other. My life as an organic being is made up of transfers of energy, movement, or heat. That life cannot be localized in a single point: it produces itself in moving rapidly from one point to another (or from a multitude of points to a multitude of others), just like a network of electrical currents. As soon as I try to grasp my substance, I feel nothing more than a slippage.

If I now envisage *all* of my life, I notice that it is not limited to this interior mobility. The currents that flow through it are not only inside but outside; my life is simultaneously open to forces directed toward it, coming from other beings. I can regard this life that belongs to me as a relatively stable vortex: this vortex ceaselessly collides with others that resemble it. These others alter its course just as it alters theirs. The movements of force or light going from me to my fellow—or from my fellow to me—matter no less—ultimately, they matter even more—than the interior convulsion of existence. Words, movements, music, symbols, rites, gestures, and attitudes are so many paths for this contagion between beings. An isolated person doesn't matter—his point of view cannot be taken up—alongside those movements that take on meaning for many men. Personally, I am nothing when placed alongside the book that I write: if it communicates what has set me aflame, I will have given my life to write it. But the book itself is little if it is constrained to some isolated domain, like that of politics, science, or art: communication can put life in its entirety at stake and trivial possibilities fall away in the face of such a grand possibility.

If we focus only on the kinds of communication, among all others, that link two beings, and if we think about the love between Tristan and Isolde in particular, then each of these two lovers risks appearing just as insignificant as any other beings outside the passion that links them. It is their love, not what they were without it, that bestows on their names the power they have to pull at the heartstrings. However, this communication that they created between one another out of their own being would not be as significant for us if we did not see that they staked their whole lives on it and that it consumed them even to the point of death. Communication matters less the more it limits itself, and even the love of Tristan and Isolde, however convulsive it was, seems narrow next to the ecstasy of a solitary individual or the passions that link entire peoples.

Each of us, in the unlimited movement of all peoples, is nothing but a convenient stopping point for the spillover.[7] Our isolation allows for this stopping point, but the stop has no meaning except in the intensity accumulated for when the movement starts up again. Separated existence is nothing but the condition of communications that are delayed but explosive. If there was nothing but communication without restraint, if eddies did not tie up and slow down the overly rapid currents, the multiple enfoldings of our consciousness would not be possible. This roughly stable order of things and the apparently definitive construction of isolation are necessary for the formation of a reflective consciousness. The movement itself cannot be reflected except with the aid of the relative fixity of a mirror. Misunderstanding occurs only when this reflective consciousness accords serious significance to this short time of rest that circumstances afford it. This time of rest is simply a time to recharge. Consciousness itself has no meaning unless it is communicated. When it continues, the intensity of the movement of communication holds only the explosive form imposed by the momentary obstacle of isolation: the pause means that communication is charged with the profound meaning imparted by the anguished consciousness of a solitary man. Deliberate consciousness and mortal anguish can both be found in the moments of communication that unite me with my fellows. They can be felt most acutely if communication puts existence itself at stake, if the life of a people and the presence of the universe find themselves joined together therein.

LAUGHTER

Laughter is a major form of communication in which everything is violently called into question. As far as it seems, it is only when death enters into play that life can burn with the extreme incandescence of light. However, the narrow and ever-strained search for such moments leads to a weightiness of spirit. The pressure of this search undoubtedly runs contrary to the need to lose oneself, which lightens the load: when an obsessive concern for ecstasy dominates my life, I can ask myself whether I would want to get a hold of this ecstasy (which I would have no hope of achieving except by losing myself) in the same way that one might possess a worthy and enviable form of power. When the need to communicate by losing oneself is reduced to the need to own more, then it is time to admit that nothing sublime can exist in man except those things that we must also *laugh* at. Yet, of all the most intense forms of connection, none are more common than the laughs that we share together. Whereas troubling over sublime connections once threatened to ensconce us in absurdity, our laughs ceaselessly give our lives over to easy forms of communication.

I must be guided by a meticulous sort of wisdom if I am to respond to the enigma of sacrifice. However—though it was not in doubt for a second—I know that such a dangerous enigma is not within the ambit of an academic method; we must approach the sacred mystery via a darker path, drawing attention to its audacity and its violating power. We must respond to the enigma on the same level that celebrants operate on. My desire is that it form part of a history of sacrifice rather than of science. In principle, this desire perhaps summarizes what I mean when I say that I am going to resolve the enigma—by laughing. I do nothing in this way but introduce a second enigma: "What becomes of those who, seeing their fellow fall over, burst out laughing? Can it be that their neighbor's inconvenience gives them so much joy?"

To my mind, the second enigma shifts the terms of the first. The person who accidentally falls over is the substitute for a sacrificial victim; the communal joy of laughter is the substitute for sacred communication. But while we have never known the emotion that the Mexicans felt while watching a man die at the hands of a priest, we have all laughed upon seeing one of our neighbors fall down. People even used to tell us that this was "nothing to laugh about": as children, being told this made us no less inclined to laugh. If we had been asked about our glee, we would not have had anything more sensible to say than the Mexican would have had about the satisfaction he felt. The only clear thing was the communicable enchantment we felt. We let out a full-throated, remorseless laugh that led us all to penetrate the secret heart of things together. We mixed the joy of laughter with the joy of living. In a decisive way, the bewitching spark of laughter became for us a sort of aurora and a strange promise of glory. We should never stop describing the dazzling things that men discover when they laugh: their intoxication opens a window of light onto a world crying out with joy. In fact, this world is so brilliant that they quickly turn their eyes away from it. A person needs considerable strength [*force*] to keep his attention fixed on this point of dizzying slippage. If an essay discusses laughter, it invariably focuses on its mechanics. Tired sages[8] endlessly dismantle laughter's minute workings as if, when it comes down to it, it is foreign to their minds: they avoid seeing what their own laughter immediately reveals to them about the nature of things and their life.

The doors of laughter open endlessly—as much in the spirit of the old savant as in that of the naïve child. Even if it is true that the laughter becomes weary and cracked (as men go sour and withdraw bitterly into themselves), those people who laugh are able to experience such a rapid movement of communication that they lose all sense of composure. This kind of bewitching radiation that we lose ourselves in when we laugh is not really located anywhere—it does not come from a precise point, and it does not move in any exact direction. But, if it takes place, the withdrawn individual all at once ceases to be separate from a world of fulgurating, instantaneous movement. A person falling over was all it took to reveal that stability was an illusion: like the person who falls, those who watched him also move from a stable world to one that slips away beneath them. All divisions fall away, unleashing convulsive movements of laughter that echo in unison. Not only does each of them share in the unfixed flow of the universe, but they all mix with the laughter of others, to the point that, in a single room, there are not several independent laughs but only a single wave of mirth. The frozen solitude of each laugher is almost subtilized, all following the course of their lives as if they were waters rushing onward in a free-flowing torrent.

Yet they take communion in a ravishment so intense that the most human among them could not act more paradoxically or profoundly if he tried. They all *know* that their destiny links the giddiest highs and the most pitiful falls. For them, such falls are like a glimmering goddess that captivates them and whom they adore unquestioningly, but in an entirely intimate and unspeakable way. There is no union more glaringly truthful than this, save that which occurs between a man and a woman when they are alone together. Even someone who arrives too late to see the fall still lets himself get swept up by the contagion: laughter has the virtue of provoking laughter. Mirth is the sign of the fall—which has just taken place—or of some equivalent cause of joy: it certainly causes perspectives that liberate the mind to be present. Resisting the invitation comes at a price. Isolation is never anything but the effect of a morose humor, of a weariness or weightiness; tempted to enter into a "mad dance of liberation," the spirit, in its first movement, rushes forth.

Say I know someone whom I rarely see and when I suddenly run into him, we recognize each other: suddenly delivered from solitude, we laugh, reconnect, and communicate with each other, even though we would remain isolated among people we did not know, people with whom we had never shared any communication. When I was a child and people used to tickle my belly, the tickling would make my belly convulse suddenly and independently of me: these movements that were out of my control made me burst out laughing; I was drawn out of my self-enclosure just as those bursts of laughter were drawn out of me. I and the person who tickled me would enter a communal convulsion from the moment when my little belly had lost the stability that I thought it had. The laughter would increase if the tickling increased, until it started to hurt, and the closer I was to crying out in anguish, the more I laughed. The moment when one is set free by laughter is not so much the point when it starts but the point when it increases so much that it reaches a marvelous intensity. It is precisely at this moment that the anguish that would normally paralyze activity increases the violence of the convulsion so that it is impossible to stop. The laughter of recognition never multiplies because a pleasant meeting is unlikely to provoke the shrieking discomfort that intensifies laughter. It is not anguish that causes the laughter: on the contrary, if I laugh when I happen to meet a friend, it's because a tension close to anguish is lifted; hearty laughter ensues if the meeting takes place after some truly anguishing experience, like if a long-term threat is avoided (in this case, it no longer matters that the meeting is surprising). Clearly, anguish does not unleash laughter but anguish in some form is necessary: *laughter begins when anguish is lifted.*

No "procedure" for relieving anguish makes laughter more complicated. In the car, if I laugh when I reach the fastest speed possible, it is because the pleasure I feel in going fast exceeds any elusive fear of danger (I wouldn't laugh if I was more used to it or if I was entirely incapable of fear). I can laugh heartily if it is not me who is afraid but another person, such as a pretentious old lady who is as opposed as it's possible to be to the world of intense movements that I love. The driver speeds up as he hears her scream: the anguish at stake is not mine but someone else's. It could reach me, it barely reaches me because of my hostility. In normal circumstances, an imperceptible anguish is lifted by pleasure. Children laugh heartily if someone they're afraid of falls down—if they knock apples from trees, for example, they laugh at the screaming owner who falls down while chasing them. What dissipates is perhaps the shadow of anguish even more than anguish itself, an anguish that we would really suffer from. However, if they were not aware of the degradation of the one who fell, the children would not laugh. The *law of concomitance* I spoke about on the subject of the gift of the self applies to laughter.*

The loss suffered by the one who falls, the degradation, does not typically make him laugh: he does not profit from it. By contrast, the child who watches him fall benefits from seeing himself as superior for having remained standing: this is what makes it easy for the child to relieve himself of the anxious thought that he is similar to the one who fell over, that he could have fallen himself. Indifference or hostility are necessary (or the fall needs to not be too severe). In the concordance that we afford it as much as in the loss itself, whatever is lost and gained must be proportionate. If the loss is excessive, and there is little to no profit, the anguish is not relieved: a concordance with the loss is not possible. A young English girl would laugh morbidly when she learned about the deaths of people she had known ( ).[9] This abnormal conduct—given the good education and kindness of the young girl—makes clear what we reveal when we laugh: the concordance, at the deepest level, of our joy with a movement that destroys us. But the rarity of this case also underlines the difficulty of this concordance.

As far as this young girl is concerned, I imagine that the reason she laughed had less to do with the death that she

---

*Note [*an expenditure is made possible by a simultaneous satisfaction of greed; by the same token, a loss provokes a gain (a satisfaction of greed)*]—but note specifically that in laughter there is not loss but harmony with loss. [This note reprises the "law of congruence of expenditures and gains in glorious acts" established in chapter IV.—Trans.]

learned about than the anguish that, in a secondary sense, was provoked by the thought that she really ought to stop laughing even though she inevitably would not be able to prevent herself from doing so. (The same circumstances sometimes cause an actor to laugh uncontrollably on stage.) This secondary anguish, which amplifies the laugh even as it strangles it, is easily stronger than the initial form. It sufficed first of all for the young girl to only dimly understand the overwhelming meaning of death. When she then understood it, she started to laugh, and laughter already begun has far more power to relieve anguish than nascent laughter. If it is true that laughter is a movement in which anguish is relieved, it will continue or redouble; the reasons for stifling it will not disappear (they may even increase), because its movement will again and again be required to relieve the anguish that is again and again renewed. Such a development is not possible in a chance meeting or a moment of recognition, both of which resolve the troubling factor instantaneously, thereby removing any possibility that it might continue. There is this possibility in laughter that comes from tickling (when a person is lightly tickled at first, it causes only a limited amount of anguish that is easy to get rid of, but tickling could quickly become aggressive). In the interpretation that I gave of the morbid laughter of a young girl, anguish freely develops on its own in her mind as she laughs. But the development is more obvious and more complicated in the pleasurable creations found in wordplay and comic scenes.

Until now, I have spoken only of laughter arising naturally: but men have cultivated laughter, as if laughter were for them what the budding flower is to the plant. They do not use subterfuges and tricks to multiply laughter and encourage its reverberation. Principally, the process consists in stoking the source of the laughter in the same way that one does a fire: we throw new fuel onto the fire which burns all the quicker as the heat increases. Generally, it is the same kind of fuel that is added—it is just about adding more. But sometimes, the convulsive force of a mad laugh encourages the person who causes it to push things as far they will go: he pushes himself to dizziness, nausea. To help me understand things exactly, I would like to provoke such states myself, right now, but all I can do is recall part of a film (*The Gold Rush*).[10]

Up in the mountains, two absurdly childish characters fight each other inside a little wooden house (so grotesquely that already no one can keep from laughing): suddenly, the house, shook loose by the brawl, slides down the snowy slope on which it was poorly anchored; it slides rapidly down to the edge of a precipice where it teeters, remaining suspended right up until the last moment, propped up by nothing but an old stump. Such a cliff-hanger—in and of itself—should surely provoke nothing but extreme unease. Granted, the characters menaced by death don't know it: unaware, they continue to behave as if they were on solid ground. Their error, the illusion of stability that they hold to as the abyss opens beneath their feet, is in itself a comic element like the others, increasing the laughter that is already underway. But in situations that normally elicit laughter, the emphasis is placed on the error and never on the anguishing element, particularly if it concerns the threat of death. This pronounced threat, which continues to renew itself as forcefully as one can imagine, even communicates an intolerable vertigo: as the vertigo increases and the rocking becomes more horrible, the convulsion of laughter reaches an intensity without limits. The measureless potential of worlds opens up to the person who is torn from their life by this crisis to the point that he *dies*. Because in this sort of beyond where he emerges—where he cannot help but emerge even in spite of himself—he has ceased to be able to recognize what frightens him the most, he is no longer separate from death, from that which kills, since an inextinguishable laugh which, ripping him apart, has made him cross the threshold, has drawn him into a horrible union.

If this isn't exactly how things are, then it's close enough. It is not exactly like this because a ruse was required to relieve the anguish: the threat introduced is not only in a fictional world (that would not make any difference—I can worry about other imaginary characters) but in the low-stakes world of comedy: it does not press upon anyone with any real seriousness (I put myself into that world to the precise extent that I laugh at them). Yet, when I was under the spell of intensifying laughter, which went too far, these differences had ceased to matter in the same way: I did not perceive anything distinctly except for the sweet and luxurious inner concordance of laughter and vertigo. In this intensification, anguish is not relieved as a result of the balancing of accounts between profits and losses. Being swept up by the movement, it is possible to go quite far in the direction of loss. When a convulsive movement that leads to a sort of loss is born, profit—the feeling of superiority—offers a necessary compensation, but when the convulsion reaches its mad intensity, this feeling can no longer perform this role. Undoubtedly, the characters threatened by death continue to be "unserious"—if this were otherwise, the laughter would be paralyzed, vertigo and anguish would take its place—but the person laughing has stopped feeling more serious than those at whom he laughs. It is in this sense that he is truly carried away into the "limitless beyond" which he first saw from on high. But his entry into the divine sphere and his own death do not take place *exactly* as I have described: they do not take their full meaning from the fact that the person laughing has stopped partaking in the serious world. They take place exactly as I described, but from the outset they are loaded with inferiority: they will be null and void when the person laughing once again becomes a serious man.

[*In the margin*: to become a god—my laughter under an umbrella[11]]

At this point I must highlight the automatic, uncontrollable nature of this course of reactions. What we have under our control, what we can modify at will, has relatively little meaning. If we could stop dismissing reactions like mad laughter as inferior, we would transform ourselves, we would build a new world, but we lack the strength to do so: we are linked to each other. We can neither suppress the weight nor modify the conditions under which we laugh: the rules are in fact so well established that if it so happened that one of us were to modify them, we would no longer be able to say definitively that he was a man—he would already be different from man, as much as a bird is different from a snake.

It would be hard to understand me without being brave enough to look closely at the moments when laughter intensifies—or at least to look at them in the way we remember them. In such moments, if he could hold onto them, a man would feel that he had become a god. But he can never exactly capture them: he would be deceiving himself if he thought he managed it. He would continue to dismiss mad laughter as something inferior rather than taking it seriously: and it is impossible to laugh and be serious at the same time. Laughter is lightness: we lose it if we stop making fun of ourselves.

In this state of suspension—at the limit between laughter and the profound seriousness of anguish, I believe I need to [*attain?*] enter—to plow headlong—into the enigma of sacrifice. At least, when I think about the moments when I was unable to stop laughing, I remember them as if seeing them at night, through eyes poorly adjusted to the darkness, still trapped in the dazzling twilight. But an awareness of sacrifice is a sort of lingering attachment to death: it cannot but bring down the spirit; however strong one's powers of bravery and ingenuity remain, an anguished silence begins.

When I used to laugh, the laughter of those around me communicated to me that all anguish was lifted: if I approach sacrifice, by contrast, I am no less dependent on the emotions of my fellow than I am when among laughing people, but the participant in a sacrifice does not communicate anything to me more than anguish itself, without relieving it. The one who performs the sacrifice and the onlookers conduct themselves as if there were one sole value charged with meaning, one sole value that counted: anguish; this anguish of sacrifice may be weak: in fact, taking in the whole scope of things, it is as strong as is possible, so strong that any increase in the number of onlookers would be untenable, the sacrifice would no longer have meaning, would cease to take place. Anguish is maintained at varying levels of tolerance: *sacrifice being the communication of anguish* (as laughter is the communication of its relief), *in principle, the sum total of anguish communicated approaches the sum total of communicable anguish.* Overly strong reactions render the operation vain: those who feel them abandon the sacrifice.

Sacrifice has a history and its various incarnations demonstrate that the level of tolerance is difficult to maintain in the long run. Men's horror at the immolation of other men has grown over time. That Calchas and Abraham slit the throats of a doe and a ram in the place of Iphigenia and Isaac signifies that those who performed sacrifices assigned the desire for them to gods, since burnt human offerings ended up being an intolerable sight for men. Although it does not make it explicit, the Bible story expresses the tragic grandeur of this struggle.

Later and in the same way, the immolation of animals also ceased to relieve the requisite amount of anguish. And from that moment an intolerance grew alongside a desire to put an end to bloody sacrifices. Men sought out less shocking religious practices. Some of them, when they saw blood flow, felt nothing but disgust. In a way, they experienced too little anguish rather than too much. Divinity for them became something less human. Eventually, the idea that Jehovah would rejoice at the smell of grilled meat came to seem revolting. At the dawn of Christianity, the communion feast, during which sacrifice was nothing but the commemoration of a death, became charged with vastly more anguish relative to that which was provoked by an immolated animal.

It is natural that at the moment when we abandoned bloody acts[12]

PRELIMINARY ESSAYS FOR *THE ACCURSED SHARE*

ECONOMY AT THE SCALE OF THE UNIVERSE

BRIEF, PRELIMINARY NOTES TOWARD AN ESSAY ON "GENERAL ECONOMY" TO APPEAR UNDER THE TITLE: *THE ACCURSED SHARE*

Basically, wealth is energy: energy is the foundation and the goal of production. The plants we grow in the fields and the animals we raise amount to sums of energy made available through the efforts of agriculture. We use, we consume animals and plants in order to acquire the energy used up in our labors. Even our inert products—a chair, a plate, a building—are subject to the conditions of a dynamic system. Using my muscular energy requires me to rest a while by sitting on a chair: the chair helps me manage the energy that I'm expending right now in writing . . .

THE EXCESSES OF ENERGY CAUSED BY THE ACTIVITY OF THE SUN

It is not difficult for me to capture the energy I need to live. As a matter of course, I have a significant amount left over and, in general, humanity, at least, possesses an immense surplus.

But it is wrong to attribute (as we normally do) our excess of wealth to recent inventions, such as the development of modern tools.[1] The amount of energy produced is *always* greater than the amount required to produce it. This is the principle of life itself, as the general activity of plants and animals demonstrates. The productive activity of a plant could be understood as, on the one hand, the expenditure of energy, and on the other, its acquisition. If acquisition weren't greater than expenditure, no plants could grow. It is the same among animals (the growth of animals is more difficult and often requires assistance from adults: in this case it is the total mass of adult and infant animals that grows). This fundamental law of life is not surprising. By expending sums of energy usefully, life is able to obtain energy from the sun, and this solar energy easily provides for the excesses of the living world.

The green parts of plants on solid earth and at sea work ceaselessly to appropriate an important part of the luminous energy of the sun. This is how light—the sun—produces us, animates us, and gives life to our excesses. These excesses and this life are an effect of this light (when it comes down to it, we are nothing but an effect of the sun).

To a certain extent, from the point of view of wealth, the radiance of the sun is unique because it is unidirectional: *it spends itself without counting and for no return.*[2] The *solar economy* is founded on this principle. If, as is typical, we consider the economy to be bounded by the earth, we isolate it. In fact, this terrestrial economy is nothing but a consequence of the solar economy that produces it and regulates it.

If, starting from this principle, we force ourselves to grasp the economic movements that give life to us, suddenly we become aware both of the energy produced in excess of what is strictly necessary, and of the general effect of this excess: if we produce more than we've expended for the purposes of producing, then the excess energy must end up going somewhere. If it is used, then it can only be toward the growth of the system that produced it. Otherwise, it must be destroyed. Whether we realize it or not, this energy at play in our activities is not severed from its original source. We are merely conduits for it—we harness the sun's rays, but only for a time. The solar energy that we are is an energy *that spends itself*. And of course, we can slow that energy down, but we cannot alter its drive to spend itself. The system of which we are a part can temporarily harness the sun's rays for the purposes of growth, *but it cannot grow without end.* After a certain amount of time, when the growth of a system reaches its limit, the captured energy is forced to resume its course and *spend itself.* The ray of light *that we are* ultimately takes back up the nature and direction of the sun: it must offer itself up, *spend itself for no return.* A living system either grows, or it must indulge in *mad* extravagances.

THE USE OF EXCESS BY INDIVIDUALS

From this new point of view, it is necessary to envisage the living world as a whole. If one looks only at a small part, then the utmost limits of that part's growth will only ever be of relative importance. The fact that an individual organism has had its fill and can no longer grow any more prevents neither the sun's rays from being stockpiled in the earth, nor the slow accumulation of all the stockpiled energy. The limit reached at the point when an animal approaches its maximum growth, in any case, allows us to observe what must necessarily occur when the excess energy available is no longer entirely absorbed for the development of the individual. A sexual explosion takes place, liberating a huge quantity of energy. Viewed from the perspective of the living world, this liberation assures the duration and extension of life. For the individual it is a loss pure and simple.

At the very least, sexual activity escapes in a flash from the stockpile of energy and prolongs the movement of the sun. The human mind views sexual activity from the perspective of the facts of *general economy*. There is a separation between the immediate impulse and its results. From the perspective of the human race the impulse should be considered accursed[3] if reproduction—the growth of the species—is the predominant objective.

THE USE OF EXCESSES IN THE EXTENSION OF THE LIVING WORLD AND THE LIMITS OF THIS USE

The activity of the globe's living creatures can only have a subordinate and provisional status in relation to the total radiation of the sun. This does not mean that life's attempts to harness the sun's rays are not constant; they are fundamental to life itself. It is the principle of life all across the surface of the globe to make use of the excess energy that the sun provides it with in order to achieve the maximum amount of growth. The limits of growth are the limits of all that is possible. Extension only stops when life has invaded and filled all the accessible space. Not only does each species—vegetable, animal—occupy on its own account all the space in which it can live, but living nature itself multiplies its forms to the extreme in order ultimately to gain access to that which had once been inaccessible (that which had previously remained off limits): trunks and tree branches raise their leaves above the grass, winged insects and birds fill the skies with life. The same process of colonization takes place in bodies of water, in the silt at the bottom of the oceans, even in solid earth. Life eventually reaches the only limit there is: complete and total occupation of available space. And when it reaches that limit—even when it draws near to it—it functions in the same way as an individual that is no longer able to put its supply of surplus energy toward growth: the surplus remains, but its energy regains its original freedom. As life is unable continuously to invest the energy usefully, it consumes[4] it *as pure loss*.

THE USE OF EXCESSES BEFORE THE COMING OF MAN

It is difficult to trace the play of energy in times that precede the coming of man. At the very least, a precise picture of all its movements would require a vast array of different forms of knowledge. The basis for this no doubt exists, but its details are yet to be established. The livable domain must have been filled, life must have almost reached its limits, long before man ever came to be. In what ways could energy be wasted within this state of nature? Only a series of in-depth studies from biologists would be able to answer this question. For now, I must make do with some general propositions. Excess is the incontestable starting point. Once extension is no longer possible, the surplus can no longer be usefully invested in growth. This implies *a priori* that great quantities of energy were available to the creatures that had the power to waste them. A certain advantage was afforded to beasts of prey. Carnivores of diverse animal classes were not simply better adapted than herbivores: the latter were ill-suited to a system in which growth is subject to limits. A world filled only with herbivores would have known nothing but famine, that much is certain. Permanent famine cannot result from superabundance. And so excess was offered to those that desired it in the form of flesh. Provided, however, that they *wasted* it. Had carnivorous animals been driven to economize, had they used up all of the energy within their grasp and ensured that it only returned the exact amount as was produced from eating animals (had they made use of the same quantity of energy produced), they would have become weak.

In the long run, however, it became clear that the wasteful expenditures of predators would never be enough. Even as those expenditures produced themselves again and again over an extended period of time, they still could not sate the relentless appetite of the living world for waste, for getting rid of whatever could not be contained.

IMPORTANCE AND DIFFICULTIES OF THE PROBLEM OF EXPENDITURE

Approaching the question of the economy against the grain in this way might give some readers pause. I do not want simply to pervert the traditional point of view, but rather to push a principle toward the point of absurdity, going as far as to claim *a need for the world to get rid of whatever it cannot contain*. It is easy to expend what cannot be contained . . . Never has such a mad problem been posed.

I must now, therefore, be as clear as possible about what I mean. Up until now, the consequences of such a simple principle have been poorly understood. *Any system that has a certain amount of disposable energy must get rid of it.* Human beings have always had an intuitive understanding of this point. Acquiring is difficult, spending is easy, no matter the resource available to us (money, for example, which is nothing but a form of energy). In the sense that the words *difficult/easy* can be used to describe split-second reactions, they are quite apt terms. But the rapid action of a sprinter involves no more effort than does the slow labor of a construction worker. In practice, the principle I've defined is as follows: given that I take in and use a certain amount of calories each day, and given that a certain portion of those calories is necessary for me to stay alive, the rest, assuming I don't get fat, have to be entirely expended. I can come and go, talk, whistle, work, or laugh. I can set aside my money, but not the energy I need to live. There are never more than a few seconds between myself and the deadline by when the remainder must be, or must already have been, spent. I only get to decide how to waste, not how much.

Without any doubt, it is a fact of fundamental importance that a given sum of calories assimilated corresponds to a determinate expenditure of energy. If this fact has tended to be neglected, it is not because it was ever unclear, but rather because it was so self-evident as to seem not worth troubling over. It is precisely because it is an ineluctable certainty that it has not been taken into account. Whereas acquisition is riddled with difficulties and carries the possibility of failure, expenditure, on the other hand, is absolutely inevitable. It does not, for all that, always make for a happy state of affairs. In any case, we must distinguish between *active* and *passive* solutions, for the latter tend to be inconvenient to those who fall victim to them (this is the solution that the carnivore provides in relation to the herbivore).[5] If one admits that, generally, there is agency in active responses, spending—when the excess can be invested in growth—is as important and as difficult as acquiring (Keynes's bottles are the illustration of this principle).[6] It is this that makes the focus on excess energy—which is what characterizes *general economy* and distinguishes it in principle from classical political economy—valuable not only to the human sciences but also to the general theory of evolution. Considerations about the extension of the space available for life have (quite recently) been introduced into biology. Now excess must have its turn as well: as we have seen, the former is nothing but a consequence of the latter.

MAN AS A SOLUTION TO THE PROBLEM OF EXTENSION

Man provided the definitive solution to the general problem of excess. On the one hand, he considerably extended the capacity of living things to make use of more than just a small part of the energy available. On the other hand, he unleashed numerous types of expenditure from within the provisional limit placed on extension. But it's not quite right to say that man "provided the solution": man himself is the solution. Humanity is the consequence of a critical point in the flow of solar energy.

Man is an effect of surplus energy: as a matter of principle, the extreme indulgence of his lofty pursuits must be defined as a dazzling liberation of excess. Free energy flourishes within him and releases endless, useless splendor. But this excess of energy could not have been set free if it had not first been seized. Consolidation was necessary for expenditure. Human activity exploits the riches of the earth with new tools. This is how it expands the domain of life. Men do not limit themselves, like trees or winged animals, to only occupying spaces that are already available. After all, it's not as if the available space was not already filled to breaking point with life long before their arrival. But by making use of new tools, they put a great deal of energy into constructions that increased their power. They uncovered, and continue to uncover, life in dead matter, something which must, when it comes down to it, be viewed as one of the many ways of extending the bounds of life.[7]

MAN AS A SOLUTION TO THE PROBLEM OF EXPENDITURE

But we should not give primary importance to the means by which man extends the domain of life because, *more and more*, this means is in and of itself what contributes to the excess. It is doubtless the periods of investment that provoke this: ultimately, these periods cannot help but speed things up. Capitalist accumulation tended to curb the sumptuous expenditures of the feudal world. Accumulation, nowadays, can operate far away from any limits: the plague of unemployment (a *passive* solution) nevertheless indicates that there is already some energy left over that cannot be invested in growth. This is why the essential problem that the life of man must resolve—actively, if possible, passively if not—is coming to a head in our lifetime.

The crisis is all the more acute for the fact that men have departed further and further from active solutions as the problem has gotten worse and worse. Sumptuous expenditures are frowned upon by the masses: they are habitually taken up by a small number, to the general misery of all. Today, it is still accepted that the world is poor and we must work. But the world is sick with luxury. A strange way of looking at the inequality of the world means that we think that we need to give back to Peter what was stolen by Paul.[8] The current scarcity is, moreover, the result of an orgy of energy. It is undeniably problematic simply to say: "If you work, it's only because, if you did not, you would not know what to do with the vast sums of energy at your disposal. You can consider working less but you cannot stop working altogether and do nothing. Never forget that you are nothing but an explosion of energy. You will never change that. What are the works of man that surround you if not a vast outpouring of the energies of life? Because the resources of the earth are all available to you, and because they cannot be endlessly extended, you owe it to yourself to *spend them actively, heeding nothing but your desires*. Otherwise, you must go passively from idleness to war. You cannot deny it: the desire is in you, it is alive; you cannot ever separate it from man. Essentially, the human being has the task of expending in all its glory what the earth accumulates, what the sun lavishly provides. Essentially, the human being is a laugher, a dancer, a holder of festivals." This is clearly the only serious language. Humanity in its infancy was given over to practices of glorious expenditure, and tragically attached to those practices the greatness and the meaning of man. The nature of humanity at a later stage has been produced through the liberation of huge swaths of energy. Let those who understand this devote themselves to these liberations. The earth has had its fill of the radiant energy of the sun—let them restore that energy to its former freedom. If they are blinded by the weakness of man's—limited—intelligence, then let them at least fear no more the heat of the sun: for whether it be willfully seized in glory, or suffered in horror, never has a task presented itself that has been so certain to come to term.

PRELIMINARY NOTES TO THE WRITING OF *THE ACCURSED SHARE*

[Dating from 1946, the same year "Economy at the Scale of the Universe" appeared in *Constellation*, these "preliminary notes to the writing of *The Accursed Share*" were likely edited for Bataille by Georges Ambrosino (cf. Gallimard *Œuvres complètes* VII, p. 23, note **):]

We propose to study, in broad strokes, energy as it moves through the entirety of the constellation formed between human beings and their environment. Some preliminary remarks concerning plants and animals will guide us in this task.

Plants with green leaves are characterized by their ability to siphon carbon dioxide from the air over the course of a day. They remove carbon and return oxygen back to the atmosphere. This process is made possible thanks to the solar energy that is absorbed by the chlorophyll in the leaves. As for the carbon that is acquired in this way, it enters into complex combinations to form the very matter of the plant itself. On the other hand, at night there follows an activity that is added to that of the previous day: it consists in systematically combining carbon and oxygen leading to the creation of carbonic gas and a release of energy.

Two contradictory phenomena confront each other in the life of the plant. On the one hand, solar energy is absorbed and stored up by the plant. On the other hand, the plant continually dips into these reserves so that it can expend some of the energy that had previously been accumulated. Because plants do not stop growing at any point in their life cycle, the total solar energy a plant absorbs over a specific period of time must be greater than the amount that is broken down and returned to the surrounding environment during that same period.

Plants absorb solar energy through their leaves; this allows them to survive and grow. We will say that they *appropriate* solar energy for this particular end, namely, existence. On the other hand, for a plant to remain in exactly the same state in which it finds itself requires a certain amount of energy that we will refer to via the phrase: *energy that is strictly necessary*. All we can say about this energy is that it is inferior to the energy that is broken down by the plant and returned to the surrounding environment.

Crucially: *the energy a plant appropriates for its life is greater than the amount of energy that is strictly necessary for that life.*

The excess energy that a plant possesses manifests itself in growth and blooming. By way of the latter, the plant produces particles capable of forming a new organism that will also be able to appropriate solar energy in quantities that exceed the amount that would be strictly necessary for it to simply keep itself alive.

Certain substances that are produced over the course of a plant's life function as food for non-carnivorous animals.

Put otherwise, animals find reserves of energy in these substances.

Similarly, carnivorous animals capture the energy that is appropriated for them in the bodies of their victims.

Animals use the energy that their food provides in order to hunt out new food, to grow during a certain period of their lives, and to engage in sexual activity. The energy that animals have available from the material of nutrition, therefore, exceeds the energy required for them to procure and break down their food.

On the one hand, they expend a certain amount of energy in order to satisfy their hunger. This energy exceeds the amount of energy that is strictly necessary for them. On the other hand, their nutritional matter provides them with an amount of energy that allows them to effectively carry out not only their basic nutrition, but their growth and their sexual activity. We will call this second form of energy: *the energy appropriated for production.* And we notice immediately that, for an animal, *the energy appropriated for production through its way of life is greater than the energy strictly necessary for that life.*

We want to show that an analogous law applies to human society.

The burning of wood, of coal, of petroleum products, as much as waterfalls and wind are phenomena from which humanity in general reaps a profit by liberating energy. One must furthermore consider the work provided by domestic animals and, above all, the work of man which lets other energies work in his favor.

But from the perspective of energy, domestic animals and men are simply motors for which food is the fuel. We may thus figure nutritive substances in the list of sources of energy.

A chief particularity of man consists in the fact that a portion of his labor is devoted precisely to the production of food. Man is in this way a motor which, by its action, extracts and puts to work its own fuel—it is a motor that nourishes itself. But this fact does not in any way change the way in which energy is released from its sources.

On the other hand, another particularity creates certain difficulties. Man is not content merely with food; he needs clothes, shelter, buildings, light, etc. When a certain state of civilization has been reached, we will admit that men on average have to maintain a particular style of life that cannot be sustained without the use of certain objects that are judged to be indispensable, even though at other periods of history these objects may well have been unknown or superfluous. These lifestyles differ from place to place: the worker in the U.S. and the worker in France do not have the same conception of what is thought of as the minimum required for life. The totality of objects and the food that a worker has access to on average, at a given moment time in a particular and undifferentiated country, will make up that which appears to us to constitute what is *strictly necessary* for the life of a man.

Let us now try and describe all of the equipment that is possessed by men in society as a whole. It is comprised of fields, residences, buildings, clothes, factories with their tools, mines, communication networks, electrical networks, theaters, etc. This equipment is brought into operation by the sources of energy that we have compiled. The energy takes leave of these sources and circulates throughout all of the equipment along various branching paths until finally it ends up disappearing completely; at least, it disappears insofar as it is no longer energy that is and can be used by men. All these uses of energy produce objects. Some of these function as raw materials for other objects, others enter into the composition of more complex objects; some allow for materials to be fashioned, and still others are necessary for satisfying the needs of human beings.

Thus, a waterfall causes a turbine to rotate and drives alternators. The current produced circulates in the wires of an electrical network whose branches end in a motor that drives a lathe. This lathe fabricates brass screws, for example. It is easy to follow the transformations of energy and its circulation along this path. The kinetic energy, having been transformed from the waterfall into the rotational kinetic energy of the turbine, is transmitted by a linking axle to the alternator. This then gives it the form of electrical energy transported along the network. One part of this electrical energy is transformed into rotational kinetic energy by the motor. After this energy has then been transferred to the lathe, it carries out the work of making the screws.

As it circulates from the waterfall to the lathe, a large part of the energy gets used up [*se perd*]. Physically, to be sure, it turns up again in another form, namely in the release of low levels of heat. But practically, in this form it serves no purpose for man as he cannot transform it into useful work again. The resting energy that presents itself in the rotation of the lathe itself creates in its totality a form of energy that cannot be used throughout the construction of the screws.

The energy pipeline that we have followed from its source, the waterfall, to its final point, the fabrication of screws, ends with the following result: not only does it transport energy, but it makes that energy serve a particular and exclusive end, the construction of screws in a specific place. It *appropriates* the energy for this purpose. We will not misspeak if we say that this pipeline "produces" energy that is appropriated for the construction of screws in this place, and we will suggest that the amount of appropriated energy that the pipeline produces is equal to the amount of energy that disappears (as energy that can be used by humans, in the final stage of production).

It goes without saying that the categories of appropriated energies are very numerous. They can be measured as a single physical unit, but this treats their specific appropriations abstractly. Finally, though they may be of equal physical quantities, economically they are not of the same monetary value, as this value is regulated by the sum total of the socially necessary labor time required to produce the two basic types of energy.

For anything that is produced, it is easy to work out precisely the amount of appropriated energy that is involved. The energy that is used up in the construction of an object, such as a brass screw, is not comprised merely of the energy that was appropriated for the transformation of a brass rod into a screw, but also of all the appropriated energy forms that were necessary for the production of that brass screw.

Similarly, when it comes to a complex object like an airplane motor, it will be necessary to take into account the appropriated forms of energy necessary for the fitting together of different pieces.

It will be just as easy to follow the route that energy takes as it leaves a coal-fired power station. All that will be required will be to take into account all of the appropriated energy forms that were necessary for the extraction of the coal, for its treatment, for its handling, and for its transport all the way into the boiler of the steam engine.

An object, ultimately, has not truly fulfilled its purpose before it has reached the person who desires it. In an account of the appropriated energy that is used up in the production of an object, therefore, one must also include all of the appropriated energy that will allow for its transportation, its circulation, and its distribution as a commodity. This point allows us to include all of the activities that are connected with commerce within the energy-flow system.

In the case of transport, the appropriated energy produced by the locomotive is the mechanical energy that is created by the wheels of the locomotive.

The appropriated energy that man produces distinguishes itself from others by its greater flexibility. It can be applied to a wide range of ends.

In sum, there exists a complex apparatus, driven by sources of energy (waterfalls, coal, food, etc.). Men are considered a part of this apparatus. This apparatus produces appropriated energies of all kinds, capable of fashioning objects for consumption [*consommation*]. It is theoretically easy to determine all the appropriated energies necessary for the manufacture of an object.

This apparatus thus conceived has the property of being self-sufficient. The production of a form of appropriated energy, whatever it may be, requires the use of different energies appropriated for diverse ends. The functioning of the electrical grid demands oversight, or in other words it requires appropriated human energy of a certain type. Motors demand constant lubrication. It therefore needs some appropriated energy to the end of extracting petroleum, distilling it, etc. Energy therefore needs to be appropriated for extracting petrol (gas), for distilling it, etc. The system meets all these needs through its own means. Furthermore, the production of appropriated energies leads to constant wear and tear on the apparatus, wear and tear that takes place, no less, even when the apparatus is not in use. The system is also capable of replacing the material that has become unusable, which is to say that it makes available all of the appropriated energy required for reproducing all the parts of the apparatus. In the case of man, the system makes available to him the conditions of life over which he previously worried and which include within them the capacity for replacing each generation with the following one.

Let us suppose that the size of the system remains exactly constant. On the one hand, it produces certain amounts of all kinds of appropriated forms of energy. On the other hand, this process of production requires certain amounts of appropriated forms of energy in order to ensure that the system will function and that it will replace the amount of material that is used up.

We affirm that: *the appropriated energy produced during a period of time is greater than the appropriated energy strictly necessary for its production.*

To see the rigorous logic of this statement, it would be necessary to compare appropriated forms of energy of the same type. The system produces all of the appropriated energy it requires; it produces that energy in greater quantities than it requires; and finally it even produces levels of appropriated energy that are in no way required by the considered level.

In an elliptical, but more striking form, we could say that: *the energy produced is greater than the energy required for its production.*

In the capitalist era, the historical proof of this law resides in the uninterrupted development of the apparatus. It is equally valid for all stages of civilization. In this sense, among primitive populations, the appropriated energies produced allow not only for the survival of the tribe and its habitat, but also for the organization of festivals that, from the perspective of production, are perfectly superfluous.

THE ACCURSED SHARE, OR THE LIMIT OF THE USEFUL

DRAFTS OF TABLES OF CONTENTS AND SUMMARY OF MANUSCRIPTS

Translators' note: In compiling Bataille's Œuvres complètes, *the editors at Gallimard used the title* The Limit of the Useful *to refer to the fragments that remain of what they call an abandoned version of* The Accursed Share. *This "text" was written and rewritten in several versions between 1939 and 1945 as* The Accursed Share, or The Limit of the Useful. *In this section, which follows the text of* OC *vol. VII, pp. 502–507, we present Bataille's different plans for this work. At the end, there is also an outline of the manuscripts used to construct the text of* The Limit of the Useful *in the* Œuvres complètes, *which we follow in this edition, save for some slight alterations discussed in the "Note on the Text" (p.* xlix of this edition).

In 1945,[1] in the manuscript entitled *Method of Meditation* (cf. *OC*, vol. V, pp. 470 and 492), Bataille announces *The Accursed Share*: "A work begun fifteen years ago, abandoned several times, most recently, as I remarked (in *Inner Experience*) to write *The Torment*[2] . . ."

In *Inner Experience* (cf. *OC*, vol. V, p. 11), we read the following:[3]

> This book is the tale of a despair. The world is given to man as if it were an enigma to resolve. My life—in its strange, disordered moments as much as in my weighty meditations—has passed in resolving this enigma. I actually went to the end of problems whose novelty and scope exalted me. Entered into unexpected regions, I saw what eyes have never seen. Nothing more intoxicating: laughter and reason, horror and light became penetrable. . . . There was nothing that I did not know, that was not accessible to my fever. Like some marvelous madwoman, death opened ceaselessly or closed the doors of the possible. In this labyrinth, I could lose myself at will, give myself over to ravishment, but I could discern the paths at will, pick a precise passage with intellectual steps. The analysis of laughter had opened before me a field of correspondences between the data of a *communal* and *decisive* emotional knowledge and those of discursive knowledge. *Losing themselves in one another*, the contents of various forms of expenditure (laughter, heroism, ecstasy, sacrifice, poetry, eroticism, or others) defined among themselves a law of *communication* ordering the play of the isolation and the loss of beings. The possibility of uniting *at a precise point* two kinds of knowledge hitherto strangers to one another or otherwise crudely confused gave this ontology its unhoped-for consistency: the entire movement of thought lost

> itself, but all at once found itself again, in a point at which the unanimous crowd laughs. Therein I experienced a feeling of triumph: perhaps illegitimate, premature? . . . It does not seem so to me. I rapidly felt what came upon me as a weight. What rattled my nerves was to have achieved my task: my ignorance turned to insignificant points, more enigmas to solve! Everything crumbled! I awoke before a new enigma, and I knew all at once that this one was insoluble: this enigma was even so bitter, it left me in an impotence so crushing that I experienced it as God, if he exists, would have experienced it.
>
> Three-quarters finished, I abandoned the work wherein the resolved enigma could be found.

These lines of August 1942, defining the origins and the ambition of the "*Accursed Share* project" (in truth of the whole work), can be brought to bear on the dossier (plans, notes, sketches) assembled later (cf. *OC*, vol. VII, pp. 519–598—cf. in particular pp. 525–534; 171–311 of this edition), where the full dimensions of this project appear.

As for this text:

We have distinguished four manuscripts, corresponding to successive versions of the text: Ms 1 (A and B), Ms 2, Ms 3, and Ms 4—to which one must add the manuscript of *La Part maudite* [*The Accursed Share*, labeled "*AS1*" in this edition, described in French in *OC*, vol. VII, p. 471]. Each new version takes up, in part, the preceding version, in the same way that *AS1* takes up the removed pages of Ms 4, Ms 2 and Ms 1A (Ms 1B and Ms 3 being separate).

Ms 1, which can be dated around 1939–1940, corresponds to two of the following tables of contents [Box 13, F: 16–17 and 18], paginated by Bataille:

TABLE OF CONTENTS A

MS 1A

MS 1B

Ms 1a (separate leaves in Box 13, G: 133–200) is paginated up to number 137, but there are sometimes three different page numbers per manuscript leaf. In this same bundle of papers, there are also the following items:

Rough drafts for Ms 1 and Ms 2 (labeled Ff)

Ms 1b (Box 13, F: 28–182), paginated 45–192.

Ms 2 and Ms 3 correspond to the two Tables of Contents that follow (Box 13, C: 309–310 and 104), paginated and titled by Bataille as follows:

TABLE OF CONTENTS B

[MS 2]

THE ACCURSED SHARE, OR THE LIMIT OF THE USEFUL

MS 3

Chapter III. The World of Private Expenditure

Ms 2 (described below), is a reordering of Ms 1a. This is undoubtedly the version that Bataille abandoned in November 1941 to write *The Torment*.

Ms. 3 [Box 13, C: 339–370] seems possibly to date from winter 1941–1942 (see the note below, p. 282 of this edition).

Ms 4 [77 sheets spread across *AS1* and Env. 4, 9, and 98], a reordering of Ms 2, corresponds to the seven first chapters of the following table of contents [Box 13, C: 307]:

TABLE OF CONTENTS C

Preface	(General description) [*crossed out*: Customs]	
Ch. I	Situation of Man in Nature	Introduction
Ch. II	The Principle of Glory	Introduction
Ch. III	Glorious Expenditures of the Mexicans	Chart of Expenditures Fixation
Ch. IV	Potlach	Chart of Expenditures Fixation
Ch. V	The Festival Economy and the Church	Chart of Expenditures Fixation
Ch. VII	The Development of Capitalism	Chart of Expenditures Fixation
Ch. VIII	[*Crossed out*: Speculation]	War
	[*Crossed out*: Establishing the Problem]	War
	The Accursed Share	War
Ch. IX	[*Crossed out*: The Impasse of Capitalism]	War
	[*Crossed out*: The Fixation of Expenditures]	War
Ch. X	[*Crossed out*: The Degradation of Forms of Expenditure]	War
	Obligation	War
Ch. XI	The Glory of Rivalry (War as a Form of Expenditure, Sports)	War
Ch. XII	Islam (ch. XI?)	War

Ch. XIII	[*Crossed out*: The Direction toward Transparency]	Transparency
	Pretexts (the City, Christ, Revolution)	
Ch. XIV	Evangelical Christianity	
Ch. XV	Romanticism	
Ch. XVI	Transparency. Beyond Fixation and Constraint, with No Pretext	
	The Gamble [*La mise-en-jeu*]	The Summit
Ch. XVII	The Gamble	
Ch. XVIII`	Communication and the Festival (Its Decomposition)	
Ch. XIX	Tragedy and Tears, Sacrifice	
Ch. XX	Laughter	
Ch. XXI	Eroticism	
Ch. XXII	Autonomy in the Gamble	
Ch. XXIII	The 52-Year Festival (the End of Days, the End of History)	

Table of Contents C appears to date from 1943 (see below, *OC*, vol. VII, p. 581, p. 287 of this edition): Ms 4 can therefore be dated to 1943—at the least, it does not correspond to the “well advanced work” of which Bataille spoke in September 1945.

The text provided in the *Œuvres complètes* by Gallimard [and in this edition] is as follows:

Chapters I and II:

These chapters follow Ms 2 (which are supplemented as needed by Ms 4 and *AS1*). These are distributed as follows in Bataille’s papers:

Pages 1–7: [Box 13, C: 311–313 and G: 64–65, 125–126]	Table of Contents B
9–21: [Box 13, C: 316–328]	
(25)–33: [p.m: 141–155]	
34–50: [Box 13, C: 329–335 and *a.s.*: 174–182]	
52–53: [Box 13, C: 336–337]	
62–67: [Box 13, C: 338 and *a.s.*: 184–188]	
Pages 68, 71, 73, 75, 77–80, 82–106 are found in Ms. 4 [Envelope 4: 32–73]	

Chapter III:

This chapter follows Ms 3.

Chapter IV–VII:

This chapter follows Ms 1b.

DOSSIER OF BATAILLE'S NOTES AND OUTLINES FOR *THE LIMIT OF THE USEFUL*

Translators' note: The following is an important dossier of notes selected, compiled, and edited by Gallimard for the Œuvres complètes, *presented as follows:*

1. Aphorisms and General Notes from 1939–1943(?) (*OC*, vol. VII, p. 519; p. 171 of this edition). Worthy of comparison with *Inner Experience* and *Guilty*
2. Plans and Notes from 1939–1941 (*OC*, vol. VII, p. 538; p. 205 of this edition)
3. Plans and Notes from 1941–1943 (*OC*, vol. VII, p. 554; p. 232 of this edition)
4. Notes from March 1944 (*OC*, vol. VII, p. 584; p. 287 of this edition)
5. Plans and Notes from 1945 (*OC* vol. VII, p. 588; p. 293 of this edition)

1. APHORISMS AND GENERAL NOTES

[BOX 13 C: 248–250]

Neither as a poet nor a sage (nor yet a philosopher), but as the man to whom nothing worth calling poetry or science would have remained foreign, who knows *more than anything* the nauseating taste that the proud individual has at the back of his throat *and who gives up nothing of his pride*, comes the *horrible worker*: on the condition that from the summit of hallucinated misery that he has climbed, he forgets nothing of what can be found there and only goes back down to go further and higher, guided by anguish. Accursed be—better yet: accursed are—those who, having visited the summit, come back down yet lower!

My generosity: those who have lost everything but who, still idle, live in hope, must be *given* a thorough despair.

The bitterest misfortune is to attack the fate of the *individual*, of *individuals*, to keep waiting.

[BOX 13 C: 257–261]

It is possible to sink gently, to drown oneself in some celestial underground: where sensations both high and low would evaporate. Sinking thus at this moment, it is time to laugh at those observers who ask us, "How do you feel? Are you nauseous?"—"Confess! Cry out! Is it horrible?"—"But speak! Reassure us!" The only answer that ever made sense was to turn cruelly away from every question: "Too late! Everything in me is spinning—in a vertiginous way. I hate all questions, I hate you. To satisfy your thirst, I would have to catch my breath again, everything would be once again immobile and dull, just like you: thought was not given to man for him to arrange the world according to his standards but to be deranged—in his standards—by the world.

The inextinguishable laughter of the gods? For you, it's a grimace!"

It is only when pains have eased and the majority are at peace that we can see life's truths. When life allows itself to shine in all its brilliance, no one becomes conscious unless they turn away from this brilliance, unable to endure it anymore: in that event, consciousness is linked to a fear of life, to a will to ease its pains. We must recognize this as characteristically human when we reflect on the countless disorders that must result from a life without restraint. But when life lacks brilliance, we become acutely aware of a lack and no desire for restraint can break it. It is under these conditions that man can become entirely conscious of his glorious destiny.

Man in his entirety.—Sang-froid, icy clarity have no meaning if they are not supported by the extremity of the *passions*.

It is difficult to combine thunderstorms with relaxation, disruptions with power, a sort of ossified, taciturn, parched concentration with animal innocence.

Only the majesty of a cold desert supports laughter, narrow-minded cruelty and tenderness. Nothing is majestic that is not childish: to *my* way of thinking, this reciprocation is true.

I must get rid of one possibility that I am lingering over—by forgetting. I will come across it again a little further on like a wreck, floating along with the current. Then there will be time to love it, to glimpse both life and power in its abandon.

[BOX 13, E: 24–29]

THE EGG OF COLUMBUS

The error of most philosophers is to begin with a simple element. The search for truth cannot be carried out if we do not already possess it, like the lost object. In philosophical speculation, we cannot perceive anything more than "what we were already seeing" *intus* and *extus*. The postulate is that we see our truth but within certain perspectives. The search for truth is nothing but a search for errors of perspective rather than a search for an explanatory principle. I admit that "what we see" could be false (by definition, in a sense that escapes us). In this case, a search for errors of perspective would still be essential to our lives. A philosopher relating these principles to their application in this book will quickly see that I have not left the approaches of the "gnosiologists" to one side lightly, but with deliberate violence. It will also not be surprising if I advance nothing related to ideas or matter and if I occupy myself as much with what the rainmakers thought as with what the makers of principle and primary cause thought.

If I speak to a particular person (rather than someone else) about a certain thing, I do not speak to that person *in the same way* as I do to anyone else. In the same way, I do not write *in the same way* at any given time, which is different from every other time. But I say *the same thing* in both cases.

Between two interlocutors, I prefer the one who is hardest hit by what I say; between two epochs, I prefer the more difficult.

If I were to [*illegible*] myself from solitude and address my fellows by giving them a book, the first sentiment that I would want to express to those who came to read me would be hatred. I have no hate for those who don't read nor write. But in anything that is *said* and understood, that which makes light of tragedy is too heavy, written, each coarse remark further debases the absent creature that we are. Man becomes an object to be haggled over.

[*Crossed out*: I cannot imagine the discovery of truth except as tragic, as if lightning and not light had penetrated.]

[*Crossed out*: A collection of circumstances and not only the war gave]

Sun-eye-sob.[1]—A sort of menacing calm, a cold dawn, blinding and as never before seen, an enchantment growing to the point of physical fear, charged with vapors of alcohol or sulfur, with lusts, with vertiginous laughter . . . one must add some signs of complicit humor, hence the feeling of a nit, of a definitive interior rotation of the globe and the eye, it is in this way that I perceive vast universes desirous of my swooning, of my sobs.

I end this hallucinated book and am almost despairing of its powerlessness. I'm begging for hope around me: [*crossed out*: no one knows what I suffer, nor why I suffer]

[BOX 14, C: 19–21]

INTRODUCTION OR PREFATORY PARENTHESIS*

The least that one can ask of a man is to know exactly the amount of sweat, exhaustion, and suffering that his existence has cost; the least one can ask of a writer is what silent tortures are tied to the follies of his pen. It is not good that the harshness of events is responsible for teaching obviousness to arrogant idiocy. . . . It is also not good that the weight of terrestrial pain overwhelms us: no doubt a fragile joy, still troubling but unrivaled in its clarity, awaits the one who overcomes it. But would he be able to if he did not at the same time sink to the lowest depths of anxiety?

I am struck by the nature of the participants in the Hegelian representation of the world. The world develops

---

*Let the reader excuse the indecision about the terms: he would be better off in principle heading immediately to the main part of the book. I have not allowed myself to place these reflections at the end, but they are by nature misleading with regard to the book itself.

These reflections are misleading about the book, but it is true that without them the book would be misleading itself.

in such a way that it is made up of men who all die without any knowledge. Knowledge hides away, and there is no doubt that Hegel was a victim of this. It is likely that Hegel would have believed that he escaped this law: a little clarity would have made him see that he succumbed to it—without even giving rise to a contradiction: can absolute knowledge exist without a single one of the knowledgeable escaping from the law? Hegel was certain of knowledge, even as he erred. Whosoever would know without error would no longer be sure of knowledge. He should, I imagine, find in the condition of knowledge—finished in time—the reflection of what is known. It if were otherwise, how could there be identity of the subject who knows and the object that is known?[2]

And how little does this absolute knowledge matter now! How futile does the overwhelming wisdom of Hegel appear! Gone with the wind. Absolute knowledge, absolute nonknowledge, who could distinguish them now? Who could even know if I sob, if I laugh divinely, if I am mad? Who could know it when I do not?

There has never been a more difficult time for speculative thought. The movement of the world has never called into question the foundations of thought with more severe necessity. This is precisely the most favorable time for speculative thought. And I know it; it's the decisive factor.

Tempted to say: misery to those whose thought does not rise to the scale of events, but how much more misery to those for whom thought does rise to that scale! In the latter case, the pain is primarily internal.

While writing this book, I would sometimes choke on my anguish. The need to write it was like that of a police interrogation—never-ending, unable to go on. I couldn't wait to be able to forget, to laugh again, to be no more like a laugh than a leaf in the wind. But I was faithful, waiting for the excess of nervousness to pass. Such a labor, it seems to me, was unlike any other, and I choked precisely when I became aware of that. It is no accident that one day I put it off until later, ultimately for no better reason than fear. In a sense, however, I don't imagine it would be possible for me to write a book in which to register more calm objectivity. And that was precisely the most difficult thing. I had to sink up to my neck into the obscurity, as I had no other hope of arriving at transparency. What was demanded of me, torn from me, was an unattainable mastery: at the moment when I should have broken down in tears, when nothing was more challenging than the project of writing a book. I had already felt the same feeling previously, but as the challenge increased, the need for mastery imposed itself as if from beyond.

Particular movements express themselves in many ways, but in the shock of numerous contrary movements, where the waves continuously collide with one another and reach their death, phenomena of interference also arise, almost independently. How, in the course of this decisive struggle, could these complex, riven expressions have more than an ulterior meaning? This must be the case with Hegel—in a less unstable time, yet nonetheless like a foretaste of our own. Could the profound reality at play complain of seeing in this way some points of reference established in anticipation of calmer times? As strange as it is, the same intention could not but go hand in hand with the acute awareness of dominant needs—which are now current.

[BOX 13, E: 30–33]

The defense of war, such as it appears in this book, seemed like an impudence even in my own eyes. Unlike many others, it was written by a man who has not fought (if it is true that Hegel, one of the most well-known apologists of war, did not fight either, it wouldn't have been common for him to do so in his time). I must go even further: circumstances have meant that I have never had to fight but, what's more, I have never *desired* to. If I didn't run away from the opportunity, neither did I seek it out.[3]

I must be clear about this: war never interested me as it interests true soldiers. Specifically, I never stopped being obsessed by *a single war*. During the long years of my youth—from seventeen to twenty-one—this interminable war had become for me the only possible horizon, a horizon that was definitively closed. Fate did not make me—at eighteen—anything but an ailing soldier, imagining each day, among the sick and the wounded even older than myself, the hell to which I remained promised. I did not trouble myself, then, with lengthy musings on the causes or political consequences. I felt disgusted at the use made of big words and grand principles that I saw in the newspapers around me: a warrior, I was sure, could only give one meaning to what remained of his life, the same meaning that a gladiator might have found (risked finding) when he offered his death to the crowd that desired it. At that time, I wrote notes each day that I titled with sad pride: *Ave Caesar* . . . My life, like those of the soldiers among whom I lived, seemed enclosed in a sort of apocalypse that was distant but also present among the beds of the hospital. In this vision, where law and justice were meaningless words, WAR alone reigned, heavy, blind, itself, it alone, demanding blood, like Caesar seated in the stands. In the shadows of this time, I searched and searched: I found only a dead night, a human absence to lament in anguish. If I thought about some departure to come, I felt no hostility, I was sweetly attracted, I loved not combat, but the excess of anguish.

This wretchedness taught me exorbitant irony, blinding nonsense: the breach opened the way to moral savagery, to *apotheosis*. My attitude toward war, the cold judgments that are linked to it, does not result from military equilibrium: I responded to the *monstrous will within me* to one day resolve the weightiest thing in the world, to conquer even if it means embracing an impudence whose horror I recognize.

[BOX 13, E: 12 AND 14, C: 1]

Undoubtedly, the object of this book, glorious life in all its forms, is beyond the concern of most people. I speak of needs, but what do these needs mean if they do not seem to be felt? If the majority of people are *strangers* to these needs, it is not reasonable to attribute a decisive value to them. But, in truth, everyone has these needs, even if they are withered and greedy and escape from people to such an extent that they do not recognize them; fear still links them to them. Giving oneself, lavishing power and wealth, has a vertiginous attraction. It is the very attraction of joy that sets one ablaze. It is why the greatest men are not those who perform quantifiable services but those who relieve fear. There is no pleasure [*jouissance*] except in setting oneself ablaze: at the same time, nothing is more frightening.

[BOX 13, G: 50–53]

FROM CORTÉS TO COPERNICUS

In destroying—abruptly, as we do an anthill—the Aztec social structure, Cortés stole life—and meaning—from the gods and beliefs on which that structure was built. For the Mexican religion, Cortés substituted the Catholic religion, which the indigenous people had to embrace. Some Catholics—glorious if not in their principles, then at least in their lives—struck the first blow: its suddenness, its daring, the terrible character of Mexican festivals endowed this blow with an extraordinary value. As if the gods of Mexico, insofar as they were showered with blood, had been the only ones who had guaranteed the harmony between the glorious world and the world of men, from the day when their idols were abandoned the will to splendor no longer had anything more than a precarious and endangered existence. The incessant contestation of all forms of nonproductive expenditure started right from that moment. The drab and rational forms of existence and thought gained ground little by little. Successively, the primitive civilizations were destroyed or lost face, humiliated by calculating civilization.

Since the destruction of the Aztec world, in all latitudes, everything that had been ruled by fantasies or dreams—customs and popular beliefs—was replaced by rational ideas and practices.

[BOX 13, E: 49–63]

FROM WHAT PRINCIPLE AND FROM WHAT MINDSET THIS BOOK PROCEEDS

The mindset from which this book flows, I believe, situates it as a change in the history of thought. This mindset proceeds from a simple principle. This principle imposed itself on my mind, one day, all at once, not as a result of deductions: "If I laugh," I thought, "the nature of things lays itself bare; I know this nature—it betrays itself. It is the nature of things that makes me laugh." This reaction supposed that, by laughing, I let myself get very carried away. This did not entail a demonstrable proposition: it could not have been otherwise; what other response could I have given? It wasn't a hypothesis for which one lies in wait: it was, more simply, a *mode of knowing* [*connaissance*] that I seized upon. The formula mattered little: I saw directly, with steady, awestruck eyes, the secret of things, and this secret was no less clear than the bright light of day; its force was incomparable, all my intelligence lived in it, radiated with it.

So as to not *see* this, I imagine that some effective objection would have been required, some bias linked to my actions; it would have been necessary for my intelligence to oppose it. But the habits of mind that I had since [*crossed out*: that time—which can be traced back more than twenty years] then, the feeling that I had about the futility of irreconcilable opinions brought me to this intoxicating and novel *mode of knowing*.[4] I want only to reject the ill-founded objection that would reduce my attitude to that of a mystic philosopher. The act of knowing that I engage in while laughing has nothing arbitrary or personal about it: *fantasy is excluded from it*. I laugh in the same instances as a large crowd does: this feeling I have of uncovering the depths of things in moments of laughter is the same for me as it is for all other men. I speak of the outburst that results from a shock, that intoxicates and illuminates. *Comic* shock and the effect it produces do not depend on a will: the conditions for shock rarely vary with the conditions of life, this setting ablaze of man is universal in nature: to the laughable, men of all times adhere with a singular, immense burst of laughter.

This mode of knowing nevertheless has some strange defects. If the group as a whole consents to laugh—and cry out in joy—it is on the condition of the denigration of the laughable. And not only is the laughable denigrated but, if it is true that it is through laughter that I *know*, this *mode of knowing* is *not known*. The domain of knowledge [*savoir*] is so profoundly separate from that of laughter that the nature of the laughable is without doubt the question that science has treated most superficially (it has tackled it only infrequently and obliquely): we fabricated each of the various explanations like the master-key of a subtle game, so many works devoted to laughter leave men in the dark as to why they laugh. From the point of view of explanatory knowledge, laughter is an occasion for humiliation. In laughing, I can do nothing but recognize my ignorance about what I'm laughing about.

All that I needed to maintain such an absurd position was the evidence crying out in me. But I recall that my conviction, from the very first moment, did not leave any room for doubt. I ultimately distinguished two modes of knowledge, one describing all things known in the classical sciences and the other, of a quite different nature, describing a category like the laughable which the first mode had no knowledge of except from experience gained by using the second. I saw at the same time that laughter is not the only path of knowing that is alien to classical knowledge. The sacred, in particular, while it is less easy to make out, is not so for any reason that differs from the laughable: if the destructions that constitute sacrifices were recognized everywhere as sacred acts, the operation of the mind through which their nature is discerned is the same type as that by which the laughable is revealed. This extension (which went still further) rendered the distinction that I made between the two modes of knowledge more comprehensible: it did not change any aspect of the first principle from which I set out, that "I know the nature of things if I laugh." I simply came to recognize other means by which I could also know this nature equally well; what I had discovered in laughing, I had to discover once more in my approach to the sacred. It is true that in this area I lost the decisive certitude that laughter gives, that this time I had touched on the arbitrariness of mysticism: that did not matter anymore since laughter remained, through which I could always return to the *consensus omnium*.

Today, I give to these two opposing forms of knowledge the names *objective* and *communal*.[5] I distinguished them as clearly as I could in myself and, from the simple fact of this distinction, I started to establish between them a conjunction that hadn't existed. The conjunction necessarily had to be made at the level of objective knowledge: knowledge of the *laughable* or the *sacred* is acquired all at once and does not create a means of extending knowledge to every conceivable domain; only objective knowledge can claim to do that. It is in fact important that when this knowledge intervenes it does so while following rigorous methods that guarantee its partial success [*crossed out*: (without this we would risk returning to the hybrid forms in which metaphysical suppositions take over)].

Moreover, the first moment of this conjunction preceded the distinction between the two forms of knowledge. The conjunction started from the announcement of the principle, when, unlike the innocent laugher, I perceived in the laughable not just the laughable alone but the laughable as a response to the problems posed in terms of objective knowledge. And the principle, in launching the conjunction, made clear the need to carry it through. It had a meaning in itself, independent of any later explanation, because it decided on the nature of things, glimpsed in the expanded moment of the burst of laughter. But this meaning was on a different level to that of objective knowledge and the demands to which the principle seemed to respond. That was why it was necessary to accomplish the conjunction in such a way that the response took place on both levels at one and the same time. The principle responded in the terms of *communal* knowledge to a question phrased in terms of *objective* knowledge. Supposing that a concordance between the two frameworks was possible, it was necessary to transcribe the response in terms of *objective* knowledge once more. It was necessary to carry the tentative explanations of laughter through to a satisfactory conclusion.

[BOX 13, E: 39–44]

Difficulty of reconciling *what* my book *is* with the refusal of the principle of causal explanation. There are not only stated facts but causes, clearly presented in a purely scientific style.

The foundation of the method is, therefore, definitively knowledge through laughter, tears, eroticism . . . I return to the principle I started with (experience engendered instead of a method described).

What remains is this: I began with the principle

laughter is an act of knowing

the real, the foundation of things, etc., is what makes one laugh

this principle must be justified by what follows

it is a sort of axiom that justifies itself

In reality, the principle of laughter having been affirmed, I sought to demonstrate it. Quickly understood that

object of a tragic emotion (tears)

object of erotic excitation

were of the same order, that the object of these emotions was always the same but of a completely different nature from the objects considered by the intelligence.

Principle:

If I laugh, the nature of things lays itself bare, I know it, it betrays itself. It is the foundation of things that makes me laugh. (That supposes that, laughing, I let myself get very carried away.)[6]

Such a principle cannot be proved, it imposes itself on the mind *from within*, if it does not impose itself, then we remain ignorant of it.

It imposed itself on my mind all at once. From then on it remained no less clear than the brilliant light of day. Its force is incomparable, all my intelligence lived in it, radiated with it. (Principle both specific and universal—all men, if they saw what made me laugh, laughed as well, were in perfect harmony with me.)

This mode of knowing nonetheless has a deep flaw. It decides in matters of knowledge. But all inherited knowledge remains alien to it. (Non-intellectual character, independent of formulation. Secondary character of extension, already an intellectual method.)

The origin of this way of seeing is the extreme freedom given to the mind by the vanity of opposing philosophies; it is, in fact, the absurdity of all thought. Beyond a certain nonsensical point, the exercise of the intelligence no longer opposes laughter but madly aligns with it. From then on it is no longer an obstacle to the revelatory principle of laughter. Its evidence emerges, with stunning force, at one blow. The mind leaps, joyously dark in the absurd [*crossed out:* the absurdity immediately resolves itself,] the intelligence is born once again from a source unmatched in its power: aligned with the absurd and the real, aligned with a *vertiginous* slipping, aligned like lovers lost in a single embrace.

(Add: more than any foundation of knowledge, more than any metaphysics of origins or foundations, there is no more a foundation to knowledge than there is an origin or causes of the world, there is nothing but a state of affairs, like the balance that results from movement—next, aphorism on the movement of waters.)

Difference with the phenomenologists (Heidegger, Jaspers): my objectivity.

I must insist on this: laughter is not knowable from within. One cannot imagine a "phenomenology" of laughter that takes into account, at the same time as the lived experience, the true reason for laughter. The reason for an anguish bares itself by way of the experience we gain of it, but less suddenly: we perceive it, or we think we perceive it, like a tail of a mouse disappearing under a piece of furniture. We do not perceive anything of the reason for a laugh, except in reflection, and the reflection disconcerts us: the origin of laughter, to the person who reflects on it, is given from outside, it is an objective given, wholly detached from the subjective result, because we can easily recognize that something comic makes us laugh but not why it makes us laugh—the link in the chain that would connect subject and object is lacking. In this way I can say that laughter, no less than sacrifice, is a gift from beyond.

It is not chance that dictates that I begin exclusively with gifts from beyond—sacrifice, war, the festival economy, laughter—and not simply from lived experiences.[7]

Phenomenology lingers over the description of phenomenological moments, which is not my goal. My goal is not a pile of descriptions. It is to extend knowledge beyond received limits. Phenomenology could not find any reason to attribute a particular value to a moment of insight such as laughter.

(Do not say *objective* for non-communal [*non-communielle*]—maybe *realist*?)

[BOX 13, C: 277–278]

We are linked to an intelligible reality, that of a street on which a dog runs, or a car drives, etc. It is possible to explain the street, its cobblestones and passersby can be *enumerated*: we tell the *story* of its form, its comings and goings. Ultimately, the street must be written into the universe of the astronomer or the calculator of *quanta*: at this moment, the naïve reality that I rely on is erased; I have reduced it to the status of a deceitful shadow. However, it is to the *cobblestone* that I owe my acute feeling of *reality*, without which the wise man's scaffolding tumbles down.

Thus, to survive in the obscure fantasy of existence, I must preside over the flight of all things toward two points, where I touch the irreducible (at least, based on its appearance): on one hand, the *cobblestone*, in relation to the raw, crude reality of which I am clearly the satellite; and on the other hand, the *numbers*. Between one term and the other: *here is man*,[8] abandoned to his unending labor of explanation.

But *communication* always remains possible. It is inserted into the realm of the explicable but is not itself explicable. I can show how it is inserted into the realm of the explicable and not explain it: it is in precisely this way that it is *knowing* and, I would say, *full knowing*. For if I *explained* it, it would not be anything more than one of those unintelligible images in relation to which the reflective surface of the human mind is the satellite: by the same token, it would immediately cease to be *intelligible* (I employ this word, here, for the first time, in a new—and bare—sense). *Communication* has its full meaning without accounting for the *why* of the *explicable* (we cannot deduce an explanation from it); it has this fullness from the fact that the *why* is superfluous. The mind explaining the reason that proves it evidently must continue to [*proclaim?*] its why, but it makes the experience of an element of displacement and of the inadmissible in the sense that continued questioning drives it mad, literally: no answer can be given to displaced curiosities when the thirst for knowledge is quenched by a single draft of ecstasy.

[BOX 23, C: 283–284]

Reasonable (or vulgar) knowledge applied in a regulated way to the facts of communal knowledge represents man's most powerful way of hauling himself up to the windows of his prison. It's pointless to make yet another critique of the foundations of vulgar knowledge on this subject, or to find other, less fragile foundations for it. We must take this knowledge with all of its weaknesses and its strengths, its problems and successes, but take it only as auxiliary.

We will bring the forms of communal knowledge into a modified field of consciousness, a field that is clarified, sharpened by reason (which amounts to saying words, sentences, figures). It is the purpose of words, sentences and even figures to find some path toward attaining the ineffable. Nothing can be *substituted* for the ineffable, true knowledge is found within it, [*because?*] the final response is ineffable, but that signifies that there is an element within it that cannot be reduced to statement, without which the statement that speaks it would be empty; it is this element and not the statement that is essential: nothing could be more certain to prevent the alignment of the ineffable and the statement.

Communal knowledge is not, strictly speaking, objective. Just like rational knowledge, communal knowledge involves a modification of the subject by the object. However, whereas rational knowledge takes its leave from this modification to conceive of the object in isolation, communal knowledge continues to have knowledge of the modification at the same time as it has knowledge of the object. No separation between subject and object is possible; we must conceptualize a *field* of communication rather than an objectal *point*. Certainly, we could project the perceived modification toward the outside, and such externalizing is a legitimate operation, but the modification of the subject in no way differs from the projection (the field of communication).

[BOX 13, E: 68–78]

The least common virtue: a vivacity beyond the self and as if fulgurating with spirit. Without an unbound, rapid, and even violent way forward, human reflection is a cesspool. The ability to come to know [*connaître*] extreme states in a single movement—the tears of laughter—and, still more, a mad laugh, an ecstatic sob—if we accede to this, all the rest seems empty.

It is not enough to try and bring two states together; within oneself, one must combine—live comfortably with—the totality of all possible states. It is the condition not of the abstract and isolated sciences but of a knowledge [*savoir*] that responds to the anguish of coming to know [*connaître*]. It is true that we ceaselessly use science to work out some particular curiosity. But no one dares to say that the thirst for knowing is not driven by human anguish: nor does anyone dare to respond to the mandate of their anguish!

My book gives me pause because it has "too little science." I should have come to know more, in certain cases firsthand. I suffered occasionally from being ignorant of what nobody can attain; but most often I have had to remind myself that others knew more about what I speak of than me. I carry on regardless, convinced that the set of forms of knowledge [*connaissances*] that I have gathered has never been encountered before. As far as I know, until now, nobody has made use of the disparate kinds of information that make up this book in the same way as me, but it is more what I have lived rather than what I have read that has allowed me to come forth and speak. He who does not burn his wings on every lamp comes at knowledge [*connaissance*] from the outside.

To give himself a rigorous certitude in his approach the man of science renounces *knowledge* and restricts himself to wanting precise answers to limited questions—questions, moreover, that have only been posed by man's traditional *knowledge*. He doesn't see that he must give up for his own sake, rather than for the sake of anyone else. Even if he can cease to want to know [*connaître*] anything beyond his charts, human existence cannot. The concealed abdication of responsibility, the trickery of science begins when it asks men to leave everything to the *men of science*, leaving each man restricted by their ignorance of everything that isn't their narrow dominion.

What escapes every man of science is the price he pays for the partial knowledge accumulated in isolation: it was only be renouncing *knowledge* that he became the man of science he is. This misunderstanding of the destiny he carries within himself makes him like a blind beast. In a strange way, what he tries to deduce through his renunciation is man himself, whom he delivers up to a new kind of bestiality.

The fundamental condition of human knowledge today is the impossibility of any one person knowing everything. The extreme development of particular fields of knowledge [*connaissances*]—the totality of which no one can lay claim to—results in a resigned mentality. If we are to believe these resigned moderns, the audacity of the skeptics smacks of arrogance. They know nothing but their own field; in fact, they have to prevent access to it, throw out the laymen, laugh at them without ever laughing at themselves since, in their chosen field, they conduct themselves with rigor. They do not see that their irony is the sign of a decline.

I am not making things easy in any way; I could not give knowledge [*connaissance*] over to delirium. Entirely to the contrary, I place an increased demand on the subject of knowledge [*savoir*]. The domain of knowledge is closed to the languor of the poet. Ecstasy or inspiration, which want to *decide*, make the air too heavy to breathe. [*Crossed out:* (To tell the truth, a kind of inspiration without heaviness, proceeding in unexpected bursts, flourishing without ever delaying, runs the risk of being too *divine* to lead to any decision: I say this, imagining that such a method could have meaning *for others*.)] Personally, I put a principle of totality before everything else. I believe that I have implemented every approach available to me (in the same way, modern [*genius?*] uses almost every technique—moral, mystical, intellectual, industrial).

In the first place, all knowledge [*savoir*] is the implementation of the sum of forms of human knowledge [*connaissances*] accumulated up to now. However, there is no better way of implementing it, from this point on, than with rough estimates.

Second, knowledge [*savoir*] cannot go without *any* of the means of questioning that have helped the sciences to develop. It is true that I have not given explicit form to these means of questioning.

I also did not want to cause significant embarrassment to myself by introducing the contradictions that sometimes result from the incompatible opposition of methods. I deliberately used the results of different methods (objective and subjective, observation and introspection) at the same time—others who have maligned this combination have done it, too, in spite of themselves. In this regard, the only principle that I have held to is that no particular result should be taken as unquestionable. The movement of thought—in the long line of men who interminably take it up again and again—and even in the life of an individual among them—can only function as an operation of war. Even in the best case, in certain aspects, things do not go as planned. Having predicted that a particular element would arise victorious, we find that it has suddenly been overturned by the enemy . . . There is no point blaming a fault in the calculations: even when a victory is achieved, it comes with many errors, meaning that it is in the nature of human knowledge to be always incomplete. Knowledge is nothing but a movement: in the sequence of wars, there has never truly been peace, but only breaks. Similarly, knowledge is never anything more than the most recent link possible between the knowing subject and the object it has come to know (given that the subject, if not the object, varies). Thus, two beings living together have never gotten to know each other, but they do not [*admit?*] that they are ignorant of one another.

[BOX 13, C: 241–247]

Attentive knowledge is born from sacrifice, but only developed by detaching itself from it: it had to make itself objective. Objective knowledge puts what is known in a closed box and, in so doing, becomes clear and precise. But if one wants to overcome the poverty of isolation, one must break the box, and in so doing return to the decisiveness of a true sacrifice. Knowledge cannot without peril encompass the universe within the closed box of objective knowledge.

Knowledge cannot stay isolated. It may have been necessary to isolate it, but no more. Man's destiny[9] ties him to knowledge but that means two things at the same time: that man is offered up to knowledge, has no human meaning other than in it; that knowledge, in exchange, cannot be separated nor distinguished from the destiny of man.

Knowledge is existence: it is the experience that existence makes of itself and the world, where making such experience and existing are one and the same thing. Of course, if the mere exercise of one's intelligence provided a result that was undeniable and satisfying, existence would be regarded as one often regards the body, as a support, indispensable but separate. This isn't the case. Knowledge does not describe something exact: the variety of men who have knowledge have not been able to agree on this. There is the man that I am living in the world and the disagreement of different forms of knowledge. The promise of a future period when the intelligence might be satisfied does not change anything about that "there is": promising this is just one possible response among others.

I suggest imagining that the feebleness of intelligence is tied to man's use of isolated knowledge (his objective coldness and his inconsistencies). Let us suppose that, now, man's destiny were to reach new limits that, for a time, could not be crossed—this destiny, this form of life hitherto unknown, should *speak* a world born in its new nudity.

(The opportunities for this nudity if this destiny, as far as the plane of knowledge [*connaissance*] is concerned, aligned itself with this principle: to reduce knowledge to the experience that man makes of the world.)

Knowledge [*savoir*] is about comprehending and not apprehending; it is about acting, not suffering. In the act of comprehending, the object ceases to be like an alien thing to the subject. Knowing is recognizing,[10] reduction of the unknown to the known, which is to say to me (this elucidated elsewhere), reduction of the object to the subject. Knowledge [*connaissance*], therefore, always requires a living subject, in full possession of life. The intelligibility of the world by life supposes the possibility of a concordance, a communication, between the object and the subject. Before that is possible, life must operate on the edge, at the limit of death, establish the strength of the subject, which is to say: fervently multiply all forms of communication.[11]

It is not sufficient that man has become what history has made him (history, civilization, the complexity of social relations): he also must destroy himself because communication demands the *loss of the self*. In particular, knowledge arises when the subject drowns himself in the object and imagines, as a consequence, whenever it occurs, the dramatic abandonment of his initial effort to understand.

These principles of knowledge cannot be given as a method, in this sense they assume a "state of grace."[12]

[BOX 8, C: 184 AND BOX 14, C: 16–17]

However, sacrifice only creates an elementary form of consciousness. It is not knowledge. It is an act distinct from the subject. But knowledge, properly speaking, bears on objects, not acts: on the subject's *isolated* spheres [of inquiry] and not on the *communications* between object and subject.

Sacrifice creates consciousness by endowing the subject with the immobility of a sensitive plate.[13] It is only much later on that this sensitive plate will be inscribed with the objective world, independent of any relation with the subject's interiority—with the subjective aspect of the subject. In turn, this ability to conceive the object in its exteriority led to a new phase of consciousness. There was man conscious of the object—and the subject—opposing one another. This man, conscious of the object and of what opposed it, could coexist—in a single subject—with the man conscious of the act of communication, but these two sorts of consciousness were superimposed and remained independent of one another. The only way to put an end to this independence is if the development of knowledge gives the meaning of sacrifice to objectifying consciousness, if the enigma of sacrifice is reduced. This would be impossible if one tried to maintain oneself outside the sacrificial sphere. And the self, in this case, is knowledge, consciousness become objectifying consciousness.

These principles have a precise meaning that on the level of the intellectual use of knowledge [*savoir*], I go very far but not farther than possible.

These principles—which we avoid saying aloud but in fact most try to follow—are discouraging for good reason, since they give no guarantee or respite, and their general result is knowledge that is empty and devoid of sense. They end in emptiness and nonsense when knowledge isolates itself and knowledge isolates itself in fear when research is made to depend on a prior response.

[BOX 13, E: 81–83]

Knowledge [*savoir*] cannot be anything but knowledge of man, hence knowledge for man.

Sum up all forms of human knowledge—and ignorance—in their relations with the life—and the death—of man.

Or rather, for man to conquer the maximum amount of knowledge—in a given time (epoch)—to abandon himself to the insufficiency of this knowledge (incompletion), this is to define, this is to *make* man who, essentially, is knowledge ([*illegible*] reaction). And as knowledge is the—comprehensible—reality to which every other kind of reality must be related, this acquisition and abandonment represent the summit. What is made is the ultimate reality. The abandonment is sacrifice. It is the moment when knowledge is no different from madness.

Atop such a summit, lost and dizzy, who will follow me? I will be the only one who remains there. If I look at my position, I am exalted, but straightaway, when I see myself perched like this, I know myself *sovereignly* laughable. Especially as a real vertigo takes over, gives me a sort of nausea, very close to convulsions. And, undoubtedly, in one way or another, I will have to fall!

[BOX 13, G: 66–69]

He whose only concern in life is what to do next is a needy person who betrays the world, even if his goals are not self-interested. Life has no meaning, it is nothing but a pile of ashes, outside the consciousness of the games that link it to the deeper world.

But this is what we suffer through today: a person who makes of his life what it is, a tearing asunder in the glorious anguish of death, is dismissed as nonsensical by the masses of those who would have no meaning if the madman himself were not part of this world. Only the cog that is "useful man" is glorified. Man is humiliated by a shell of himself and we, we suffer the shame in a stupor.

It is blindingly obvious that the fate of the human being, today, depends on us, on the choice that we will make—it depends on intractable pride, and who could have such pride if we were not proud? But what might a person want to say about pride if they were not prepared to bind, not prepared to build a community based on strength and hardships? The wretchedness that makes it so that *we* are thus is now desperate and, desperately, in the depths of solitude, I would like to let it be heard like a cry.

The time is coming when we will have to play flawlessly: when the storms rage and redouble, we can no longer rely on the benevolence and abilities of yesteryear. From this point forward, life will keep a rigorous record of our errors and our lazy timewasting.

At issue, specifically, is the being that we are, our glorious destiny, our triumph or fall. This destiny, this triumph or fall is in our hands. The indecisive have never been able to fulfill man's destiny: it demands the gift of the self and the audacity that *chooses*. It depends on our gift and our choice that man should truly become the glorious mirror that he is in the world, no longer the unhappy cog in a machine.

Now nothing can be done except by men who take on the meaning of their community: the most weighty event, full of chaotic shocks, would just be a small number of beings linking their "community" to the communion of man with heaven and earth.

[BOX 13, F: 300-308 AND G: 122–124, 127–128]

Recognizing that the world has no meaning unless it is sacred is the province of a select few. That means that the world in which we live, the human world if it were to attain its plenitude, is composed of a multitude that will only be brought together through sacred bonds. But these sacred bonds cannot be regarded simply as cords that only have to fulfill an exterior role. What is sacred does not bind men from the outside the way a cord would bind the stalks of a corn-sheaf. Every sacred reality links itself to men by asking them to give the gift of their being unconditionally. Such a reality even merges with the gift because it lives within it: what comes from the gift of the self must be ceaselessly nourished by the gift of the self. Sacrifice founded the sanctuary; renewed sacrifices converge on it and the sanctuary is the same thing as the convergence. The "communion of saints" holds to the sacrificial life of those who found it: furthermore, to live it demands each of those who want to find themselves therein to be initiated into sacrificial life. The multitude does not have to dedicate itself to this task: a select few would be sufficient, but this supposes that this select few have a different attitude from the peasants who bind their sheaves. A peasant who binds his sheaf is satisfied if the binding is solid and maintains [*a page is missing*] Christian binds the sheaf, he binds it effectively, but he does not know that he is doing so and, moreover, he does not worry about it. All of his practices are linked together as if they were part of a drama played out exclusively between God and himself. On the contrary, we know that sacred life is the necessary link in the life of all men—we see this life reduced to a state of moral poverty that is near laughable—bands of isolated beings, a dry dust, ignorant of the hidden depths of the life that animates it, ignorant of itself and of everything in the Universe that is magic magnificence—we suffer from this disintegration and isolation—we hide among the crowds like mockingbirds, and a stormy sickness empties us out—but, however lucid we are, our lucidity leads to nothing. We ourselves have no sacred life. We speak of it only to become aware that it is lacking in the world, that the world lacks it and we lack it. We would like to bind together a world that is falling apart but we have no rope, and we know that if the rope is not in our hands, it is because life no longer tightens its knots in us; it is because we are lacking in life itself. The Christians, like those who came before them, were not aware of the need to bind the world, but they bound it, they knew how to bind it, they had only to live, and they lived; we are keenly aware of this, but this awareness means that the world is no longer bound together, it is falling apart, and we do not know how to generate the strength [*force*] by which we would live and which would save the world. And yet we must live, and the world be saved. Hesitating would be of no use. The Christian approach has ceased to make sense for the manliest among us. Action, in bringing the masses into its fold, sends a heroic tremor through them: it has no knowledge of the slow spell that weaves lives together in their intimacy and aligns them with the silence of the heavens. In truth it is as if this world is dead because the profound values that have brought it to the point where we are belong to a past that we cannot revive. We cannot remake life and carry it forward except through a new birth. It is likely that this lucidity that we are so proud of goes further than we would have ever believed in the first place. What do we have to complain about, bitterly recognizing that we are missing life's secret? That is not the question. We don't know what to do, but what does this ignorance matter since we are constrained by knowledge [*savoir*]? I will go further still: we should bless this ignorance that is linked to a constraint: rarely do such formidable fairy godmothers continue to watch over an empty cradle on their own. But their presence should appear like so many signs of life, or rather like the signs of a love raised for life. Life delights in destruction, violence and, still further, leaps into the unknown. When a new being is born, when he comes into the world, what does he know of himself? He knows nothing, but life nevertheless comes into his head. We must be like a newborn who throws himself into life without knowing anything about it beforehand.

It would be absurd to leave these undoubtedly dramatic conditions in the dark—they belong to those haunted by the nostalgia for a sacred world. They are inevitable but nothing about them should be surprising: existence, as soon as it ceases to be chatter or routine, is a convulsion near madness—it is itself located at the limit between life and death, at the limit of madness. Moreover, it is necessary that these conditions are like this nowadays so that they seem proportionate to the circumstances. However, I have not articulated them in a strange and unfavorable light with the sole intention of claiming a pathetic quality for a new work.

Regarding the constraint that I spoke of previously, which requires a new world be born within us, I can say precisely what it demands, even if I am still incapable of following the constraint through to the end. Anyone who decided to carry on regardless and then give an answer with his life must at least know *exactly* the question addressed to him, he must know the extent of the demand. I proceed in a certain sense like a monstrous riddler, and yet I will formulate a sort of program.

Here is the first problem that would have to be solved by anyone who suffered the constraint I am talking about.

He knows that in the past, men had the power to create existences before them, shades or forms that seemed irrefutably sacred. They knew how to make the presence of a terrifying reality present to those around them, how to communicate a feeling of terrifying grandeur. The means they used are of secondary importance: in fact, it is necessary, temporarily, to wipe clean the slate of everything we know of these means and the narrow ideas that were linked to them. The moment is coming when it will be imperative to no longer know anything about what other people thought about what went on behind the sacred powers they possessed. Because it is not what they put behind that we must discover but the powers themselves—whatever they may be. That is why we must not keep talking about multiple gods or one God or even society. It is only in his nudity that a new man will be able to regain access to these powers. He must rediscover them only because they exist and because, in the presentiment that he has of them, his heart already cleaves to them. But he must rediscover them, even if they leave him broken. Would he really be able to take on anything meaningful before having acceded to what the earth hides in its deepest depths?

Now, here is the second problem that that he is faced with.

It is not enough to have found, by some path or other, a way of gaining access to what was once present, long ago, in every sanctuary. It is not enough that some furtive communication becomes possible again between our life and the forces that animate it. This life aspires to *contemplate* a reality of ice and fire, to slowly annihilate itself before it. The mystic union of man and the forces he sees within to the outside is necessary for man to fulfill his destiny. Nothing would continue to make sense if his mind did not reach a point of ecstasy from which he is finally of the same stuff as the magnificence of the Universe.

[BOX 13, G: 133–135]

// to have exactly this meaning. Among primitive humanity, an entire population would rediscover the profound sources of life in the chaos of a festival. The festival entailed the derangement of the senses, drunkenness and sexual exuberance. But this disorder was linked to the tragic feelings and the anguish caused by sacred ceremonies, touching beings to such an extent that they would crumble. In our day, the festival remains accessible in a popular form, considered base and separated from any tragic meaning: death and extreme joy no longer meet in an explosion where human existence would rival the brilliance and intoxication of light. The constraint that I mentioned leads us to bring man back to the elementary conditions of the festival, because this is the only way in which a sacred world can be rediscovered. The sensual elements of festivals are present for us only to the extent that they please us: it is enough for us to desire them and to happily place ourselves on the level of popular jollities; above all else, it is enough for us to know laughter. But we must know how to link the tragic feeling that we find in solitude to this drunkenness that unites us to all people. As is natural when one speaks of the sacred, without having anything other than sentences available, I have had to make do with allusions and I have only been able to insist on the fact that none of this can take us any further than up to the leap into the unknown. But when I began to show the solitary individual linking together his life with everything that these days is separate, I did not stray far from a fundamental inquiry: the point is to link men, to retie the knots that bind them together //

2. PLANS AND NOTES, 1939–1941

[BOX 13, F: ON THE COVER OF THE DOSSIER]

Part I: Expenditure

III

Text from August 1938 on expenditure (III*a*)
And ch. IV of Joy Before Death (III*b*)

[BOX 13, F: 15]

General Plan of the section on Expenditure

I. Universal principles
II. Expenditure in general in economic history
III. Wars and revolutions as expenditure
IV. Religious sacrifice and joy before death
V. The opposition of expending to acquire
acquiring to expend

THE SACRIFICE OF LOVE (IV AND V)

(Before this: the major contemporary forms)

In general, there is a balancing of accounts. However, in the reality of war we see the birth of an ordinance dictating a shocking approach to death.

Organize: joy before death as a return to sacrifice in another form.

Second part: return to the balance of accounts in another, more profound form.[1]

[BOX 13, F: 13]

Division into sections

I. The glory of the universe and the meager condition of man.
II. Glorious acts and economic activity.
III. The mundane world of utility.
IV. War.

V. Sacrifice (in this part, the point of rupture must come at the end).
VI. The brilliance of day.

[BOX 13, E: 150–151]

5TH PART (POINT OF RUPTURE)

In war, the "point of rupture" is very [*illegible*]—it is the "object of communication" that counts; highlight this precisely to show the meaning of the book.

The game-like character of points of rupture: reason makes points of rupture equivalent with one another, there is no sacrifice, a naked woman is absurd, etc. Anything that establishes difference must be placed on the side of the game. The difficulty—so that I can represent everything together—is to fix what is meant by "game" here in opposition not to reason but to the real (or necessary). The game means sticking to the rules and the sense of luck. It is life, symbol of life. Similarly, life is game and luck, beginning with isolated individuation. There is nothing artificial about when a point of rupture ties itself up in me subjectively. All points of rupture are subjective. It is the coming together of a large number of subjectivities that gives such a point of rupture a character of objectivity. Nevertheless, this coming together can be the result of objective conditions.

The point of rupture (the difference) cannot, therefore, be formed arbitrarily. It only makes sense if the objective possibility of coming together is carefully handled.

Beings are composed around points of rupture. The core of composed beings is a communal point of rupture.[2]

[BOX 13, F: 184]

	action	*subject*	*object*
sacrifice	ritual destructions	sacrificers	that with which we comm. direct. sacred world goods exploited but not profane
war	fighting	those who fight	other combatants, including the general
love	union	male lover	female lover
laughter			
ecstasy	exercise		

[BOX 13, F: 185–187]

5TH PART (ANGUISH)

Determining role of anguish in the *Menschwerdung*,[3] anguish of greed.

Festival: greed satisfied because we eat, but the principle of the festival being anguish, greed does not follow suit.

Interpretation of what survives: after the death of efficacious belief, the festival can subsist

there is: profound reason (anguished concern)—exterior belief (economic effect)—rite (glorious act)

if the rite survives after the death of belief, it loses all dramatic character (anguish).

But the possibility of survival shows how unimportant belief is; it is nothing but a middle term between profound reason and the rite.

anguish	***point of rupture***	***closed comm.***	***open comm.***
death	killing	society	God, etc.
death	real deaths as threatening images	army embodying the nation	combat in and of itself
obscoena	nudity	communal life	love for love's sake
	image of the fall of a non-serious person	Laugh of exclusion	
death	nocturne: explosive diurnal images: images of radiance	God	

It is highly important to take these facts into account, but they are only a point of departure.

At the most acute moment of suffering, something like a change of charge occurs in the quality of feelings. We see the thought of death, considered as a return to nothing, appearing; when Madeleine[4] speaks about it too much and starts to desire it, these statements that make you think about the idea of suicide signal oncoming ecstasy (following the statements of Madeleine herself)—*From Anguish to Ecstasy*, I, p. 194.[5]

From Anguish to Ecstasy, I, p. 195, fig. 27:

[BOX 13, F: 189–190]

5TH PART (COMPASSION)

Communication generates pessimism when it communicates suffering (compassion). Against this sort of communication,

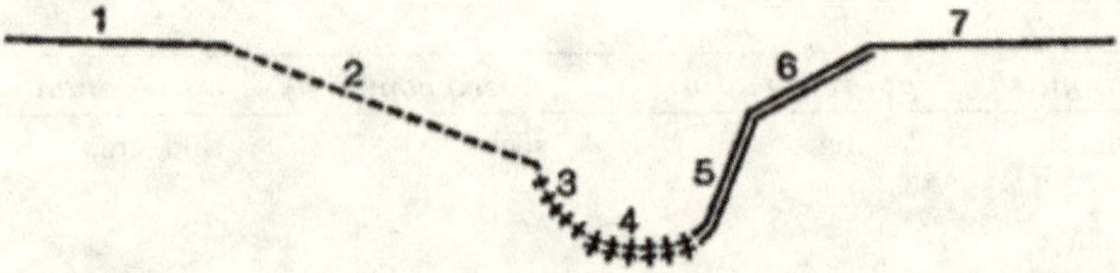

Schema of the succession of states: 1 and 7, states of equilibrium; 2, state of temptation; 3, state of barrenness; 4, state of torture; 5, state of ecstasy; 6, state of consolation.

isolation is necessary: such an isolation can ensure the most liberated form of communication. Isolation is necessary in sacrifice so there is no compassion for the victim.

The principle opposing compassion has a crucial moral value.

If I consider a human sacrifice, hoping to see within it a *communication* between men, I cannot fail to see the opposite at the same time. There is a link of *communication* between my neighbor and me, a link that touches on the *sacred* part of myself and others. This link *exists*, all that is left to do is to consecrate it through ritual acts. But when men sacrifice a man, they swear this sacred line did not exist for them. I alone felt the absence of this sole link.

[BOX 13, F: 199–212]

5TH PART (SACRIFICE)

Push to the maximum the possibility of delay, of calculation, all that is represented by a greedy disposition, because consciousness itself is greed, greed of possession—but delay only to better experience this vertiginous movement, calculate only to be stirred more deeply by the incalculable movement of giving—in the end, this is the only sense that this consciousness can have, a sense radically contrary to its own sense.

The completion of consciousness that Hegel represents is the most appalling. Because, in Hegel, consciousness possesses the world. Because delay was the condition of consciousness, Hegel believed he could bury the moving world in the fictive immobility of the earth and in the consciousness that remains lurking therein. Without any doubt, for a consciousness condemned to think, the world cannot be thought except on the condition of achieving a consciousness that reflects it, the world is not conceivable except as reflected, even though that should require the world to stop at the point when consciousness arises. To me, this stop evokes the fall of the body from the top of the sacrificial pyramid, and also evokes the contrary: the bloody heart raised up.

In sacrifice there is delay, slowing down, but no stopping, not even the attempt to stop—quite the opposite. There is no feeling of stopping, but rather one of movement.

Throughout life—everyday life—there is a will to stop (unconscious) (laughter is involuntary). There is no real stop, but the feeling of stopping.

This feeling of stopping is necessary for consciousness, but if it takes place without an opposing force, consciousness becomes consciousness of *nothing* (consciousness of things).

In sacrifice, the thing is objectified but destroyed.

There are nothing but delays, breakdowns, and reversals. Like how light breaks up in a prism and throws back an image—explanation of the stars.

Articulate here:
At the beginning sky opposed to earth
At the end communication to isolation

hence the position of the problem at the start, including the opposition expenditure-acquisition, wasn't correct

sacrifice is the means to define an absorption as a communication, in opposition to isolation.

"I propose to define religion as follows: *a collection of scruples that hinder us from using our faculties.*" S. Reinach, *Orpheus*, 4.[6]

Dussaud, *Introduction to the History of Religions* (Paris, 1914):[7] religious practices from the lowest to the highest degree, "cult of the principle of life." Show the equivalence with the principle: glorious act[s].

> We do not fully appreciate that the Christian myth of salvation supposes that God, the creator and master of humanity, can still consider the immolation of a human victim pleasing, like the old Yahweh; that the death of Christ was able to destroy sin, in the same way that the sacrificed scapegoat cleaned Israel of its impurities;[8] or even that the blood of Jesus erased the sins of men, just like how, for the Greeks, spreading

> the blood of an animal victim over the hands of a murderer would erase the stain of his crime. And the authors of the New Testament found it natural to compare Jesus to the Paschal lamb. The moral lesson behind God being pleased with Christ's willingness to accept his death does not stop the death of Jesus from being seen as a kind of repayment that satisfies God, from whom humanity buys life in exchange for the death of its celestial representative. Nothing fits better with the general economy of sacrifice, and what characterizes Christian sacrifice is the faithful, though largely unsuccessful, effort to give a moral to an idea that has nothing to do with morality. The economy of Christian salvation is undoubtedly founded upon a myth of human sacrifice, and it is through this myth of human sacrifice that the eucharistic sacrament must be interpreted. Thus, the force of universal religious tradition manages to impose, through dogma and imagery, the most horrifying kind of sacrifice on a religion that avoids any bloody immolations. (Loisy, *Sacrifice*, p. 115)[9]

5*TH* PART (EXPLANATIONS OF SACRIFICE)

For Christians, "animals are put to death to signify that man deserves death for his sins, sins that only his death can expiate" [*Lesèbre?*], art. sacrifice

"A sacrifice that is offered outwardly represents the inward spiritual sacrifice, whereby the soul offers itself to God as at the beginning of its creation, and its end by beatification . . . So what matters, in sacrifice, is not the value of the victim sacrificed, but the sense of honor given to the sovereign Master of all the Universe." Saint Thomas, *Summ. Theol.*, II*a* II*ae*, q. LXXV, *a*.2.[10]

[BOX 13, F: 192–196]

5TH PART (LAUGHTER)

In laughter: Hegel, contradiction in itself in tragedy, struggle of two contraries

two contraries in sacrifice—it is only at the moment when two opposites are posited that there is sacrifice—no totemic sacrifice

in laughter there is also a victim—the victim is not affected by a distinct force that intervention overwhelms

Pair the parallel laughter-sacrifice with comedy-tragedy.

The relief of anguish through laughter is total due to a displacement—sudden passage from a point of anguish to a point of satisfaction. Wordplay is the prime example: sudden difference in tension, in level. There is none of this in sacrifice, or in tragedy; there is also relief of anguish, but without the rapid release.

Stability Isolation

lack of stability = lack of isolation

laughter chases us out of our personal isolation, puts us in communication with others (even the laugh of recognition)

the laughter of death the only example to cite

anguish relieved? or rather there must be no anguish due to its insignificance—it is the same whether it concerns others or myself

finish the chapter with the theme: *vertigo, not fall*

laughter: same case as sacrifice: essential enigma

identity with sacrifice

meaning of life, profound meaning

however, that goes against everything that it is possible to think about seriously

in this case, would there not be something improbably insidious in all of this?

p. 157: The error begins only when reflective consciousness takes seriously the small amount of rest that it is afforded by the circumstances.

Big fault (appendix?):

To define laughter through communication is to define it through an abstract generality. It would be better to define communication through laughter: its ability to break things up and tear them apart would emerge. As long as we say: *laughter is communication,* we risk making nothing out of a beatitude that is common and devoid of magic. If we are to choose between the true image and the pernicious one, we must have full knowledge of the facts—at the scale of our true reason, the world is entirely perverse and bent.

Even Nietzsche, in canonizing laughter, purified it.

Liquid nature of laughter.

[BOX 13, C: 262–269]

6TH PART (THE GLOBE OF THE EYE)

Sun eye of glory

Galaxy, Sun and sky = glory

radiance and glory identical

The glory of the Sun offers itself to man as the very meaning of his life. It is, nevertheless, quite the opposite.

Each being situates itself at the extreme end of a breakdown that leads to an endless division of small, powerless particles [*petites parties sans force*]. They tend to fold in on themselves in a miserable isolation.

The question of human radiance

"the look of one who gives has the brilliance of gold"[11]

the gleam in the eye

the pitfall of glory, that it becomes the object of property (in a military context particularly)

the eye as glorious body

When the fact of seeing is taken as an exercise, how much of it is glory and how much is utility?

There is this final response to man's wretched situation on a cold earth and even to his general wretchedness: this illusion of a stable ground on which to base ourselves, this icy slowness of things, the atmosphere in which we live, I want to compare them to the prism that breaks up light. The world that produces us, this terrestrial surface, is like an interference fringe. The image of the universe is slowed down within it, broken down and inverted: in the same way that light from a sun breaks up in a prism and gives an explanatory picture of itself—instead of just shining. The immensity of an astral body, the incredible distance traversed by light, and the laughable smallness of the prism are the data of an operation that we see going only in one direction. The image of the star that we sense with our eyes is a spectrum composed of colored rays. Turning the process around, if we consider the star itself, we no longer have an image that can be sensed but an arbitrary construction in which numbers come together to determine the size, the density, the temperature, along with names for atoms and molecules. In the same way, life on earth breaks up the game of the universe which is reflected on its surface: it

In reality, the earth is the mirror of the universe, and the myriad eyes of animals and men are essential to its surface. However, what is immediately noticeable is that the eyes that make up this mirror do not look at the world at all: they look around. What they perceive, therefore, is not the splendor of the sky. (Note on standing upright.) This splendor would blind them—it would, moreover, be monotone compared to what they see. What they perceive is light detached amidst its [*fall*?] and, from its instantaneous movement, captured by agglomerations of immobile matter. They seize hold of a play of brilliance and dizzying rapidity in a petrified reflection.[12]

But two sorts of light exist for these eyes: gray daylight captured in clouds (gray day, day of truth—the utilitarian aspect of objects emerges—it is the inverted image).

On the other hand, the light of a clear day throws us all of a sudden, by comparison or by opposition, back into the game of the heavens (equivalent to beautiful monuments, beautiful landscapes—the utilitarian aspect no longer has any meaning)

fantastical moment
moment of singing and drunkenness
moment of illusion as well

the return to the gray day is death, and the clear day takes on a meaning in relation to death

thus, inversion and return

It is this play of inversion and return that is seen by human eyes. In the glory of the clear day, sacrificial splendor is seen.

But the moment of the festival is death surpassed

It is, at the same time, the only chance that eyes have to see. [*Illegible*] of death for a time but looking at it

As if at the image of the sun

ocular globes turned from the sun but aspiring toward it

[BOX 13, F: 218–222]

6TH PART (FESTIVAL OF 52 YEARS)

The Aztecs divided time into periods of fifty-two years that they called "sheaves." They believed that the earth would one day be annihilated and that this end of the world would coincide with the end of a "sheaf." When a "sheaf" was nearly finished, they entered into a prolonged anxiety. On the final night, everyone was seized with terror and waited anxiously for what was to come. In this anguish, they imagined the end of the human race, the darkness of that night becoming eternal: "the sun would not rise again, and the Tzitzimimeh, repulsive and terrible figures, would descend from the heights of space to devour the men and women." Pregnant women were gagged and locked up in pits because people thought they would be transformed into ferocious beasts. At the same time, the fires in all the hearths were extinguished, and "blocks of rock or wood that were worshiped like household gods" were cast into the canals and lagoons. At sunset, the priests "dressed up in the ornaments of their gods, so that they resembled them absolutely." Then, in this terrifying night, these "gods" took to the streets, "marching slowly, gravely, and in silence." They went to the top of a mountain near Mexico City, which they reached just before midnight. During this time, the people of the land, all mired in anxiety, climbed to nearby vantage points to look toward the mountain. When the priests arrived at the summit, "they immediately fixed their eyes on the Pleiades, to see if they were in the center of the sky. If they were not there yet, the priests waited for them to arrive." For them, that was the critical moment when the world could end. But as soon as they saw that the constellation had passed the zenith, they knew that the movement of the heavens would continue. They then proceeded to the sacred action that the whole crowd was waiting for: as a sign of deliverance, they lighted the new fire.

"As soon as it was lighted, it was seen from all the surrounding mountains. Those who were waiting for it then let out a great cry that carried their joy up to the heavens." Because the signal told them that, once again, the world was not being plunged into darkness, and they could be sure of fifty-two more years of light ahead of them (Sahagún, I. IV, appendix and I.VII, ch. 10).

end of the volume

men bewildered [*erased?*] by anguish and the night: all that remains is the light (the fires) to which men, as *mirrors*, cling completely

finish on *life* and *light—vertigo, not fall*

If sacrifice avoids the death of the person who carries out the sacrifice, it is because, when it is looked at from an impersonal perspective, from outside the selfish point of view of the one carrying out the sacrifice, life is all that matters; the hypocrisy of sacrifice is first and foremost a hymn to life.

[BOX 13, C: 253–256]

[*Crossed out—cf. preceding p.*: "As soon as it was lit [. . .] fifty-two years of light.]

What I wanted to show in this book: that a consciousness not bound to "strong feelings" was a fallen consciousness. Practical knowledge has the privilege of treating its object like a dead thing, but this only realizes one part of the will to knowledge: I am anxious to find out the secret of this universe to which I am abandoned, whose every element arouses me so much that I am lost, *as if it were a girl, full of life* [*in the margin*: link between wanting to know and wanting to undress]. If I imagine the detached limbs of a cadaver spread out upon a dissection table, and a professor pontificating to his students in front of this table, I feel a sense of comedy. Because there is no naked knowledge that is free from anguish, there is also none without a cry of release. It is easy to laugh if one of us suffers long torments for a woman we do not love, who leaves us cold; even more so, the fear that arises during a moment of change appears laughably naïve as time passes. However, it is fear that goes far down the path of understanding the universe, not the equation of an astronomer. A living man who looks at the universe without anguish knows as little of it as the professor knows of a woman from looking at her disarticulated cadaver. The astronomer does not enter into the universe except through the abstract data of his calculations. The Mexican, who nowadays is no more, is comparable to the dead lover of this dissected woman, to he who once knew the passion that she brought to life: what he knows of the universe is nothing but its brilliance (or the interruption of this brilliance), but he knows it insofar as he reproduces the image of it through his search for glory or his celebration of his harmony with it. It is through the communion, or through the anguish that took hold of him whenever he feared that the communion might cease, that this primitive [*naïf*] man came to know what the wise man did nothing but cut into pieces.

[*Crossed out*: Primitive knowledge [*connaissance naïve*] could never obtain the harmony of reason.]

APPENDIX (GAME)

(do not use as is)

"The game changes an equivalence into a difference." I should have developed this definition: my appetite for it is taken away by what it opens my eyes to. It took shape for me when I was almost asleep, in one of those vague moments that mark the end of a dream and waking. Sleep brought it to me, not my waking thoughts: a dream resolved itself in disjointed reflections on horse racing (which I have never taken any interest in); that small phrase was the conclusion. It left me awake and immediately aware of its significance. I had laid down with the intention of writing down what I had thought during the day about the principle of the point of *rupture*. I did not doubt that I would find the right phrasing. But it was 11 o'clock, it was cold: I put my arms under the covers and I slept. I awoke near 2 o'clock: I vaguely tied the thread of my thoughts back together, I combined the opposition between quantitative science and its object. In this half-sleep, "Carnot's Theorem"[13] seemed to me a blatant absurdity: it single-handedly proved the weakness of science. Out of the world's diversity, reason takes hold of nothing but equivalences. [*Crossed out*: at this moment, I was not worrying myself with Hegel, Meyerson, or Nietzsche.] In this "theorem," I saw science personified—stupid and easy to eviscerate: it made me deliriously happy, and I fell asleep again immediately. I dreamt of an elegant stranger suddenly possessed of an animal lust for me. She led me to the terrace of a café and wanted to sit at the occupied tables there: I objected, stunned. The terrace was located at the entrance to the Bois:[14] I supposed that my dream, riven with delays and uncertainties, led me to the racetrack at Auteuil. I woke up, formulating the "little phrase" that clearly [*laughably? Crossed out:* obviously] responded to "Carnot's Theorem."

[BOX 13, E: 90–91]

APPENDIX (TOTEMIC ORIGINS)

In totemic society, no individuality is possible. Individuality—including the individuality of nations—is a fact of the post-totemic period.

In the state of *Gottwerdung*[15] there is a disappearance of individuality—even in communion, there is no more subordination.

Laughter and madness. Fire of joy. Absence of inhibition due to a beyond in laughter. Two related possibilities: *a*) closed laughter, the hat on the head of the goddess[16]—the beyond is unknown, unconquered; *b*) open laughter—the beyond is conquered.

In totemism, there is body and spirit but there is no distinction other than what distinguishes between species.

In totemism there are the ancestors

People (Frazer) interpret totemism as a form of magic. Actually, if one looks at *Intichiuma*,[17] it is only proximate to magical operations. Its goal is the reproduction of the totem. But in principle those who reproduce the totem do not eat it: only other men eat it. The *gift* is therefore essential to human behavior . . .

But there is more, there is exceptional consumption of the totem, festival consumption: in these instances, greed is given an opposing meaning.

(Maintain this theme independent of the *hypothesis*; include consideration of religion linked to the economy but on *an economic level*—at least, more linked to the economy than sociology. If it is social, it is due to communication. Religion links the economic and the social.)

[BOX 13, C: 285–295]

APPENDIX (TOTEMIC ORIGINS)

text from winter '41
to be introduced as a general hypothesis, particularly fragile when it comes to the beginning

Everything we know about man's oldest ancestors is conjecture, but we can say that they were not conscious of being men; they were such before they knew anything about it. They lived off animals and plants and the forces of nature. They absorbed meat and plants, turned themselves into hunters and then into shepherds and farmers—they exploited what lived through the action and labor of their hands. In some way or other, they destroyed the animals and plants, killing them or picking them or, subsequently, domesticating and cultivating them.

We do not have clear consciousness unless we destroy: to learn the existence of an object, we must seize hold of it, abuse it, possess it: the only way we can understand existence completely is by putting a stop to it.

Every act of understanding resembles the appropriation of an object, but it is only a fictional appropriation: the intelligence incorporates that object's image. Primary understanding must involve true appropriation. The animal was first understood by a man who killed and ate it. Before, the play of images would appear like water flowing—none of them arresting the mind. The absorption that destroyed made visible what it had destroyed. Distinct understanding is different from the feeling of similitude (or of contagion) that two beings feel when looking each other in the eye. Regret and the impossible desire to see the dead brought back to life began to take shape in the dark mechanism of representation that living beings possessed. But it was not so much death as the *abuse* committed on a living being for whom one felt an immediate sense of fellowship that inaugurated the *anxious concern* necessary for knowledge. The *greed* which compels us toward the *exploitation* (to the incorporation) of another lies at the origin of our consciousness of that other as a fellow being, but only insofar as it collides with the contrary tendency. Reciprocally, this other tendency—immediate *communication* of living beings with one another—only led to consciousness once destructive greed made it impossible. I do not believe that this conflict, which is essential to man, had any other sources than an acquired intensity, a relative imbalance in the contradictory movements that are unique to each . . .

Man's recognition of living things as similar to himself implied the consciousness he had of sharing the same essence as animals. Man did not recognize himself first as man but only as a living existence. At the deepest level of his reflections, he counted himself on the same level as the birds that he killed. At the same time, he counted himself on the same level as plants, or the other things that pleased [*jouissait*] him and that seemed full of life (water, the wind, the sun, clouds). This primary consciousness that man had of himself differs from the one that has come down to us in that there was not, beyond his own existence, another, more perfect existence that exceeded his own. Animals, men, plants, rain, and light played and blended together in the unity of a nature at once destructive of and prodigal with life. Beings shared terrors and joys equally. If one wanted to enjoy an abundance of rain or animals, one had to conduct oneself generously. At this time, we cannot really call it sacrifice; men did not kill any victims. They mutilated themselves, pulled out their own teeth, sliced their foreskins or their fingers, slashed at their chests or their penises. It was their own blood that they religiously spilled across the ground.

[*In the margin:* one creates abundance with what one eats at a festival! How far removed this is from magical egotism]

In this they conducted themselves differently from animals. With the work of their hands, with their weapons and tools, they transformed the world around them, seizing and destroying. But they also used their hands and sharp tools in the opposite way: as they absorbed, changed, and captured for their own uses everything they needed, they also murdered each other in turn, destroyed themselves in exchange for what they destroyed in others, gave in order to receive or in recompense for what they had taken.

The religious attitude of men—which clearly distinguishes them from animals—always had this precise meaning: that they could never take out their greed on others—destroy them for their own use—without the consciousness of those others as fellow beings. This consciousness is why men engaged in mutilations and generous outpourings to satisfy the needs of their brothers and sisters—the animals and plants, the light and the rain—just as they all satisfied the greed in man. But these strange acts not only revealed man's consciousness of others: it also revealed his consciousness of himself. Men conceived of others in their own image: this image was therefore present in them.

However, while it implied a difference from animals, the image that men made of themselves was not, in the very beginning, a human image. The oldest human beings were not conscious of being men in the way we understand it. Today, we distinguish men for being in possession of rights that elevate them far above animals. This consciousness of superiority entails moreover a consciousness of inferiority, at least when it comes to deep desires. Men should feel that the superiority that they attribute to themselves over animals is imperfect, causing them to suffer because they cannot free themselves from the alleged flaws of animals. Those who ceased to understand themselves simply as living beings, in discovering that they were men, managed to do so only insofar as they imagined the existence of beings who were superior to them. The notion of man is opposed as much to that of angel or god as to that of beast.

Essentially, the consciousness that man has of being a man is linked to the rapid distinction between bodies and spirits, to the deep dualism that still forms our natural milieu. Originally, animals, plants, and natural phenomena did not seem less possessed of spirits than men. But little by little, spirits began to appear distinct from these corporeal things. The body represented everything that was part of nature and man, although he belonged to nature, appeared distinct from it in that he was not only body but also spirit. This distinction gave way to several, superficially different representations of the world. For some, spirit transcended nature, and for others it did not. These problems are important for those who enclose themselves in their datasets. But seen *from the outside* (and from a distance), all philosophies (and religions) form a profound unity. They all gravitate around a principle of opposition: to this principle is linked the consciousness that man has of being man—different from a pure spirit, just as he is different from a beast.

In all this *hypothesis*, nothing is said on the nature of things in a mathematical sense.

[BOX 13, C: 286–303]

There is also communication among animals, but it is unbroken. Human communication is intensified by the anguish that disrupts it: it is in this way that man is the loyal expression of the Earth.

Man is distinct from animals in that he gives as well as absorbs.

Animal communication is weak and constant.

Man suppresses communication and then finds it again with a sort of explosion.

He can absorb much more, through his hands, through labor.

The living being greedy for life absorbs dying life. He starts to become conscious of the destroyed life that he has absorbed.

He recognizes himself as perishable life and dwells on this recognition through sacrifice.

This man who recognized himself as perishable life kills other men and eats them, or enslaves them, as he kills, eats, or enslaves animals.

He absorbs them, exploits them, and *recognizes* them in the exploitation.

The subject is first of all an animal for whom consciousness discriminates nothing. Then an animal conscious of being a living being among others (plants, animals). Then man conscious of being man.

He becomes man conscious of being man:—in human sacrifice; then in the abolition of sacrifice; then in the celebration of the death of Christ, where sacrifice and its abolition coincide.

What distinguishes man from animals is perhaps communication, which may be the effect of sacrifice. In this case, the end of sacrifices would signal the withering of man, his return to a new form of animality. This may happen to the masses—if a small number of men, who are so "new" that the name of man no longer applies to them, separate themselves from those masses.

More often than not, a supposed moment of progress is nothing but an urgent remedy to a problem that has just appeared or got worse. It brings a new duty with it, a new task that will lead to more changes a bit later on. A civilization is no less the symbol of growing problems than it is of an ability to solve them. Population, needs, weaknesses, and anxieties increase to the extent that resources increase as well. If these resources come up lacking, the great weakness acquired is put on full display.

In the *act* of sacrifice, an act is contemplated, reflected, echoed: as the subject acts on the object, they both take something away from the other, the object sinks into death and the subject sinks into anguished contemplation of its *act*. The only power that continues to exist is that of the *act*, which affects the inert consciousness of the one sacrificing or the one in attendance in the same way that light affects a photographic plate.

Sacrifice is D. H. Lawrence's "Morning Star."[18]

At a point, which is to say, at several points in the biosphere, excess energy must be expended toward a goal other than growth. In general, animals respond better than plants to a necessity of this kind, but among animals it is the most powerful that will necessarily dispose of the excess energy of this biosphere when that biosphere cannot expand any further. In general, the most powerful animals seem the least fortunate: they cannot just dispose how they like of the riches that their superior power puts at their mercy. They do not just get to eat more than they need and rejoice in peace: this superabundant energy is like an explosive; it does not resemble a fertile plane but rather a //

APPENDIX [BOX 13, E: 18–19]

Communication in nature seems inaccessible to anguish: so too does light . . . But we only have knowledge of nature from the outside. If we were able to penetrate, other than just in our minds, the horrible depths of the sun, if the secret of this incandescent terror were delivered up to us, the intimate truth of day and light might seem harsher to us than the sacrifices of Mexico. But the knowledge that we have about the truth of the physical world is so external that we cannot imagine anything emptier: a vain mockery, so flatly ignorant that rude myths seem preferable.

We do not enter further into the understanding of nature by *denying* all anthropomorphic character in it. In so doing, we create an abstract appearance, an algebraic phantom and not a world. That nature's "intimacy" is not the same as human intimacy does not mean that it is reducible to the *appearance* that it takes in the human mind. It is pointless to never grasp what tears the mind to pieces: the anthropomorphic image, at least, avoided emptiness.

APPENDIX [BOX 13, C: 251–252]

If men withdraw into themselves in inertia, it is for a laughably short time. Collectively, men are as mixed together as a mass of waves across time: united from one end to the other as echoes of a single, lost agitation. What fades away when looking at the whole is everything that is solitary, weary, and deficient. By contrast, the moments of fulguration, necessarily standing out from the flow of this single and liquid movement of existence, have a full and redemptive expressive value.

In everything, look always at the *relation* between two or more beings, what passes between them, what they tear from each other or bring together: currents, ruptures, sparks.

APPENDIX [BOX 13, C: 275–276]

Roughly, communication is to the mind what matter is to the "isolated being." In this game, "mind" has lost the character of *personal* immortality. It takes its *impersonal* character from the old world of matter. But *matter*, *mind*, just like *isolated being*, *communication*, only have one reality. Nowhere are there isolated beings who do not communicate, nor is there "communication" that exists independently of points of isolation. Let us take care to separate two concepts that are poorly developed, residues of childish beliefs: at this price will this most tangled problem be cut through.

APPENDIX [BOX 13, C: 279–282]

[*Crossed out:* I speak of the origin of capitalism, but I am not looking for its *cause*.] If I drive in a nail, the *cause* of it is my decision to drive it in. Everything else is a set of passive elements that make my action possible. This set is never a *cause*. There is no true *cause* except in a man's deliberate decision: other active factors that appear similar to a decision—because they "decide" on exterior changes—cannot be considered *causes* except arbitrarily. If lightning killed me, why would lightning be the *cause* any more than my position in a given place: I would not be dead if I had been somewhere else . . . But if some other man killed me, his decision would be clearly different from the other factors of my death: my death would have been *desired*.

To speak of a primordial cause is to regard the Universe like the nail that I drive in.

The idea of cause dissolves entirely once I envisage all the elements necessary for my decision—that is to say, the passive aspect of my action. Theoretically, the only things that remain are constant associations and the reduction of particular phenomena to the appearance of a general phenomenon.

Practically, however, a human decision requires a sense of causality. We must therefore acquire a mobility of perspectives. In a decision, moreover, there is the power and discernment of constant associations: the perspective of causality is not false, therefore, as long as we recognize that this causality is actually the final result (the opposite of what we thought when we looked for a first principle).

Envisage it as we wish, the origin of the world is, by necessity, *marvelous*.

3. PLANS AND NOTES, 1941–1943

[BOX 13, C: 106–107]

The Accursed Share, or The Limit of the Useful (final outline)

I. Customs
   1. Man and the universe
   2. Unproductive expenditure
   3. The world of private expenditure
   4. The glory of rivalry

II. The gamble [*mise en jeu*]
   5. Transparency
   6. Sacrifice

[BOX 13, C: 102–103]

I. The sphere of the gamble
   (A) general principle and the sphere in total
   (B) the festival
      1. opposition of the festival to other times
         (a) to the time of work
         (b) to the time of war
      2. the totalizing nature of festival
         (a) eroticism
         (b) heroism (representative side)
      3. breakdown of the festival and the sphere of representation

II. Different forms of the gamble in the sphere of representation
      1. definition of the sphere
      2. enumeration and brief definition
      3. mode of relation at different periods and in a given period

III. Different phases of the gamble (in sacrifice)
      1. the natural given or the stake
      2. raising the stake
      3. the gamble

4. surpassing the given
5. waste or the appropriation of the result

IV. Sacrifice
V. Mythology
VI. Tragedy
VII. Poetry
VIII. Comedy and laughter
IX. Philosophy
X. Ecstasy
XI. Dialectic of knowledge and the gamble

1. religious knowledge
2. philosophical knowledge, essentially Christian knowledge
3. scientific knowledge and nonknowledge
the negation of nature
the generality of the gamble
gambling and putting into action
the natural given or the stake
remark on the lack of difference between what is given and the result
necessary reality of the stake
the expressive form of the stake or the face
death of the stake
representation
the domain of representation
link between the real importance of the stake and its figurative value
raising the stake
examples of raised stakes
the idealization of language
idealism and the negation of the gamble
increase through laughter

[BOX 13, C: 115]

FUNDAMENTAL THESIS OF THE BOOK

(to be expounded for the first time in the Preface—by a citation from ch. V[2])

From a psychological point of view, nature has a meaning. *Die Geistigkeit des Natur.*[3]

In the sun, energy is expended, purely and simply.

On earth, part of the available energy must be invested in the work of producing energy. Endlessly.

But:

the sum of energy produced is, in a practical sense, greater than the sum of energy necessary for production.

This precise naturalism is necessary for the naturalist interpretation of natural attitudes.

(Discuss Loureiro and alcohol here)

In the classical theory, man is represented as eating, other consumptions of products are represented on the model of food, we cannot eat and consume in general unless we produce. Therefore, man produces to eat. More precisely: man produces

(a) the energy required to produce (to subsist)
(b) a surplus

[BOX 13, C: 108]

PREFACE

1. The current need for a politics of expenditure.
2. Natural basis (cf. Fundamental thesis of the book).
3. One of my friends told me that Hegelianism led him to the unknown (unlike positivism) (cf. Essential trajectory of the book).

4. The need for a down-to-earth basis for speculation (departing from Hegel) (no claim to have covered everything. I wanted to come to an end whereas the trajectory of the book covered everything).
5. But the rock fallen from the sky,[4] no opportunism. That's the way it is, no matter what. A deep-seated axiom that no agreement could lay to rest. Man is this axiom in the movement of his bones, no matter what he says.

[BOX 13, C: 105]

ESSENTIAL TRAJECTORY OF *THE ACCURSED SHARE*

Given the separation between the natural attitude and the rational attitude, we must rediscover their harmony.

The separation will be described in ch. III.[5]

The fundamental difficulty of the harmony will be described in ch. IV, whose main idea that the alienation of man has been dependent on the opposition between *Herr* and *Knecht*[6] (the *Herr* considered as *evil*).

The harmony, its possibility, must appear at the end of ch. V (§ on the unknown): it is linked to growing conscious, rationally, of the natural attitude and the underlying elements, which will also come out in the analyses in ch. VI (on laughter, sacrifice, and communication). This growing conscious is linked to the failure of speculative thought (which implies that active thought reaches its full potential). Only speculative thought can glimpse this moment of fulfillment in the unknown and, beyond this fulfillment, something different from an object that must be transformed into something known: to perceive in an agonized inner experience what can naturally be perceived through laughter, sacrifice, etc.

(The essence of Nietzscheanism is that this spiritual process is not possible unless we stop denouncing the *Herr*. It involves rediscovering the accursed share.)

[BOX 13, C: 110–114]

III. THE WORLD OF PRIVATE EXPENDITURE

Mature capitalism is impersonal—its rapacity (its will to expand) works indirectly. It puts all the available resources into a project. But not as part of a will to improve: simple extension. The gamble that attaches itself to the enterprise is like an opposition that is also a traditional supplement. The gambler (player) is nothing but a sterile hybrid who embodies the final movement of capitalism: suppression of glorious expenditures, diverting wealth for the benefit of expanding the forces of production, but eventually annexing wealth for private expenditure, for the sordid individualism of enjoyment [*jouissance*].

If we consider in detail the tableau of unproductive expenditures during the Middle Ages and those of our day we undoubtedly see a reduction, but this is not guaranteed; what emerges most clearly is individualization.

Individualization arose, moreover, as a form of political activity of glorious, heroic expenditure, which helped to compensate for the general reduction of glorious expenditures. This activity became partly confused with romanticism, which, as we will see later on, was in fact the exact opposite. It led, in any case, to the complete suppression of the shared solidarity of expenditures and, in this way, to the suppression of living solidarity. The links of solidarity become impersonal in the State, and the individual is reduced to drift idly in a world with no moral compass. The impersonal system of enterprise pronounces its sentence on him: no enterprise, no bread.

IV. MILITARY GLORY OR THE GLORY OF RIVALRY

The surplus of energy set free by the machine of capitalism (the accumulated forces of production, the drive to reduce expenditure) can only be expended through more and more violent wars, which end up devaluing the spirit of expenditure, leading to a deep and justifiable suspicion of all expenditure.

This suspicion is applied to expenditure in general because the *means* of expending have, since the earliest of times, been placed in the hands of the most powerful, the warriors and masters, leaving the weak with the *weight* of expenditure. This leads to a fundamental conflict between the ideology of the festival and that of labor. Since the alienation of man is linked to the exercise of power by the elite, and since that exercise is linked to expenditures, labor tends to deplore the spirit of the festival as well as the elite's appropriation of the means of expenditure. As such, misery tends only to produce more misery.

In fact, the critique of miserable labor goes against the *alienation* from glory itself which, in the hands of the powerful, transforms into *glory of rivalry*, which can either be to the benefit of individuals or groups. Potlatch, gods, etc., are expressions of the exercise of rivalry in expenditure; in fact, they signal the construction of two opposites, with rivalry implying a greed for power, a form of potlatch: we expend with a view to acquire. In the seventeenth century, glory is acquired by the individual. There is little difference between the glorious individual of the seventeenth century and the commendatory abbot.[7] The glory of rivalry is merely a step on the road to capitalist individualization, in which glory sinks in the mire of private expenditure and industrialized war.

The easiest way to understand this alienation is to focus on its origins. To begin with, expenditure basically took shape in the form of the festival. The festival is, theoretically, the expenditure of everything without reserve, expressing as completely as possible the unity of men and bringing about communion between them. In this sense, the festival was the most meaningful social form: executing the king separated his existence and prevented men from communicating with each other. But when royalty was primarily military, the king bared himself: there were substitutions (festival [*sed?*], slaves, carnival kings). The idea of the reversal of roles is still present as a theme in the dream of the golden age. All these themes reappear in Christianity, but the essence of Christianity is the condemnation of murderers, and consequently of sacrifice, which is evil (do not develop the topic of Christianity here, which should take place in the following ch.). The most remarkable thing is that in Islam—which is less a religion than an army—sacrifice disappears; military spirit and sacrifice are incompatible. At its core, Islam is the simplest thing. There is only one God, so he can have only one people; everyone must submit to this one true people, so this gets translated into military action. When it comes to the glory of rivalry, the most important thing is for everything to be reduced to a single God, which is to say to the universal (this will primarily be developed in the next ch.). Instead of doing away with the king, we make him into a universal, which comes to the same thing from the point of view of the glory of rivalry: men are all equal and commune with each other easily: the communion that they no longer find in the act of sacrifice (show in ch. VI the general virtue of sacrifice-rupture), they now find in communal military action.

V. TRANSPARENCY (THE AFFIRMATION OF A WORLD OF UTILITY NECESSARY FOR TRANSPARENCY)

How "Mexican acts" seem neurotic to the individual. Anti-bourgeois romanticism as an intermediary form, individualist but not entirely limited to the individual.

1. *Geistigkeit des Natur* (cf. Fundamental thesis of the book) introduced by the principle: no decadence possible, the need to arrive at a glorious existence flows from a very simple law.
2. Intermediary role of Christianity. It already started to negate the accursed share but, ultimately, it tends to make it appear more transparent, though in hateful forms like humility; God's absorption of all the glory of rivalry; there is a struggle against the glory of rivalry without glory being abandoned, thanks to some concessions.
3. The move toward transparency is necessary and mainly appears as a kind of decadence; sense of romanticism in opposition to the degradation of the bourgeois world. The meanings of romantic terms are limited by this opposition:
   —nature
   —love
   —poetry
4. The unknown. A final term, but one that can clothe unforeseen forms.

The unknown is encountered in the total failure of speculative thought, but not indifferently or as something that must become known: as an irreducible thing sought out in the ruins. (Cf. Essential trajectory.)

VI. SACRIFICE

1. The principle of circularity and laughter. In the unknown that is not indifferent, speculative thought regains its natural attitude, the attitude of laughter. The failure of speculative thought is matched with an immediate kind of reaction. The natural attitudes: laughter, tears, sacrifice, tragedy, heroism, eroticism.
2. Theory of communication. The natural attitude is an attitude of communication which presupposes a break with the world of action or the world that is known and reduced to action . . . what is unknown to natural attitude is necessary for the rupture.

Relation between the gamble and project

the Aztecs' own disgust with sacrifice (the need for harmful punishments for those who avoided attending child sacrifices).

Final paragraph. Tears. The summit of knowledge in the night of 52 years.

[NOTEBOOK 5, NOT PAGINATED[8]]

THE ACCURSED SHARE

An Economic [*crossed out:* Poetic and Philosophical] Account of the Glorious Condition of Man

First Part: Customs
Second Part: A Man at the Summit of Knowledge
First Part: description and interpretation of human customs in relation to man's situation in the universe.
Second Part: Change through time—man is not only in such a position, he moves from one point to another, as from a lack of knowledge to knowledge, until two forms of knowledge coincide:
(a) knowledge resulting from his place in the world
(b) objective knowledge, instrumental [*ustensile*]

(1) interpretation of the change in the forms of knowledge in relation to the change of position in the universe (more or less [*greed?*])
(2) success of consciousness through the union of forms of knowledge
laughter
the other forms (identity between them)
ecstasy
identity of knowledge and ecstasy
Discursive knowledge, received knowledge.
Hegelianism—unimportant uncertainty.
Science, equally.
Need for the extreme degree, the only thing identical to non-knowledge.
In the end, the unknown.

For the unknown is not just the result of the coincidence, its content, it is also the object of man's primeval quest throughout all time in sacrifice, etc.

it is in the unknown that human communion is established.

Possibility to close here, but no, the unknown is at the same time the impossible (instead of the good)

fall in the night, thunder and lightning

in the place of sweet and succulent chains of the person

General arc of sacrifice

<table>
<tr><td>animal
man (an other)</td><td>}</td><td>others apart from the self</td></tr>
<tr><td>of the self

ecstasy</td><td>}</td><td>of its joys (asceticism): Christ., Budd.
of reason
of words</td></tr>
</table>

tragedy
poetry
laughter
heroism
ecstasy
eroticism
no abuse of the self before consciousness of the self
as soon as self-consciousness is born, the sacrifice of the self begins
moment of birth: sacrifice of the king
an impossible execution
the impossible enters being
theory of sacrifice abuse in the first part
take up totemism again

The arbitrary: why knowledge at the summit? In any case, this is a long way from Hegelianism, which makes an analogy between knowledge and a flower at the end of a plant's growth—or, more precisely, which makes knowledge into a teleology. Strictly speaking, the teleological trajectory is also present in desire, desire for knowledge and more generally for satisfaction.

World of humble utility

Need to feed capital to feed oneself.

Mutual compensation, on principle, between greed and glory. Disruption of the balance.

New compensation, the individual.

(a) individual combat, glorious combat
(b) negation of glory by the individual, but the need for the alliance between the bourgeoisie and the individual to be revived

The individual needing to take on the functions of the gift of the self, of sacrifice, and of fusion with the world

political combat, its limits (here simply: bourgeois leader)
the individual imagining the State
reason, science

Other compensations at the individual level

Romanticism,	poetry	neurosis	nature
	nature		love
	love		poetry
			(later, ecstasy of non-knowledge)

Return to the social aspect, revolution and war (following chap.).

What does it mean for an individual to search for glory?

for the individual, the actions of the Mexicans are neurotic
first development, capitalism breaks social links, disorder
second development, the growth of businesses encounters the result of the disorder that has been caused, each reacts to the other

It is important to bear the following principle in mind: businesses are machines that long to seize power. To understand this well: we cannot eat if capital does not grow.
The individual's state of inferiority in relation to industry (while the aristocracy ruled)
What the game had transformed into differences, reason strives to turn back into equivalences. At its core, glory is nothing but difference in action; sacrifice is the sum of energy that must be expended to carry out an external action
Add this development onto the individual

The goal of individual wealth: reaching the end of the Christian trajectory (salvation, etc.—starting with potlatch) but potlatch was only a sketch—a sketch of the union between rivalry and glory? No. All the glory of Christianity is formed in the same way. Could we not consider Christianity as a stage in the depersonalization of glory? Individualization would play the same role, exhausting the possibility to the fullest extent.

The situation of romantic poetry in this regard.

Depersonalization in love since the person is the society. What one desires in love is the transparency of beings. Nudity.

Depersonalization takes over the strongest personalities. Transparency instead of resemblance.

Modern poetry as transparency.

The need to sing it. Just as in love, social situations have no value except in being destroyed (but a destroyed social situation is not the same thing as the absence of a situation). The same thing can be said of words in poetry.

Poetry is produced for everyone in the sense that it satisfies other needs than those of the poet, needs that the poet satisfies for everyone

by destroying himself as a person.

Review inner experience on this subject.

The poet facing the impossible, in contrast to Christianity. Otherwise, he would not have the capacity for destruction. Poetic cynicism, the poet on the side of evil.

The poet, like all other forms, is transitory, but he was particularly tarnished by the false situation of the eighteenth-century liberal (cf. phenomenology of spirit), which has already been written.

All this should be considered a simple overview, a lover of the impossible needing to go further, complete transparency demanding consciousness.

Nature, poetry, and love are like preludes to the impossible, [part?] *of the unconscious turning away, but the rupture with the glory of rivalry, not total in love, the situation is only destroyed.*

In the glory of rivalry, the impossible was directly confronted (sacrifice, war, potlatch, sumptuary expenditures in the face of poverty, etc.), in poetry, nature, love, on the contrary, the possible (rivalry) is neglected, but the impossible is hidden, embellished with flowers, disguised in the potential, in pure potential, the potential makes itself invisible, pretends to be disinterested, ethereal, denies any self-interest, any natural greed.

Christianity in the middle.

But in this direction, no systematic obstacle to the glory of rivalry: undoubtedly, some occasional obstacles, but leaving quite freely open the possibility of a return to rival glory.

SECOND PART

A direction in time. It is essential. If there is a direction in time, man has a "why," man's purpose is this or that. For example, knowledge, in Hegel, then knowledge of what is not known or of the zenith of knowledge. Could this be put better: either it's an error, or it's finally *the truth*? Unless the goal is created arbitrarily by man, rather than defined in advance. It is not possible to say anything when it comes to the model in which a lack of knowledge takes on knowledge; we cannot choose between three hypotheses. We only perceive God in the slippage from the possible to the impossible, and this takes place at the level of general observation as much as at the level of the final and most internal self-interrogation: from something possible closing in on itself, having started with something impossible that has been confronted and clothed with this new knowledge, which is composed of ecstatic non-knowledge, I am brought back to the previous impossibility.

SECOND PART

The essence of the book. As I explained to R.C.[9]: at the height of knowledge, we see only non-knowledge. And yet (this may have been noticed previously), we see that the unknown we arrive at is, for man, neither something new, nor a detachable part of it; we see that this unknown, before being encountered at the level of pure knowledge, has been encountered in various forms of human activity; we see that the unknown has been hidden inside man himself in the form of what is funny, tragic, heroic, sacred, poetic, erotic; that the unknown actually plays a major role, that it is necessary for communication. All this means is that men cannot communicate when it comes to knowledge, which locks them up and squeezes them, but whereas in Hegelian teleology knowledge was the only thing at stake, we can imagine a teleology in which the unknown would play a part. We could ask of the unknown that is necessary to communication: is it not God? (If God existed, man's goal would be to reach the unknown.) This would be an insecure hypothesis if we did not add the following here: that the unknown is the same thing as the impossible, and therefore the same as evil.

CHAPTER III

One could say that as chapter I is the general account, chapter II is required to introduce ch. III—then I return to the general facts, war and sacrifice (war itself being introduced as an attempted [*escape?*] from the world of ch. III, sacrifice being the central theme).

On principle, ch. II should have included the critique of the glory of rivalry, but it [*will fit?*] just as well in ch. III—in any case it is ch. II that introduces and develops the theme.

An overview of Christianity will also have to be included somewhere.

For me, really, there is essentially:

For the second part	(A) The world of the master (priest-king) and the slave = war of sacrifice, glory of rivalry, potlatch (B) The world of the slave becoming the master for the second part (the bourgeois) = glory is contested in all its forms right to the end. (C) The world of man, neither slave nor master and a kind of hybrid of A and B. (D) World of the priest alone, trying to save glory by creating a false version of it, taking the concept of rivalry away from it = the world existing inside others.

The themes of rivalry:

essentially war then sacrifice potlatch	themes of ch. I

In ch. III, we first have the development and the individualization of the concepts of rivalry—at the same time there is the individualization of tragedy, but nearly everything is comical

then the birth of the depersonalized themes—love (depersonalized), nature, poetry critique of these themes, the impossible does not show through them except in a warped way.

Domain of depersonalization

reason	language	poetry
science	things	nature
State	h. beings	love
reason-poetry	authority and counter-authority	

Capital absorbs power, not with a view to expenditure but rather to ever more absorption.

The opposite of the stomach, man's intelligence (his mind) digests itself (the mind's first action is to enslave, then it enslaves itself). Enterprise (the totality of the means of production) does not set anything free as it develops. The tribute to glory is no longer paid. [*Crossed out:* Versailles was in no sense an excessive expenditure, neither were the wars of Louis XIV, rather, Versailles and these wars were the share that capital already claimed in advance to allow it to grow.] Sumptuous expenditures are reduced progressively in the eighteenth and nineteenth centuries, in Catholic countries and in others. Capital (the means of production) also digests man's intelligence.

If capital does not grow, it stops providing its minor distributions. That means that a certain part of capital's circulation stops; since the minor distributions are the condition of possibility for capital's growth, it can no longer grow if it stops providing them.

If it can no longer grow = if it can no longer provide major distributions, in reality it is: *if it no longer dares to grow*, from fear of not having the power to make any major or minor distribution.

Fragmentation, the individuality of businesses is a necessary part of this fear. Otherwise, the inability to make distributions would be less important.

So that a large-scale factory (industry for production) can live (pay its workers), new businesses (or extensions of old businesses) must be created—or a war must break out. It cannot produce merely for profits since the expenditures of the war of the State are theoretically profitable.

There is absolutely no room for expenditure in commercial enterprise. For each product a business must pay for labor, and if it cannot pay it dies.

What stops the machinery is that money no longer risks being invested.

If the surplus of money were expended sumptuously, it would lead to production—

[*Crossed out:* even] destroyed gloriously?

distributed to the consumers?

Be that EE, capitalist enterprise in general

PP, the producer for production
PC, the producer for consumption
pc, the product for consumption
pp, the product for production[10]

for the worker at PP to buy pc, he must produce pp. If PP slows down, some of its workers cannot buy pc anymore, so PC slows down.

There is, therefore, absolute interdependence between PP and PC. PC can only produce if PP produces. PP cannot produce unless enterprise in general grows. EE cannot grow unless there are forces it can take hold of, and these forces come not only from first substances that can be transformed into pure power but also from power that can be sold. Taking hold of forces means producing a substance that can be sold = that which has been produced is immediately transformed into a force of production. To produce the forces of production, commercial enterprise must grow in general, which is to say that producing the forces of production means taking hold of the forces.

Since every being on earth is simultaneously a being of greed and a being of glory (which means that they expend themselves willingly, and never despite themselves), they are also different from capital. Capital is the only entity that refuses to feed those who comprise it if it is unable to grow, and even if it separates itself from them, it rejects them

glorious expenditure of capital is idleness

capital is earthly existence reduced to the state of an all-encompassing machine, but as it has no knowledge of glory, it resembles a being that is entirely voracious, amoral, and devoid of glory.

Not only does capital not want to waste; it *cannot* waste. If enterprise in general cannot be expanded, PP cannot deliver pp, so the workers lose their jobs and unemployment extends to PC, since PP is no longer producing anything and so is no longer absorbing its share of pc.

C must make endless distributions but can only distribute in service of growth. This is because C = PC + PP.

This places the vital movement of the system—its soul, in a way, or its will—in CL, free capital [*capital libre*], capital which has not yet been transformed into means of production—the essential feeder of PP. Moreover, this soul cannot be neatly separated from businesses; it is part of what they constantly emit, the emission that they live for. Clearly, this is the spirit of capitalism, which is greedy for production, but this also involves distributing, being paid, extending the spirit of capitalism through the productive increase of money, and as such the productive increase of the spirit of capitalism itself, which is greedy to go even further.

The spirit of capitalism is produced in the form of stock market profits (which are real insofar as we believe that they will increase). It is undoubtedly in the stock market that the spirit of capital dwells, there where profits are evaluated and where this evaluation is a function (in times of peace) of the general possibility for expansion, whose general evaluation underlies particular stock market evaluations.

The spirit of capital returns to glory through the gamble, but it is only a kind of escape when it has reached its highest point.

There was
at the beginning
Franklin's principle
it is the basis and the rule of the game
and the fundamental spirit of capital

We must distinguish
an impersonal will
following Franklin's principle
representing greed pure and simple without any concern for, or even any possibility of, expenditure
this is puritan capital
the growth of wealth in itself

Law: capital cannot in any measure escape its puritanical form because it is the production of the means of production.

But the principle of personal enterprise moves into a general and impersonal state.

Given a productive enterprise, A, its greed does not directly affect its own expansion but rather the expansion of enterprises in general and, in a mediated way, through the mediation of an enterprise, N, that does not yet exist.

that which "does not yet exist" is the source of speculation

the avidity of puritanical capital is incarnated in its [*illegible*] by speculative capital. It is speculative capital that has become the heir to Franklin's idea, and it remains puritanical insofar as, in its fundamental form, its movement is impersonally conserved, but in its personal form it is completely opposed to its puritanical origins—it becomes glorious.

Take it up again as follows:

The spirit of capital is present in a single Puritan business, whose owner has dedicated his fortune to production and saves his profits for the expansion of the factory. Puritan enterprise is emblematic of the movement that creates capitalist industry, which divides up productive activity and glorious activity. But as institutions develop, one business on its own does not matter. Today, the spirit of capital is embodied in the entire collectivity of business: it no longer has a personal form.

Nevertheless, I want to discuss *puritanical capital* as the expression of the will of all enterprise: this will runs in completely the opposite direction to glorious activity, but without even a hint of moral compunction. Capitalist enterprises can be split into two sections: the section that produces the means of production, and the section that creates products for consumption. If there is no increase in capitalist enterprises in general, the first section can no longer sell its products, and from that point on it can no longer buy the products of the second section (which are consumed in part either by the workers or by the businesses themselves). The system, therefore, has to slow down to function, and significant disorder ensues. In capitalist enterprise in general, therefore, there is a will that exists by utmost necessity and that is impersonal in the extreme—a will to develop industry indefinitely. This will gives capital its puritanical nature: the bourgeois capitalist's aversion to the glorious use of riches. But in this developed form, the greed of businesses is indirect. It is not possible to say of any one business, nor of the collection of businesses in general, that they, in and of themselves, long to take hold of the productive forces. Their only wish is to sell their products. Their greed for growth requires a middle term, a new enterprise, *not yet existing,* which will need to arise autonomously (in normal circumstances), or at the very least it requires the growth of old enterprises that are only slightly dependent on the will of those that precede them. This kind of indirect greed, greed for which the middle term, by definition, does not yet exist, is the *speculative* will of capital. It is the *speculative* will of capital which makes the entire world vulnerable to exploitation, which tends to bring all the available forces within reach of exploitation.

This speculative will is in one sense localized: it is the result of free capital, which has not yet been invested and which generally comes—directly or not—from the profits of businesses. Free capital, moreover, makes up the largest portion of capital in general since wealth can be more easily and sufficiently captured by businesses if, through the sale of equity, it can be recuperated at will, taken out of one business, and invested in another. It is the freedom of investments that makes money flow on the stock market, but at the same time that freedom also introduces speculation—that is, the endless hypothesizing about the potential future profits of businesses. In normal times, this speculation is a function of the possibility of the expansion of businesses, which are evaluated in general terms as a basis for specific evaluations. Understood in this way, speculation is the spirit of capital itself—its limitless voracity is contained within it.

Any chance for expansion that appears on the field of speculation is immediately followed by an activity of seizing that fuels an influx of money. Moreover, two types of will express themselves in this activity:—the *impersonal*, puritanical necessity of capital, which commits it to infinite greed;—the free activity inscribed in this necessity but particular to *personal* speculators. Strangely enough, it is not important for the general meaning of impersonal *capital* (which remains a stranger to glory) that the activity is led by speculators, and that they partake in it because they have been fired up by their own rapacity and vainglory, because they are heirs, to a certain extent, to the spirit of potlatch. To overall speculation is added the thrill of losing felt by a small number of players gripped by "gambling fever," who sometimes gamble away their life. That does not change the spirit of capital in any way, which simply makes use of a spirit that runs counter to it. Capital uses the wagers to drain the surplus of available resources, making money flow as quickly as possible and with all the fluidity it requires;

it even makes use of the spirit of the wager to double the power of its vision: a raptor always has good eyes; speculators are the eyes of capital.

Too bad if, as often happens, the speculator is personally nothing but a glorious being, squandering his gains in sumptuary expenditures. Capital, fueled by the principle of nothing ventured, nothing gained, unquestioningly pays for the services of those who make resources run rapidly to where they need to be. The one caveat being that those who continue to embody the spirit of capital, the true heirs of the Puritans have a shade of contempt for speculators. On the other hand, they cannot help but fear the fever that speculation sometimes provokes.

It is not the case, incidentally, that all speculators squander. A solid speculator tends to enrich himself and then give back to capital the personal plunder that he took on credit, reinvesting it, at his own risk, in other businesses. A very small part of the profits from speculation feed the way of life of the rich. In a general sense—contrary to what took place in the agrarian economy, whose fruits could be expended gloriously*—the profits made from the use of capital must in large part be employed in the expansion of enterprise, so that the producers of the means of production can continue to operate, and as such, so can the entire system that depends on them.†

---

*Almost everything disappears in wars.

†If what I say is true for money, it would be necessary to show that this results in a question of the utilization of labor time. Proportion of

But what happens if we reach a point where development reaches capacity?* if the means of production, in the form of raw materials, machines, factories, are suddenly irrelevant? In theory, the industrial economy would need to be stabilized, would need to find the relative balance of the agricultural economy. But there would be no more chance for glorious expenditures that were commensurate with the situation. We would try to make profitable expenditures. We would need to build sumptuous social structures, but we have forgotten the meaning of sacrifice. There are no

---

workers employed: *a*) in the consumption of subsistence; *b*) in the fabrication of the means of production; *c*) in the consumption of luxury, ways of life like those who work for luxury (artists).

Plus, a chapter for war.

On the other hand—the idleness of one class, of all classes—the number of festivals given in the Middle Ages.

Finally, the moral question, the harder we are the more we expend for luxury—in opposition, expenditures for comfort, idleness, rest.

Relation between capitalism and sluggishness: due to a lack of solidarity of classes between each other, a general slackening of motivation, because there is not even any "luxury" so there are no great systems of moral, vital tension, but rather an absurd system of exploitation from which everyone is trying to escape (comfort, flight from life).

Hardness as a fundamental condition of luxury linked necessarily to religious or military sacrifice.

In the preface, my life and the principle of the extreme. Nothing beyond a shaky competence on any of the matters discussed—scientific training, however.

*Beforehand, the principle of the note: I can only consume if the factories etc.

longer any "motives for expenditure" that are capable of setting fire to wealth somehow, in the way that it continues to burn right before our eyes in the cathedrals of Europe or the temples of India. There are no longer any true festivals where we might consume the long-accumulated reserves of straw through fire. The sense of sacrifice (the mystery of the gift of the self and of death linked to an unleashing of human joy) is now so profoundly lost, so well erased by the centuries of puritanical morality, followed by rational and utilitarian morality—that nothing could be vainer than to look for escape routes in this direction. Furthermore, the return to equilibrium would require a transformation of industry, a reduction of heavy industry that would imply a break with the capitalist system, arresting the movement that drives it. In the current system, the only way we can consume is by paying not only for the cost of the consumed commodity but also for a corresponding part of the cost of the expansion of capital. Each expenditure, even if it is unproductive, is subordinated to the acquisition of new forces of production. It is the exact opposite of the economic system of the festival, in which every purchase contains a reserve that is destined for the squander of the festival, is subordinated to squander, has squander as its final goal. In any case, instead of directing his glorious ends toward the heavens, man renounces them, is reduced to necessity, to his limitless greed for growing his forces; he only expends so that he can—on the condition that he will—grow those forces. And what if the possibility of growth ends up going wrong? If the monster ends up consuming the very thing that might have comprised it? We see then that the monster only nourishes those whose labors sustain it on the sole condition that they increase its volume. It is not enough for the workers to make what is necessary, that is, useful objects: if they can no longer respond to the greed for the growth of capital, they will stop (or, at least, some of them will stop) receiving their share of the consumable commodities. But this share exists, is available, and in fact the failure to consume it is disastrous. Thus, the inverted system ends up the same way as the first system: in squander, in the loss of consumable commodities, whether through a loss of value or through real destruction. The accursed share, which at its core is nothing but the "superfluous," is rediscovered in this way—but instead of us "sacrificing" it, it obstructs the circulation of goods. Sacrifice is active in the first case and passive in the second.

If we want a clear idea of these bizarre results, we must reduce the objects under consideration to their essentials: *when it comes down to it, it is about the way time is employed.*

Men can work, or rest, or follow their passions (when it comes to communal activity, festivals are the unleashing of the passions). They can also make war.

The time for work can itself be split into three (or four) parts: the first part is put toward the consumption of the needs of subsistence; the second to producing the means of production; the third to responding to the desire for luxury (the fourth is reserved for outfitting war).

We must envisage under the heading of the third part: works of art and their [*pageantry?*] (edifices, gardens, sculptures, furniture, paintings, music, literature, and publications), festivals, spectacles, cults and the maintenance of the clergy, games, sports, adornments, certain [*diamonds?*], certain drinks, cafes, gambling houses, dance halls, many restaurants and hotels, all that is necessary for leisure trips, for tourism, beautiful cars, horses, prostitution, and, finally, tobacco. In numerous cases (prostitution, literature, etc.), it is sometimes difficult to say where work ends and where the play of passions begins. Science itself is at the same time passion and work, and insofar as it is work it is sometimes on the side of luxury, sometimes on the side of the means of production.

In comparing the society of the Middle Ages with our own, it is difficult to obtain any simple data except:

—the number of people not required to work (nobles, clergymen) was considerable;
—laborers worked longer days, but festivals where people were unemployed were more numerous;
—in the past, a much larger proportion of the available time was dedicated to the construction of glorious buildings; imagine a building in New York with no commercial purpose, towering over skyscrapers to the same extent that a cathedral towered over the houses of the Middle Ages, with the main object of concern corresponding to the sculptures on cathedrals that practically nobody could see;
—in the past, the time available for the creation of luxury objects was considerable: we spared nothing to perfect their quality; it is not certain whether the quantitative ratio of luxury objects to useful objects was different from ours; nowadays, in exchange, we lend a false air of luxury to many useful objects;
—in the Middle Ages, the largest share of unproductive expenditure followed the rules of the gift: it is the opposite

today; the festivals, tournaments, and mysteries of the past are opposed to today's cinema, theater, and sports matches—the cinema is the second industry of the United States[11]: apart from a few stadiums and churches (the sumptuous buildings of our day), most cinemas, theaters, and amusement parks are commercial operations.

Nothing is clear overall, but there is a tendency toward degradation, the generalization of tacky luxury, tobacco, individualization [*going?*] through private riches:

1st stage: collective spectacle for all
2nd stage: unequal distribution
3rd stage: individually equal distribution
Two sorts of degradation:

(a) individualization
(b) commercialization

More seriously, commercialization corresponds to the growing importance of interest, the impossibility of giving oneself over to sumptuous expenditure if it does not lead to savings—from which stems the loss of the idea that man lives for a glorious purpose and the predominance of economic goals.

Would Carnot's principle play a role here? Would there be loss of energy?

Expenditure is indeed comparable to the production of energy, the type of energy expended is solar energy, which is captured when it comes to earth—because it is captured it can be regarded as working energy (work of water). Life can take hold of it, life is essentially glorious in principle, but it can be enslaved, like solar energy, *a*) by consumption, *b*) by being put to work, the work of horses, of carbon

Different sorts of labor

—of the sun, which doesn't notice it, remains glorious
—of water, which takes no more heed than the sun
—of plants consumed, total destruction, not an alteration but a suppression of its glorious nature
—of consumed animals, the same
—of animal products, milk destined to be extracted for use, a teleological and non-glorious substance that has only one purpose: to be drunk, the glory of milk is in being drunk
—of the beast of burden, laboring for others, loss of its wild, glorious nature (opposition: the lion, the steer)—the principle is a labor that diminishes the share of glory
—free labor above all, but almost all the development of labor in the servile sense, servile labor is that in which expenditure is destined for the glory of others
different from the labor of the plant or the dead animal
wretched type, working in the library represented as useful, not glorious
capital is still a particular type
I must find the names for each type and precise formulas for each
sun, water exuberant labor
manure, plant, dead animal
beast of burden, slave

labor for capital
labor of capital
free energy, captured energy or labor

Energy is captured in order to be set free—at the very least in a gradual way. The capture of energy corresponds to the decomposition into greedy particles.

First of all, there is emission of free energy, as with solar energy (and even terrestrial energy). This free energy can be captured by one or more systems that will set it free again at the end—thus, a plant absorbs solar energy, is eaten by an animal that works on men's behalf, and then is eaten by them in turn. As energy, men's food is transformed into labor. Human labor is absorbed in two ways—essentially, under our current conditions, by the capitalist enterprise, the factory.

In the labor of the plant, there is accumulation of energy—the plant forms itself, accumulates [*resources?*], then flourishes and bears fruit—the flowers and fruits are the glory; the food and absorption represent the labor of the plant.

In the same way, feeding and absorbing make up the essential labor of the animal.

In both cases, animal and plant, labor is opposed to the emission of energy. It is the absorption of energy. If there is expenditure, it is for the benefit of absorption.

This is not a definition of labor: a man can labor at the theater. There is payment, to work is to earn money. In fact, we can distinguish between:

labor for the self (the plant)
labor for others

labor for others is partly labor for the self, in the form of payment or food for livestock

and yet, labor for all.

In labor, the energy expended by the worker is absorbed by the product. But the absorption of energy by the product is always divisible into two parts

nutrition acquisition
assimilation transformation

on the one hand, there is cultivation (production with a view to harvesting) or extraction (fishing, hunting, foraging) of raw products and transport instead of consumption

(cultivation is the capture of the labor of another with a view to harvesting the product) second element: assimilation, transformation of the raw product with a view to its use

man produces
light
heat
food
clothes
edifices (works of art)
the tools [*ustensiles*] of consumption
the instruments of labor

the essential part of production hinges on nutrition that is either

(a) positive, food and heat
(b) negative, conservation of food, clothes, buildings—which is to say, transformation of nourished beings

buildings, clothes, tools, instruments are those things that are added to the human being to help with various functions absorbing energy, consuming

conserving the energy absorbed

laboring (producing energy necessary for consumption, for the conservation of labor)

beings transform with a view to gaining more and more power

capitalism as activity of metamorphosis, necessarily temporary

we already knew that, but without recognizing all the ins and outs

—normal state of society, glorious man—whose nature is in no way ruled by the fate of *metamorphosis*?

necessity that it ends in a relative point of saturated capacity, return to glorious man

capitalism itself is a crisis

In the agrarian economy there was slow change, but not crisis.

We say that all our needs are not satisfied, it is a fiction: needs are limitless. In any case, it is time to dream about normal existence without returning to it—by normal, I mean an existence ruled by the conditions of the play of energy [*jeu énergétique*]. We are forever and always determined to capture more energy—we must recognize that captured energy must be expended, capture is nothing but a transition, what is absorbed must be given back. Earth and man are nothing but loci of transition, loci that split up the sun's rays—but this idea of man as a locus of transition must be linked to the meaning of death.

(end of the chap. on sacrifice

somewhere, metallurgy: the taboo on blacksmiths, not observed by us)

labor changed into glory

labor changed into power

The energy that we expend in labor is absorbed energy. Labor is emitted energy. Emitted energy always comes from captured energy. We labor by capturing the energy we have emitted to grow our power.

Labor:—as emitted energy, labor is tied to a being who has had to capture the energy he emits;—as captured energy, labor is still tied to a being who needs to capture energy; the being is not the same in both cases.

Each laborious task increases a being's power; but the power makes itself felt through an expenditure.

Simple case of a farmer feeding himself from the products of his labor.

Perhaps the labor of producing flour.

The flour in the farmer's mill increases his power—but he eats it in the form of bread so that he can make bread next year.

In reality, eating is the actualization of power. To eat is to expend, in the same way that to put oil in a car is to expend.

Double aspect of the fact of eating:—expenditure, emission of free energy, eating well on Sundays, drinking well, festival;—acquisition, emission of energy captured by work, pleasure of eating reduced to nothing.

In the agricultural economy there is a surplus to consume via:—festivals;—armed men.

The fields produce more than is necessary for the emission of energy required to plough them, at least from the moment when we began to use the labor of beasts, being frustrated by subjugated labor—slaves—that is the glorious condition.

The glorious condition disappears with capitalism because the surplus becomes used for the production of new instruments of production.

We have the following circuit:

being emitting energy, slave

the master acquiring power

nourishing the slave so that he produces

wasting the rest, unable to do anything else with the rest

the remainder is the amount of slave labor time put toward the creation of luxury, nourished by the peasants

in capitalism, those slaves fed by the peasants will be used to grow the means of production

before the division between master and slave, the festival, saturnalias, golden age

emitting being

capturing being

capturing and emitting being (the same)

emitting being and capturing being separated through domination

emission of energy—work = growth of the power of the capturing being

the acquired power is actualized in expenditures

the capturing being emits energy in feeding the emitting being (simple continuation)—in creating new means of production;—in emitting free energy

in reality the capturing being is always emitting—but for him, working means feeding a worker

the hard thing to understand about labor is that it is always a master who works—by expending money (giving out food, positive and negative energy in general, nourishment, clothes, places to live) this means that labor is linked to the use of arms and the spirit of decision.

The growth of the power of the capturing being has a bearing on:

(a) capture with a view to captured expenditure—the ability to buy labor, to emit energy, by dint of owning food, clothes, houses;—possession of the instruments of labor;—possession of the means of producing these instruments;
(b) capturing with a view to the emission of free energy.

Before this development: matters related to rest, idleness, etc.

Distinguish between emitted energy captured in preparation for free emission and emitted energy captured in preparation for captured emission

The many ways of putting energy at stake in a single action. The purchases made by someone with a salary

money is available energy, it is, in principle, gold; the army holds the truth of it since gold is what is at stake for the armed forces. Gold attracts armies. Gold is quite precisely obligation but can be moved from one form of obligation to another.

Obligation is the control of energy. *Money is an order given to x*, impersonally.

All energy is placed under obligation.

Those in possession of an army are the only ones who can demand free expenditure; all others need everything to remain captured.

There is a constant emission of energy in any possible form, available for the emission of captured energy.

sacrifice chap.?

In any case, the excess of energy is the accursed share.

In the oldest system the circle of morality is already circumscribed by daily activity, by labor: the moral is the profane. The elaboration of morality is the reconciliation of the sacred and profane domains.

The sacred is necessary in the profane at the moment of sanctioning, the moral is necessary in the sacred to make the sanctioning possible.

Whence the reconciliation of the possible and the impossible.

The domain of the sacred is that of the impossible. The moral problem is to make the impossible possible, to reconcile God and reason, Christianity, intercession.

On the one hand, to attain a morality free of all sacred elements. On the other hand, to attain a moral expression of the demands of the sacred.

The accursed share in the crises of overproduction

The accursed share without judgments on luxury, wars, excess energy, must go before the impossible, the necessary wavering of man, the rough appearance of everything

Fundamental question

Could we not labor less, rest, expend less energy?

Is the sum of energy captured from labor not a function of obligation?

Is it not the army that captures energy?

If we got rid of armed force, would we not also get rid of the excess?

Does the excess not come from the fact that it costs the army nothing, that it is precisely suited to the army?

Excess among the Eskimo.

Or is it excess that makes the army possible?

In other words: energy in men exists in relation to need—how can it be that it exists in excess?

Energy exists in excess in plants.

If it exists in excess in men, it is not as a result of their will, their caprice.

It is nevertheless remarkable in this regard that armies have been constituted through need, that wars have often been provoked by need (invasions).

In the emission of energy, need and the particular form of need that results from obligation play the role of primary cause and regulator. But all the available energy is set free in one way or another independently of needs.

Obligation works as a multiplier. It is obligation that causes the production of part of the excess, because it demands it—but there is still an excess produced of the part dedicated to obligation.

Obligation is added again and again, increasing the excess part but not creating it.

There is, however, a sort of link between the obligation and the excess because imposing the obligation is linked to the excess of virility.

Virility is the true expression of excess.

It is doubtful that that alters the balance very much.

Australians, Eskimos

It seems that we never get to know the conditions in which the sun emits energy without capturing that energy.

But every particle detached from the system needs to capture energy.

To capture it, it is necessary to expend it first of all; this is the principle of labor.

We could say that a particle has two immediate goals:

(a) to acquire as much as is expended = conservation
(b) to acquire more than is expended (at first)

(1) to increase its power (2) to expend the excess

reproduction
(one and the other)

It is the interplay of detachment, isolation, stripping away [*dénuement*], and recuperating that makes up the game of being human, in which anguish is attached to glory.

Communication reunites (in part) that which had become detached—return to solar fusion or the direction of this abandoned fusion.

What is clear, in any event, is that once energy is emitted, the capture of type *a* and the same goes for type *b1*.

But it is still necessary to consider the different possibilities that might ensue in each case

there is always a question of domination, of reliance
herbivores reliant on plants
plants reliant on the unmoving earth (?)
carnivores reliant on herbivores
men reliant on everything

certain men reliant on others.

Nevertheless, expenditure does not increase regularly, one step at a time: the dialectic of domination and communication is Hegel's dialectic of master and slave. Through domination, one gains the power to expend what is necessary for communication, but one also gains isolation.

It remains the case that it is not possible to imagine a system free of obligation—but still it must be destroyed.

No system without obligation—but reciprocally, no system without excess

change over time

sadness of capitalism

reduction of expended energy—in accordance with the reduction of obligation, itself a function of capacity and of the lack of interest in accumulation and in the requirements for freedom from capitalism

return of obligation at the point of saturation

of growth

absence of obligation = less expenditure, less excess all the same

capitalism is against obligation because obligation leads to excess

what is obligation if not the expression of will?

it is oppression that is linked to capitalism, let's at least call it that

it is a defense to get out of a stalemate, no positive character

capitalism is apathy

there is only one way to get it out of a stalemate: invention

Essential theme for the overview of the chapter

for the individual, the actions of the Mexicans are neurotic

from the glory of rivalry, via Christianity, to transparency—depersonalization linked to individualization

evolution over time and the dialectic of the master and the slave

Christianity resolves the themes of rivalry to the benefit of God alone, salvation is like a gift made by royal prerogative

depersonalization in reason, science, the State—then in poetry, nature, love

the autodigestion of spirit (in. exp.)[12]—autodigestion is the general fact linked to the development of the bourgeoisie

take the difficulty up again in a general fashion—tendency toward a balance between emissions and acquisitions

capital as apathetic, divided, powerless

capital linked to Christianity, sign of fatigue

what is the point of producing for consumption if it is not directed toward free expenditure, but the confusion must be introduced first

difference between a bourgeois and a great lord: equal wealth, different modes of expenditure—difference between a worker and a petit bourgeois with equal wealth—the worker spends more for pure enjoyment, the petit bourgeois spends more for the glory of rivalry

the shift is tied for the first time to the dominant bourgeoisie, art against the dominant class—the dissociation of taste, general ugliness in the end—a bourgeois art that is opposed to the type of art that must lead a cautious life, preserving itself like Ariadne's thread.

Idea of the accursed share and the theory of sacrifice repairing an abuse—this means defining abuse as the start of a cycle of equivalences

Once history has ended (it is difficult to imagine that it will carry on without end), man will be alone with himself

PLAN

simple entry into subjects

—explanation of the mechanism of capitalism, speculation
—question of the chapter: would there be a transformation

[*In the margin:* at this point invention, assessments of value, rest]

(a) evaluation in relation to the Middle Ages (before capitalism)
(b) posing the problem in general terms: that energy must always be liberated

principles of the capture and liberation (contrary to Carnot's principle) obligation

—general sense of the transformation

it is the critique of the glory of rivalry

the individual against institutions but the individual as a negation of individual glory and even individual liberty (fundamentally)—transparency

(a) negative struggle, reason, science, the State

benefits of the struggle from the point of view of glory
philosophy (of the 18th c.), the wise man, the politician

(b) neurosis as waste
(c) positive struggle, poetry, nature, love

[ENV. 65: 1 TER]

Clermont-Ferrand, January '42

1st totemic situation
The rule: we sacrifice what we appropriate, what we unduly absorb. There is a feeling of guilt.

Whence human sacrifice when man is a slave
Sacrifice-madness, when intelligence is servile
(conjectures in contradiction with . . .)

2nd In composing himself, the greedy being ends all communication, withdraws from it. The king no longer has slaves nor subjects; he is executed by those close to him.

3rd The military chief, *der Herr*, opposes his enemies, does not attain universality but *is* in opposition; he cannot be killed, those close to him are the *Knechte*, he has slaves. He himself has withdrawn from communication (pyramids, obelisks). A substitute is executed, but slaves are rejected due to dissatisfaction; they can no longer accept the fact. Conquering wars only delay the problem by extending subjugation. They satisfy a few people but increase the number of unsatisfied people even more. (In the Roman system, part of the lack of satisfaction develops outside, leading to catastrophe.)

Brahman Rajah
China

[ENV. 65: 15-17[13]]

THE STAKE [*LA MISE*]

essential part

The entire share of surplus energy is staked

3 portions of energy

(a) put on hold
(b) put at stake (α) in anticipation of production, therefore canceled, held back from the game
(ß) really put at stake

α = put into action; ß = put into question

difficulty of distinction

in each direction, we find a *waste*

precise terms:

(a) put on hold (b) put into action (c) put into question	} put at stake

but although it is put at stake in the case of putting into action, we must reserve the term "putting at stake" for putting into question, "putting into action" being reserved wherever possible for *taking out of the game*

definition of game?

in theory = expenditure

but there is not loss pure and simple in the same way that there is, so far as it seems, in the sun

energy is changed into something else which exceeds the fact of nature to which the wager is reducible

the stake's essential element, ourselves

sometimes totality—risk of death
sometimes partial—expenditure of energy

ORDER TO FOLLOW

1. General principle, putting the surplus at stake
2. Definition of the game
3. Definition of the stake

Essentially the surplus of energy, which means:

ourselves
the more energy we have available
= all wealth except the means of production

nevertheless, what is expended is fundamentally the energy that was necessary for production
examples:

an object of luxury
a life in its entirety, in part dedicated to representation
the food etc. necessary for this life
the objects necessary for representation (churches)
the objects necessary for eroticism
the objects necessary for the glory of rivalry (war and ostentation)
all the objects that are not—the means of production
—objects linked to production

in laughter, eroticism and tears, real energy; also in war

physical energy properly speaking: eroticism, laughter, tears, dance, songs

in death there is no deployment of energy, but the energy available is cancelled out insofar as it is possessed by the dead man

festival: physical energy
foods consumed in large quantities—drunkenness
objects of sacrifice
gifts
buildings, the tools and clothes of festivals

all the above is put at stake in service of representation
leads to the representation of the world
representation is necessary for surpassing

when something is put into action, the gamble has a dual nature: *a*) labor, *b*) natural given

when something is put into question, there is: *a*) energy of the gamble = γ, *b*) natural given

continually distinguish between γ and the energy put at stake

laughter

there would be	(a) γ (b) energy put at stake (c) state implied by γ	} expenditure of laughter

(same when it comes to putting into action)
γ consists of overcoming anxiety (x)

[ENV. 65: 22–26]

The gamble is not an immediate excess of energy. It is, *at its core*, excess, but the excess appears as energy put at stake. It is, moreover, difficult to be specific without having determined the way that terrestrial energy moves in its stages. There is:

(a) *simple*, immediate expenditure (without a plan)—laughter, tears, eroticism
(b) mediated expenditure (work) following a plan. For food, mediate expenditure goes all the way to the kitchen (inclusive).

Every product of labor must be conceived as an expenditure of energy, but expenditure split across two periods: period of *labor*, period of *consumption*. If consumption serves production, it is cancelled out as expenditure. It is a *neutralized* expenditure, limited labor. On the other hand, there is *open labor* and delayed expenditures. But since the consumer is distinct from the producer (the worker), open labor is a limited expenditure for the worker in which his salary allows him to continue his work.

Vocabulary: simple expenditure
delayed expenditure (labor)

(a) neutralized or limited labor
(b) expenditure or servile labor

An unconsumed product (or one that is intact or still usable) represents energy put on hold.

For each of these products, energy has been spent in a certain way, but the expenditure is unconsumed.

Now it appears that labor is not an expenditure properly speaking but an accumulation of energy. The product of labor is energy put on hold. To consume a product is to consume the energy that it cost to create it. Money is the form in which energy that has been put on hold is made available. Money is a product representing the energy it took to earn it. As money is also accumulated energy, the seller of the product exchanges one amount of accumulated energy for another.

Energy is not really accumulated in an armchair, but a sum of energy has been expended to make the armchair and this energy has not yet been consumed.

warriors α

erotic value of the combatant
sacrificial value of heroic death

feminine body ρ

relation between prostitution and war
sacrificial value of prostitution
comic value of obscenity

sacrificial victim θ

combat sacrifices
comic value of the sacred

comic object or . . . β

tragic, mythic, epic heroes, words and thought

creation of language ω

α, ρ, θ, and β are creations of ω by magnification
ρ and β have something of θ, and even of α and ω
all would be reducible to θ considered in its relation to ω

[*Crossed out:* In eroticism]

Dignity declines into animality (infancy)

the infantile, the animal, the indefinite of laughter is like sacrificial death, like the moment of nudity in eroticism

the interpenetration of two spheres

major sphere

minor sphere

(The following pages [Env. 65: 66–68, 72–80] seem to date from 1943 and correspond to table of contents C)

BEGINNING OF THE SECOND PART OF *THE ACCURSED SHARE*

A book whose subject matter is a form of knowledge presents itself as a finished whole—when it is nothing but a link in the chain! Not only does it have its origins in other, older books, but it has its conclusion in books that will emerge out of it, books that have not been written yet. This conclusion already challenges the book in advance. Nevertheless, an author normally disguises the incomplete nature of his work. Like a house, a book is built on a plan: once the plan has been executed, the edifice remains in its rhetorical isolation. The lie of a book is that it looks finished, dressed up in the literary artifice of the author. In truth, it is nothing but a construction site.

This method has its advantages. A reader, like a book, gives an impression of calm authority. Malevolence itself profits thereby (critiquing this would mean recognizing that the author is an accomplice). The author himself yields before the fiction of a finished work just as he yields to a necessary subject matter. It would be impossible to relieve the significant tension that is attached to the anxiety of finishing without causing some harm.

When it comes to the general effort, it is true that it requires the greatest possible will. But it is more about the form. To write a work by carrying out the intended plan seems strange to me: that supposes that the results can be acquired independently from the execution, that thought stands immobile during all the time of execution.

I may use plans but no longer tolerate being bound by them. Carrying out the work becomes a time of anxiety for me. I never stop changing. I have been [*dragging?*] this work out for years. I intend to continue it in a different way from how it began. Up until now, I have tried to express something known: I have had to begin what came before again. From now on, I will try to translate an unfinished movement, such as it is.

VIII

Immediately after the main body of the text on Franklin, it is necessary to introduce these general considerations:

Capitalism resolved the problem of excess by putting it toward the development of the forces of production. All it has done is increase the difference between the two amounts.

Two things remain unclear: the uncertainty over what is *necessary*; the role of obligation, the labor time could be decreased. Put the question of obligation in the chapters on war. But treat the reduction of labor time as a possibility.

The growth of excess is remedied in three ways:

(a) individualization of expenditures
(b) fixation: transformation of superfluous expenditure into necessary expenditure[14]
(c) reduction of labor time

IX

Capitalism develops individualization

Chapter on individualization in which the general picture of the types of expenditure from the Middle Ages to today will be presented

Maintenance of rivalry, of waste

disappearance of the feeling of common value: loss of awareness.

Individual expenditures are unproductive for the personal chapter but productive for the general chapter.

X

Effort to fixate superfluous expenditures.

By setting the minimum standard of life way above the level attained, it should develop.

(no chapter on the reduction of labor time—combine fixation and reduction)

XI

The permanent nature of excess.

The accursed share

Necessary failure of capitalism as no balance possible.

However, beyond capitalism (but within its limits) it would be possible to reduce labor time.

All one can say is that capitalism introduces a fluctuation, an uncertainty. It interferes with the primitive givens that have already been altered by obligation. At a certain point, it is difficult to judge where we are, where we are going.

The consideration of the animal world encourages us to think of it as a foundation.

Eroticism and rivalry, procreation.

In the human world, festival and war.

Accursed nature of eroticism
of the festival
of war

Capitalist accumulation is added to it

Accumulation completes the curse.

Only the festival has disappeared. War and industry remain.

(BEGINNING OF THE THIRD PART)

XII

OBLIGATION

Another part begins.

One could say that labor is no less a curse than the festival (the Bible).

Essentially, obligation has to do with the need to survive.

We cannot consider as obligations the consequences that arise from the concern for glorious expenditures. (In an economy without classes.)

But in a hierarchical economy, the weakest are required to provide the glorious expenditures of the most powerful; the most powerful have an existence that is purely and simply glorious.

It is the impossibility of what obligation alone has made possible that gives obligation its false appearance. The only freedom that is suppressed is that of obliging.

In an intellectual sense, the most openly free time is that which precedes the removal of obligation and implies it will be loosened.

XIII

THE GLORY OF RIVALRY

The pretexts. In the first movement, glory is given to the city.

In the second movement, it is given to God, and utility is given to man in general, independently of the city.

The law that all expenditure must be justified by a gain.

XIV

ISLAM

Removal of any expenditures that are not for the benefit of war

read the Quran

Sacrifice disappears in Islam, which is an army.

Incompatibility of sacrifice and military spirit.

But if we don't suppress the king in Islam, we make him universal, which comes to the same thing from the point of view of the glory of rivalry.

XV

EVANGELICAL CHRISTIANITY

Direction toward transparency, suppression of the glory of rivalry, its absorption into God.

XVI

ROMANTICISM

Nature. Love. Poetry.

Nostalgia for the past.

XVII

TRANSPARENCY

It is lucid consciousness.

Suppression of the glory of rivalry

Autonomy accomplishing itself in a renunciation of the self

4. NOTES FROM MARCH 1944

....

[Ms 6, unpaginated *On Nietzsche* manuscript[1]]

THE MOVEMENT OF WORLDS

This being that we are, coming from nature, is not just the product of nature. Because we tear ourselves away from nature. We are not in the universe in the same way that a sponge is in the sea. We emerge, or try to emerge, from this universe. In some sense, man wrings himself dry from the universe or nature. He forces himself to be autonomous.

It seems to me that man's rupture with nature is no different from our normal way of being when we experience fear or anguish, when we experience a lively pleasure, when we laugh, when, in general terms, we live. It is not the effort of a conscious will saying: "I exist and there is nature opposite me; I want to separate myself from nature." Before reflecting on anything, we are inspired by a certain amount of autonomy and the desire for more autonomy. Animals themselves—each one seeking out pleasure for itself, fleeing pain or death—possess this relative autonomy and are in search of greater autonomy. I think it makes sense to imagine that this animal autonomy extends the even more obscure autonomy of the infinitesimal particles of matter. The most noticeable expression of this autonomy is the desire to endure, which is given a tragic meaning by the frailty of the animal.

The truth of autonomy is precisely that of being oneself and not anyone else. But every form of autonomy, no matter how entrenched it is, is precarious. In this sense, being an animal is, in man's view, rather a comedy of autonomy. In fact, the animal is not aware of its relative autonomy. It is its own self and wants to be so: it flees death, but if it is generally aware of its existence, it does not know that it is itself rather than anything else. It seems to feel isolation, its real, desired isolation, in the combative exploits it successfully undertakes to avoid dying. But unlike me, the animal is not haunted by death. To tell the truth, I must let myself be haunted by death all my life: without this shadow thrown over everything in me, I would have no *consciousness* of being myself, the autonomy I would enjoy would be that parodic version which irritates me in beasts.

There is, in fact, no difference between autonomous existence and conscious existence. More or less consciousness signifies more or less autonomy in man. An autonomy which is not clearly conscious of being autonomous can be perceived as such in relation to full dependence, but in relation to clear consciousness I can recognize it as a clownish pretension. If a beast, such as a penguin, reminds us of a human being by dint of some exterior characteristic, thereby allowing us to see the impoverished drive that gives life to it, then there is something comic about it. Knowing that I am autonomous is not enough for me to be autonomous: but this knowledge, even if it is partly wrong, makes my relative autonomy as effective as possible, fills it with existence.

In this way, all aspects of human consciousness are linked to the notion of autonomy. Insofar as it is fundamentally the same thing as consciousness, this notion is extremely simple. But autonomy, existing more or less as a kind of effectivity, is linked to the entire development of consciousness through the experience it has of the world. We cannot, therefore, draw out an understanding of consciousness that is separate from the knowledge we have accumulated. We do not draw it out solely from within but from without as well. Or rather, it results in us from the relation between what is within and without. The notion of human autonomy is in truth the most complex of notions: everything contributes to its formation. It makes use at one and the same time consciousness as a foundation and the experience that consciousness has of the world around it—which is to say, all of history. And not only history in itself but the fragmentary knowledge we have of it. Other notions imply this use. But in this instance, it is total use. To the extent that one among us provides himself with an autonomous existence within nature, he has his eyes fixed on the whole of the universe and the scientific knowledge that we have of it, on the whole of history and historical knowledge, at the same time that he is conscious of himself.

In itself, man's autonomy is questionable, but the same can hardly be said of his desire for it. I do not even doubt that this desire has been continually important throughout history. But I find that it is linked, precisely, to two conditions that I discussed previously.

The first is the error of the immobile ground.

The second is the requirement that a (relatively) detached particle must enrich itself at the expense of others.

But the desire for autonomy (the hunger for liberty) that fuels me does not only have *conditions*. It necessarily has this *consequence*: the acquisition of autonomy cannot be separated from a contestation of its truth—that is, its reason for being. Would I be autonomous if I did not have the power to question my autonomy? To doubt it: it may be imaginary. To doubt its legitimacy: it may be bad.

Second consequence.

I perceive human existence clinging to the slopes of a mountain it is trying to climb. As it seeks autonomy, it laments its lost dependence. Nostalgia for nature.[2]

But regret and nostalgia merge with the contestation of autonomy.

The situation becomes stranger the moment that man perceives that his possibilities for autonomy are founded on an illusion and a weakness. Ambiguity is introduced as a result. We magnify the immense universe. We immediately perceive its grandeur and prodigality, and we place them in contrast to our greedy small-mindedness. We annihilate ourselves in every way. The nostalgia for the universe is the same thing for autonomy as the nostalgia for death is for life.

But the desire for life is not suppressed in the desire for death and, in the same way, the desire for autonomy is nothing but exhausted in the magnification of the universe. In fact, the nostalgia for death puts life into question, the nostalgia for nature puts autonomy into question.

What happens first and foremost in regret is the transformation of an autonomy based on error and greed into an autonomy that is more completely based on a renunciation of stability and on putting itself at stake.

At a certain point, we perceive that the nature in relation to which we would like to be autonomous is the stable earth and the obligation to enrich oneself. It is the share of nature that was required for the development of the necessary conditions for autonomy, which is to say the part that we depend on immediately and whose specific characteristic, due to its isolation, is that it is kept back from being put at stake for a period. It is this share of objectified nature to which we relate all the rest by chains of identity, which we deny by affirming our autonomy. But the universe that science discovers is tainted by the fact that it is linked by identities to the objects that surround us and whose representation is linked to the stability of the earth.

One last operation of rupture is necessary. It is from the world that he created for himself—and "he" here is man in his actual situation, not man as an autonomous being (or a being striving for autonomy)—that he—now "he" refers to the being striving for autonomy—must tear himself away.

Autonomy requires greed to be stabilized and satisfied, but it cannot stop there. It is greedy autonomy. There is, beyond it, autonomy that is linked to loss. The freedom that is the freedom to give and not to take, the freedom to lose oneself and not accumulate riches.

In the end, the consciousness of being oneself must be joined by a renunciation of being that self (the only possible culmination). No asceticism, which is still just the fear of being oneself.

But this clear consciousness that I have of myself and on which my independence is based shows up the limits of that independence at the very moment it establishes them. What is the meaning of this being who will die? Moreover, once my clarity has developed, it shows up all my frailties. My existence in particular, its autonomy, both depend on the situation that I have described: they are engaged in a struggle against the existence and autonomy of the other, in the limitless monopolizing of riches; they are defined by the evident stability of the earth and by the illusion of fundamental stability. I become more aware of my autonomy as I become richer (more powerful) and as the things around me become more solid or appear to be.

CHAPTER I

Human existence is placed under conditions of isolation within which: 1st the reality of the universe's (or nature's) movement cannot be sensed; 2nd being is divided into particles striving for the greatest possible autonomy, condemned to capture (to the greatest extent that each can) all available force—contrary to the sun or the stars that are not divided up and which radiate force.

CHAPTER II

Man is a natural being who tears himself away from nature. This tearing away is part of the complex development of a consciousness that is autonomous or that wants to be so, which is constantly contesting and being forced to contest the grounds of its autonomy, while having to contest, finally, the fundamental conditions (described in chap. I). This is this book's message, showing that the necessity, so that it can exist, to question autonomy (to put it at stake) requires a free *expenditure* of force accumulated with difficulty, just like the stars.

This chapter on autonomy should be moved either to an appendix or to the end of the book.

In all likelihood, *the sum of energy produced would be*, as I have said, *greater than the sum necessary for the production.*[3]

This truth is drawn from experience. In different types of societies, an appreciable share of the labor can be used for ends other than the production of what is necessary. It is true that the notion of the "necessary" introduces, on the one hand, something vague, a variable state that it is impossible to define generally, and on the other hand the intervention of an obligation without which society would not be able to limit workers to what is "necessary."

5. PLANS AND NOTES, 1945[1]

[BOX 13, C: 154–167]

THE ACCURSED SHARE
OR THE LIMIT OF THE USEFUL
AN ESSAY ON GENERAL ECONOMY

PLAN

PRELUDE TO THE SUBJECT MATTER

Difference from other studies of the same subjects

opposition between *general economy* and *restricted economy*;
difference from Marxism
radical removal of psychological elements as independent factors.

The principle of the vaudevillian meet-up

the question is the one posed by the drama of human life; all the characters of the play are necessarily featured in the response.

SECTION A: HISTORICAL INTRODUCTION
(description of historical effects as a way of positioning the problem)

Sacrifice
Potlatch
The festival economy
Capitalism
Reason (principle of capitalism and socialism)
Military constraint (excess linked to suffering)
Christianity (will to suffering—where Buddhism negates the meaning of effort, Islam reduces the expenditures of excess to military expenditure)
Demographic growth
Reduction of labor time and unemployment
Armament
Romanticism (principle of imaginary expenditures and ambiguous confusion)

SECTION B: THEORETICAL INTRODUCTION
Excess energy

general definition of energy;
basic energy;
the law that the energy produced exceeds basic energy;
the theory of surplus value according to Marx;
necessity for energy to be completely used up.

The effects of different movements on one another

principle of energy to be expended and of its use leading toward the maximum increase of energy in general;
limit of this effect: principle of the maximum development of military possibilities, diverting an important share of production toward useless ends;
limit of military effects: (*a*) possibility of the system being exhausted, (*b*) historical variation in the points where military energy can be exerted;
limit of the growth of energy.

Overview of useless expenditure

general summary of the volume;
expenditures through physical activity: (*a*) muscular, (*b*) secretional;
production of useless objects, those that are: (*a*) consumable, (*b*) mobile, (*c*) immobile;
expenditures of mental energy: the principle of contagion and the vital *continuum*, principle of the *notion of activity* and the *external sign*
general description of stimulation and stimulants.

SECTION C: GENERAL ECONOMY OF ENERGY
Man's place in the biosphere

growth, sexual explosion, and growth of the species;
the general limit to the growth of the nonhuman biosphere;
the requirement for the most powerful animals to expend excess energy (*disastrous* character of the power of this expenditure);

the most powerful animal is the one that appropriates energy the best: tools (Neanderthals).

General specificity of man

erect posture as an emergence from the animal biosphere (the most liberated and least servile way of being);
the rhythm, expressive of the excessive flow of energy;
labor, the rhythm in work and effort;
war;
consciousness as anguish and consciousness of death.

Tragic expenditure

the rupture of the continuum, tears, anguish, and sacrifice;
the theory of the gamble and of gain;
the sphere of activity (opposition between immanence and transcendence);
general description: sacrifice and evildoing, laughter, dreams, and childish immanence, poetry, eroticism, pleasure in nature, mystic effusion;
glory (opposition between communication and the glory of rivalry) and overspending through expenditure (limit of the idea of pleasure);
principle of what cannot be said.

Historical variations of excess

Study of the curve of variation of free excess and capitalist accumulation: the meaning of the world wars.

SECTION D: CONCLUSION

Position of the political problem

the problem as fundamentally nonsensical;
dialectic of the manager and the managed (the manager demands a maximum amount of work for a minimum amount of consumption; the managed aim at a minimum amount of work for a maximum amount of consumption);
historical development of the opposition; that it is irreducible once management is reduced to reason;
principles of the self-assertion of the managed: the voluntary rejection of management, the return to what cannot be said.

GLOSSARY [BOX 13, C: 209–216]

production: mobilization and conduction of energy

destruction of energy: expenditure of energy in an activity whose results do not respond to the needs of the dynamic system

useful: responding to the needs of the dynamic system, thus serving production, which is to say the mobilization and conduction of energy

appropriation: not the fact of acquiring, but of directing a certain amount of appropriated energy toward a certain end

labor: act of changing the state or position of an object in response to a goal

linked expenditure: the expenditure of energy that is useless but that a wage-laborer claims he cannot do without. Although it does not itself fulfill the needs of a dynamic system, on account of the worker's refusal to go without it, it becomes one of the conditions for the system to be set in motion. An example of this is the production of tobacco. Insofar as an expenditure becomes one of the general needs of a certain group of workers, it must be considered as linked; as a result, it is reduced to the scale of an expenditure that is also linked when it is expended by non-salaried workers in the same place, unless we are dealing with individuals whose entire life is useless.

DYNAMIC SYSTEMS [BOX 13, C: 168–170]

A *dynamic system captures*, *conducts* by *accumulating* or not accumulating, *appropriates,* and *expends energy*.

A productive system is a dynamic system that expends its energy in the production or transportation of objects.

Appropriation is the method of conduction.

The goal of an expenditure may or may not be the *transportation* or *production* of an *object*. This object can satisfy the *needs* of any productive system: it is then a *useful* object. On the other hand, it must be called *useless* if it does not satisfy the needs of any productive system. In general, any expenditure wherein the goal is not to transport or produce a useful object is useless.

In the human sphere, the *residence* with its *residents* is an elementary system whose expenditure is often external since the residents can spend a large amount of their time outside the residence. More often than not, the residence is immobile, but the tent, the trailer, and the boat are mobile.

Each resident makes up an isolated system entire unto himself. He can remove himself from the residence but, under threat of wasting away, he cannot leave it for another.

The transportation and production of a system's objects occur partly in the residence. The lands and facilities where the rest of the residents' work is performed are combined with the residences. In some instances, the lands and the facilities are linked to the residence and form a complete system with it and its residents. In this case, individuals living in other residences can come and add their labor, for a wage, to that of the residents. In other instances, the lands and facilities where the residents work are connected to another residence. Finally, the lands and facilities can form relatively autonomous systems (kolkhozes,[2] nationalized factories, limited companies), which do not depend on any particular residence and which rely solely on a group of nearby residences housing individuals who can come and expend their labor there.

SIMPLE EXPENDITURES [BOX 13, C: 176–177]

I.	Immediate expenditure		
	(a) active:	jumping and dancing shouting and singing making love laughing crying	
	(b) secretive-excretive	sperm, eggs (useful for others), ornamental tissues, tears excrement, sweat, ear wax	positive negative
	(c) total	death (useful for others: those who eat)	
II.	Useful expenditure:	secretive: all internal secretions walking and runing, working (changing the place or state of an object)	

LINKED EXPENDITURES [BOX 13, C: 217–234]

The inevitability of industrial development does not progress without the effort of adaptation.

The capitalist reaction to the system of glorious expenditures arises in a human context, in the same context that produced the glorious system. It establishes itself as a response to the general feeling of poverty and to the expenditures that represent an affront to this feeling. But on all sides, active desire plays a role in expenditures. The capitalist system cannot suppress this desire. Capitalism makes use of it, moreover, whenever it allows it to realize its goals.

But it tends to transform it; where possible, *it changes it from being a master that must be satisfied to being a servant, an assistant*.

Unproductive expenditures that are tolerated or, better, developed by capitalism have the following characteristics in common.

In the festival economy, some payments correspond to them but they are not the starting point for further surplus value. The labor required for unproductive expenditure may be paid for. The labor of the architect and those who work on a cathedral is normally remunerated. In the same way, the choristers, vergers, the embroiderers who make the ornaments receive a wage. But the cathedral differs from a theater and above all from a cinema insofar as the work produced [or] destroyed within it was considered to be such (as it was for festivals and ancient games) by the person or persons in control of the buildings and the services (cf. *Inn. Exp.* Where I indicate that we motivate and then arrive at the loss of motivation). Whereas a film producer approaches his work as if it were any other industry producing useful objects. A factory that produces tires for trucks (find the name) and that prolongs the rubber industry contributes—to a degree that is quantifiable—to the mobilization and conduction of a certain amount of useful energy. This amount must in principle be greater than the basic energy required for the production of tires (food and upkeep of workers, fuel, loan repayments, maintenance and updating of tools). Of course, it is not the same for the film producer: the energy expended for his initiative is entirely dissipated. It does not satisfy the needs of the dynamic system that is productive society. But the film producer tells himself this: "If I had carried out the production of tires, rather than films, I would have provided society with a useful service that would have represented in possible payments a sum greater than my expenditures. I can expend my labor power just as well in producing films (to begin with, that power exists only as an undefined form of capital). But only on one condition: that in exchange for my service, and even though that service does not help to produce any energy, society gives me a sum equal to or greater than that represented by the useful service. In other words, only if the public (conceived as a mass of isolated individuals), and not me, takes responsibility for the destruction of energy."

In the capitalist economy, it is no longer the ones who demand an expenditure and decide the form it will take who assume the expenditure as a loss: the ones who do this are the passive spectators. Producers provide these passive spectators with the chance to essentially spend the share of energy that was necessary for production: money allows for this since possessing it supposes either a paid service of an equivalent amount of energy or the capitalist appropriation of the share equal to the excesses of energy that were mobilized. In a sense, the value of the money paid by the spectator is not destroyed: it returns to the producer (or to anyone who made the production possible: distributors, projectionists). In the hands of the producer, it is turned into a quantity of energy that he can put into action as he sees fit. The destruction—the production of a film—thereby enters into a useful cycle. This simply required those who possess energy, on every side, to take responsibility for it and replace it by providing a greater sum than the sum destroyed. But, in this way, expenditure is *subordinated* and differs, as a result, from *sovereign* expenditure (the service in church is still a *sovereign* expenditure). I prefer the film to the service: nevertheless, I remain disappointed by the servile nature of its projection. Thus, when it comes to unproductive expenditure, whatever satisfies my *taste* is the most suitable.

Our inability to satisfy a taste for sovereignty (that remains in all of us to a certain extent) allows me to view *subordinated* expenditure as relatively deteriorated.[3] However, we will see in what follows that an authentic liberation proceeds from this deterioration.

This deterioration, here, has to do with the substitution of a great number of spectators for the hierarchy that rules in the festival economy. The great number altogether—which does not exactly refer to the community but to the average man considered in isolation—is the judge of what is suitable to them:* his judgment, however, is interpreted

---

*Note on inquiries, films initially projected in rooms.

by a capitalist producer and his natural propensity limited by the state's censorship.

(a little later on—end of the chapter—the fact that the absence of sovereignty over expenditures has another meaning: to the extent that a salary gives one access to them, expenditures contribute to the growth (?) of production, in any case they are not sufficient to destroy the excess).

The reduction to average taste, the interpretation of this taste by a man for whom money is the measure of value, and the intervention of a public morality hostile toward anything that does not conform to the principle of utility add to the relative blandness of productions. The rule of the *happy ending*,[4] which applies to all but a few exceptions, is diametrically opposed to Greek tragedy.

(if the market wasn't already saturated with absurdities, no good film would be possible—following chap. about the rights of those who are managed)

There is a degradation of expenditure, also responding to a dispersion in time that corresponds with the distribution among the masses. We enter the cinema like we do a café, at any hour of the day. We used to condense possible expenditures into a point, into a given time: there was a relatively rare break in the ordinary course of life (life dedicated to useful work). Modern expenditures which, by contrast, have been inserted into this monotonous course of life, have lost the power to break from it and become subordinated to its dull repetitions.

This degradation can already be seen in the useless expenditures that capitalism, by following its natural inclination, imposes on or proposes to the largest possible number of individuals. Not only is an old form of expenditure—the spectacle—degraded, but new forms of release are better suited to the dominant principle of the economy. From this point on, everyone is worried about every form of useless expenditure: this sort of expenditure is no longer proudly affirmed, we search on the contrary to justify it, to cloak it in some rough comedy of utility. It becomes essential that the chain of actions eventually leads to some kind of emission of energy whose final goal is not the production of different energy but that simply responds to

(from the moment that we can pretend that it is useful, and thereby make it part of the [*payment?*] for labor, a useless expenditure is no longer sufficiently useless)

our tastes (if, as I said, the energy necessary for production is less than the energy produced, then this is the case). But we will prefer to satisfy a taste that is justifiable, on the surface, from the point of view of utility. A bathtub is presented as useful. So, it is not, in fact, an object whose luxurious nature we proudly affirm (as we do of a painting or a vase placed in a ceremonial hall). After all, a bathtub is convenient and, without it, I would live less comfortably. My parents, who did not have a bathtub, did not know that they lived less comfortably.

They [expenditures] are distributed differently from those of the festival economy

in theory, these are not public, collective expenditures (with the exception of equipping the army), these are individual expenditures within reach of the greatest possible number and in the same way that they tend to be divided between individuals, they are also divided up in time, it is a process of degradation

moreover, they have a hybrid nature (negative nature as well—holidays), are no longer frankly unproductive

these expenditures are occasionally superfluous but useful (bathtub), sometimes completely useless (tobacco) but linked

these expenditures satisfy the instincts that are implied by unproductive expenditure, but they degrade them, minimize them, subordinate them to:

(a) the principle of utility
(b) a payment (war is not paid)

Linked expenditures also are useful in a real sense. The affirmation of utility is not merely formal.

They allow and solely allow a high level of technical development. Man expending gloriously is not capable of serious technical development, nor is the man who is unable to expend unproductively a good technician, at least by the standards of modern technology. To read a blueprint, one must know how to read and write; it also helps to live in conditions of relative comfort. Undoubtedly the comfort of American workers is the effect, not the cause, of American prosperity, but it is a factor in the growth of this prosperity because it provides a greater number of American workers with a greater level of technical skill.

In this way, capitalism organizes a neutral environment, without true unproductive expenditures, but at the same time without unproductive expenditures being prohibited.

The process of these linked expenditures is costly:

the number of hours necessary for each hour of production increases but this surplus is made possible by the fact that the accumulation increases the quantitative value (the yield) of the hours of production. Moreover, it tends to make this yield larger.

On the whole, surplus value thus increases through evolution.

In no case can these linked expenditures fulfill the goal of the outlets sought by production.

There is a moral result, balance, and subordination, creation of a favorable (ambiguous) environment.

but the expenditures of wage-laborers are in no way able to resolve the problem of division posed by the development of industry.

In the capitalist system, it is out of the question for there to be fewer hours of production than necessary—surplus value cannot be suppressed, the gap cannot be closed. On the contrary, it is increased: this is what is expressed by the fact that superfluous expenditures are given an air of utility.

From the moment that a wage-laborer can engage in an expenditure, it ceases to be unproductive, or it ceases, in any case, to be sufficient to satisfy the need to expend the surplus. Undoubtedly, we must consider certain relative exceptions in this regard (the cinema), but we cannot define unproductive expenditure in the strong sense unless we note that its essential nature is the destruction of surplus value. What is at issue is not the more or less expensive or destructive nature of the cost of production. It is not a matter of identifying whether some minor destructions have become necessary or have helped production.

SIGNS [BOX 13, C: 181–197]

An active expenditure is doubled, in a certain way, as an expenditure and a sign, and the sign is simple, like the expenditure itself. Excretive expenditure and death also end with objects. These objects, like the acts, have the value of a sign.

Every immediate expenditure creates a *sign* that expresses to others the *meaning* of the expenditure carried out.

Expenditure is contagious (someone else's leaps can make others want to leap, someone else's sobs can make people want to sob, the drip of a faucet can make others want to piss). The signification of an expenditure is the same thing as its contagion. The signification of a dance is provided by the fact that I dance in turn, or at least that I want to dance. The sign is a phenomenon that accompanies an expenditure as it spreads. But contagion cannot take place if an expenditure is not signified. In the same way, a sign is at least the rough sketch of an expenditure.

A leap, a dance, a cry, a song, a sexual act, a burst of laughter, a sob, interpreted through sight or hearing, signify the *expenditure* of others to those who perceive them. The meaning of an expenditure of energy is related to the fact that this expenditure spreads. Something discharged by one or many individuals, if it is not met with willful resistance, is echoed by those nearby.

A dance is the simple sign of an explosive release of energy. A dance in the theater is reduced to this simple sign that is not actualized (it is not a more or less durable object). When I see dancing on stage, the expenditure of others is communicated to me in this way in the form of a sign. My participation is thus reduced. A given quantity of energy is used up before me, but I do not use any up myself.

A non-vital tissue—a mane, a crest, the tail of a peacock or the hair of a human being—are more completely separated from what they signify than a dance or a cry are. They are the signs of an excess of energy that is being expended within them. If the energy had not overflowed in them and been ready to flow out, we would not have these ornamentations that do not satisfy any of the needs of the dynamic system. But the excess energy that was destroyed within them can no longer be seen to be used up except in a weak way. That is, through products and objects, rather than acts. And these products are the signs of previous expenditures.

The sign of a previous expenditure, which has taken the form of a stable product, whether it be one made by human hands (the pyramids, embroidery, a gold coin) or a biological tissue, has properties similar to those of the sign of a current expenditure (dance, song). In both cases, the sign of expenditure *signifies* expenditure itself: this means that it is the contagious form of it.

A church is the sign of how a religious state of mind has been appropriated. This state of mind expresses itself as wealth, but this wealth has a limited signification. A dance and a song are limited ways in which energy can overflow.

We talk of energy overflowing, but it is not a simple kind of flowing like that of a stream, which cannot take up many different forms. Rivers flow differently depending on the slope, the size of the bed, and the volume of water. Men have a thousand ways of letting energy overflow: expenditures can be explosive, sad, gay, revolutionary, religious, sadistic . . . The possibilities are endless.

Every sign of expenditure generally signifies expenditure, but specifically a particular opportunity for expenditure. A church is a religious sign, just as dancing is an erotic sign and music a militaristic one. Furthermore, any domain can be subject to several different modes. A thousand sorts of churches or temples express the wide array of religious states of mind.

But the sign, every time, is *interpreted* by the one who perceived it. And interpretation varies widely. A pyramid or a cathedral do not have the same meaning for us as they did for the men of Ancient Egypt or those of the thirteenth century. And we ourselves, like people of every era, are divided in our individual tastes, our intelligence, our different occupations.

These differences, from a general point of view, are hardly important. A definite sum of energy consumed [*consumée*] in an object gives a theoretical *value* to this object. The *value* is the quantitative meaning of the object. The *value* of the objects, the signs of expenditures that have been made, is generally measurable in terms of movable wealth, more rarely in terms of buildings (the value of a palace, a chateau, is composite, some parts of them respond to the needs of the dynamic system).

STIMULATION:

All expenditure stimulates expenditure or, we could say, all expenditure is contagious. A cry stimulates crying, a dance dancing, a burst of laughter laughing, a yawn yawning. A certain expenditure stimulates, in theory, the same expenditure. But any expenditure can increase the stimulation of a given system of expenditure. If we dance together, we shout and our shouts further stimulate our dancing. Moreover, we can also be stimulated without joining in the dance immediately. Stimulation on its own is already a consumption of energy. It is the first hint of the expenditure, the tingling in the nerves that triggers it. The stimulation can be inhibited but some problem may stop it from reaching its conclusion (if we do not know how to dance, if we do not have a partner, if the dance is only for professionals, etc.). If the dance continues before us the persistence of stimulation is an important expenditure to the stimulation on its own.

(Consider sexual stimulation in this framework)

SIGN, SIGNIFIER, SIGNIFICATION:

A sign is the figure that can be sensed and that is formed through signification. An expenditure of energy is signified, which means that it is rendered sensible. An expenditure of energy stimulates but in theory it is the expenditure of energy itself that stimulates, not the sensible figure. Nevertheless, only the sensible figure, which looks like an expenditure, stimulates as well. It is associated with the reflex of stimulation. But we do not *understand* that there is expenditure. The stimulation to expenditure is not provoked by the fact that we perceive expenditure through its sensible signs.

Systems that communicate are said to be immanent. I can speak of the immanence of nerve cells. I hypothesize that nerve cells have the ability to transfer a movement of energy caused by an expenditure across the tissue that they are composed of. I receive the shock of an expenditure, say the excitement of a dance, not only as a sensible figure but as a dynamic shuddering. The animal organism is defined by the power of its nervous system to change the shock it receives, the movement it perceives, into a similar movement that the receptive organism carries out. Reproduction is in no way the result of an intellectual operation. A newborn child who urinates when he hears the drip of water issuing from the tap is nothing like an apprentice reproducing the work of his master.

In this way, the sensible figure in the dance (even supposing that it is perceived by a deaf person) is not limited to a series of pictures, each one being simply a static image. The nerves are also sensitive to the explosive discharges of energy involved in a dance. This is in fact the essence of representation developed in consciousness: it is precisely what the dance *signifies*. It is not received as series of images deprived of meaning but as the *expression* of a state of mind: in each case, that state may be one of giddy joy, or drunkenness, or angry hostility toward those who dance.

TRANSLATORS' AND EDITORS' NOTES

INTRODUCTION

1. Alexandre Kojève, *Introduction to the Reading of Hegel: Lectures on the Phenomenology of Spirit*, edited by Raymond Queneau and Allan Bloom, translated by James H. Nichols Jr. (New York: Basic Books, 1968). Published in French as *Introduction à la lecture de Hegel* (Paris: Gallimard, 1947).

2. Commonly referred to as Léon Chestov in France.

3. Georges Bataille, *Expérience intérieure*, in *Œuvres complètes* (hereafter *OC*), vol. V (Paris: Gallimard, 1973), 11. All translations from the *OC* are ours unless otherwise indicated.

4. Bataille, *The Accursed Share*, translated by Robert Hurley (New York: Zone, 1988 [1949]), 20.

5. Max Weber, *The Protestant Ethic and the Spirit of Capitalism and Other Writings* (New York: Penguin, 2002 [1905]). Maximilian Karl Emile Weber (1864–1920) was an early sociologist, and a principal early theorist of the development of western modernity. His work shaped Bataille's understanding of the relationship between religion and the social.

6. Bataille, *The Accursed Share*, 134.

7. Michel Surya, *Georges Bataille: An Intellectual Biography*, translated by Krzysztof Fijalkowski and Michael Richardson (London: Verso, 2002 [1992]), 560.

8. Mathilde Girard, Preface to Georges Bataille, *La Limite de l'utile* (Lignes, 2016), 14.

9. Bataille, "La Notion de dépense," in *La Critique Sociale* 7 (January 1933); *OC*, vol. I (Paris: Gallimard, 1970), 302–320. "The Notion of Expenditure," in *Visions of Excess: Selected Writings, 1927–1939*, translated by Allan Stoekl, Carl R. Lovitt, and Donald M. Leslie Jr. (Minneapolis: University of Minnesota Press, 1985), 116–129.

10. Surya, *Georges Bataille*, 308.

11. Stuart Kendall, *Georges Bataille* (London: Reaktion, 2007), 157.

12. Bataille, *L'Expérience intérieure*, in *OC*, vol. V (Paris: Gallimard, 1954), 73.

13. Christian Limousin, "Vue d'ensemble," in *La Part maudite de Georges Bataille: la dépense et l'excès* (Paris: Classiques Garnier, 2015), 26.

14. Bataille, in *The College of Sociology (1937–1939)*, edited by Denis Hollier (Minneapolis: University of Minnesota Press, 1988), 90.

15. Ibid., 334.

16. Bataille, "Corps célestes," *Verve* 1, no. 2 (Spring 1938); *OC*, vol. I (Paris: Gallimard, 1970), 514–20. "Celestial Bodies," translated by Annette Michelson, *October* 36 (Spring 1986): 75–78.

17. Kendall, *Georges Bataille*, 94–95.

18. Bataille, *OC*, vol. II, 550.

19. Kendall, *Georges Bataille*, 155.

20. Cf. Surya, *Georges Bataille*, 297–298.

21. Bataille, *The Accursed Share*, 10–11.

22. *OC*, vol. VI, 421.

23. Georges Ambrosino and Georges Bataille, *L'Expérience à l'épreuve: Correspondance et inédits (1943–1960)*, edited by Claudine Frank (Paris: Éditions les Cahiers, 2018), 297. All translations from this text are ours.

24. Ambrosino, cited in *L'Expérience à l'épreuve*, 9.

25. Frank, Introduction to *L'Expérience à l'épreuve*, 20.

26. Ambrosino, cited in *L'Expérience à l'épreuve*, 297.

27. Bataille, Lettre 3, in *L'Expérience à l'épreuve*, 87.

28. Ambrosino, Lettre 4, in *L'Expérience à l'épreuve*, 89.

29. Esther Ambrosino, quoted in Frank, Introduction to *L'Expérience à l'épreuve*, 42.

30. Bataille, *The Accursed Share*, 191.

31. David Émile Durkheim (1858–1919) founded the first department of sociology, became the discipline's first professor, and established its first scholarly journal—as such, he is commonly understood as the chief architect of modern sociology. His work was a formative influence on Bataille. *The Elementary Forms of Religious Life* (1912), in particular, profoundly shaped Bataille's own theories of religion and communication. In this work, Durkheim proposes the concept of "collective effervescence," which designates the collective experience of similar emotions, thoughts, and actions as a result of ritualistic gathering. Marcel Mauss (1872–1850) was the nephew of Durkheim and the founder of modern ethnology. His seminal work, *The Gift: Forms and Functions of Exchange in Archaic Societies* (1925), explores the role of gift-giving and reciprocity among a multitude of indigenous cultures and is a principal influence on Bataille's central theory of expenditure. As mentioned, Max Weber's *The Protestant Ethic and the Spirit of Capitalism* (1905) influenced Bataille's understanding of the entanglement between religion and capitalist development.

THE LIMIT OF THE USEFUL

CHAPTER I

1. Translators' note: The editors of Bataille's *Œuvres complètes* (Paris: Gallimard, 1976–88, hereafter *OC*) give the following note about the manuscript, which is relevant to our edition as well: "The mark '/'" indicates that one or more pages are missing. In the first two chapters, the fragments given between two lines of ellipses correspond to edits made at an earlier or later date that fill in gaps in the manuscript that we principally follow." As mentioned in our introduction, the editors of the French edition removed passages from the manuscript that also appeared in *The*

Accursed Share. We have restored these using the translation by Robert Hurley (New York: Zone Books, 1991–93). They are placed in square brackets in the manuscript with a footnote referencing the relevant passages in French and English. Also in square brackets and footnoted are passages that Bataille crossed out, along with any gaps in the manuscript and changes made by the Gallimard editors. Alternative versions of some sections of the manuscripts are also footnoted.

2. Gallimard editors' note: The text that follows, until p. 191 [*OC*, vol. VII, p. 12 in this edition], is that of the article "Corps célestes," published in *Verve* (vol. 1, no. 2), in Spring 1938, cf. *OC*, vol. I, pp. 515–520. "Celestial Bodies," translated by Anette Michelson, *October* 36 (Spring 1986): 75–78.

Trs. note: *Verve* was a short-lived, lavishly illustrated quarterly journal that featured articles written by intellectuals and cultural authorities such as Paul Valéry, André Malraux, and Paul Claudel. The issue in which "Celestial Bodies" appeared featured, appropriately, imaginative depictions of celestial bodies by artists such as Wassily Kandinsky and André Masson.

3. Trs. note: Sir Arthur Stanley Eddington OM FRS (1882–1944) was an astronomer, mathematician, physicist, and philosopher of science who wrote a number of works on the mechanics of the universe for a general readership. Among these was *The Rotation of the Galaxy* (Oxford: Clarendon Press, 1930), which Bataille read, likely at the suggestion of Georges Ambrosino, around the end of 1934 or the beginning of 1935. *The Rotation of the Galaxy* is referred to explicitly in "Celestial Bodies," and much of the material for this chapter is taken from that article. Additionally, Eddington's works often contained reproductions of photographs of outer space—these are likely what Bataille refers to when he writes of "long-exposure photographs" of galaxies and nebulae. Eddington was among the first to theorize how Albert Einstein's theory of general relativity applied to cosmology, and he also anticipated the discovery of the production of stellar energy via the fusion of hydrogen into helium. Eddington luminosity, or the Eddington limit, measures the maximum luminosity a celestial body can achieve when accounting for the force of radiation acting outward and the gravitational force acting inward.

Eddington would remain an important touchstone for Bataille, providing the scientific substructure for many of his cosmological ideas. As late as 1947, Bataille requested that Ambrosino write an article on Eddington for *Critique* (cf. Ambrosino and Bataille, *L'Expérience à l'épreuve*, p. 232).

4. Gallimard eds. note: Lacking Ms. 2, folder 8, this section has been completed with the last lines of the first chapter of Ms. 4, entitled "Situation of Man in Nature" [Envelope 9, pages numbered 1–6]. Ms. 4 [Envelope 4: 82–84, numbered 7–9 and the manuscript for *The Accursed share*, hereafter a.s.: 141, numbered 10] then gives the following:

The Principle of Glory

The goal of human activity is production. Men must, from the very fact of their condition, capture forces, either in the form of animals as food, or by organizing nature through civilization. Value, anything worth desiring, expresses itself commonly as a quantity of captured force. In theory, a product could be regarded as the equivalent of the sum of energy necessary for its production. When that product is used, the producer is able to recuperate an equal or greater sum of energy at the point at which it is sold. Money unifies evaluations and facilitates exchanges.

It is obvious that force isn't captured except with a view toward a particular use, that is, the expenditure of that force in another way. Absorbing food is necessary for the worker, employee, or manager to produce their labor. Work is expended to create products—theoretically, useful products. Products are necessary for the productive forces. They are sometimes given to the labor force (to maintain the workers), sometimes to the machines of industry [*outillage*]. In this way, human activity seeks to determine how the captured energy flows. It can obviously increase the global sum of available energy, but any new contribution must in turn enter into circulation. Theoretically, the circuit that comes to be defined should close upon itself. But that would suppose an equivalence between the portion produced and the portion necessary for its production. If there were an equivalence, we could use all the energy produced; we could put every expenditure toward a productive end. But if, as it seems, the sum of energy produced is always greater than the sum of energy necessary for production, then the excess must be *lost*, expended in pure loss, dedicated to energy emissions that serve no purpose.

Expenditures made on the condition of capturing energy anew are *productive expenditures*. Free emissions, like those of stars, of the sun, constitute *nonproductive* or *glorious expenditures*. In the minds of the uncultivated peoples, glory is associated with the sun. We can use that association to define the notion of glory, which has remained obscure. Glory is the effect of energy expenditures that are unconcerned with utility, or at least that present themselves as such, or that surpass utility in some way. In this sense, the light of the sun is rightly regarded as glorious, and it is equally right that in the popular consciousness, the sun has been assimilated with certain aspects of human life: prodigality, measureless courage, sacrifice, poetic genius . . . In general, glory is seen as the aftereffect of a glorious emission. It is reduced to its favorable consequences, which are worth obtaining even from the nonglorious point of view of utility. It is not far removed from the fame of a celebrity, the common notoriety of a criminal, businessman, lawyer, or hero. However, the notion of glory adds to that of notoriety a sort of bad quality, a useless tawdriness, which continues to afflict its original sense.

I will try to elucidate this notion by associating it with the subsequent description of nonproductive expenditure. To this end, I will consider the different forms of these expenditures in different economic systems.

Glorious Expenditures of the Aztecs

The Aztecs, whom I will speak of first, are as removed from us as it is possible to be, morally speaking. The general consensus is that their civilization was far below ours. But they had astronomical knowledge, architecture; they used writing.

The search for glory was clearly of crucial importance for this people. The Aztecs joined the glory of the earth to that of the heavens. In their eyes, the sun was the expression of a sacrifice. A god similar to man had become the sun by jumping into the flames of a brazier.

The Spanish Franciscan Bernardino de Sahagún . . .

[This would return the manuscript approximately to *The Accursed Share* (*AS*, vol. I, p. 46; *OC*, vol. VII, p. 52) or *The Limit of the Useful* (*OC*, vol. VII, p. 192; p. 13 in this edition.)]

5. Trs. note: Each use of the word *primitive* in this chapter corresponds with Bataille's use of *naïf/naïve*, a word whose English cognate bears a connotation of absentmindedness that is not present in his usage. Bataille employs the word in its literary sense, referring to that which is close to its origin, possessed of a natural simplicity, or newly emerged—childlike, perhaps, but certainly not childish in a pejorative sense: *naître*, to be born, comes from the same root. Bataille is here developing what he conceives as the emergence of a human consciousness from what he will later describe as a state of being "in the world as water is lost in water" (*Theory of Religion* [New York: Zone, 1989], p. 29). He will further develop variations on this theme in publications such as *Lascaux: Or, the Birth of Art* (Geneva: Skira, 1955) and "Terre invivable? United States Line" (*OC*, vol. XII, pp. 514–516).

6. Trs. note: We translate Bataille's term *déchéance* as "fall," but it also has connotations of forfeiture, decline, degradation, and decadence. As implied in "the part of myself that has fallen from the sky" in this paragraph and a "fallen god who recalls the heavens" in the following paragraph, the implication of a literal fall is also present. This sense will take on additional significance in Bataille's reflections on slapstick comedy in chapter VII.

7. Trs. note: The reference is to Genesis 3:19. The full verse reads: "In the sweat of thy face shalt thou eat bread, till thou return unto the ground; for out of it wast thou taken: for dust thou art, and unto dust shalt thou return." These words conclude God's curse on Adam for the sin of eating from the tree of the knowledge of good and evil, that is, the fall. Adam and Eve are thereafter cast out of Paradise, condemned to labor for their survival.

8. Gallimard eds. note: In Ff [Box 13, G: 143, paginated 20]: // "serves for nothing," it is vile and valueless: however, that which serves is never more than a means . . . Utility refers to acquisition, to the increase of products or the means of producing them: it is opposed to unproductive expenditure. If this morality wears off, men dress themselves in their

decadence: a greedy and cold world closes on the surface of the ground, in which everything is measured at the smallest size. The sun in this world matters because of the increase of goods that it procures, and solar glory no longer makes sense. [*In the margin:* hat, goddess*—last chapters]

*Gallimard eds. note: Cf. *OC*, vol. VII, p, 10, p. 12 of this edition, Ms 1, *in the margin*: Modern man generally conducts himself like a commoner in a palace, one who would hang up his hat on the head of a goddess.

9. Gallimard eds. note: Ms 2, folders 22–(25), missing or mixed with a.s. We complete this passage with Ff [Box 13, G: 144–146, paginated 22–24], then (cf. note 11) with Ms 1.

10. Trs. note: Bernardino de Sahagún (c.1499–1590) was a Spanish missionary to what is now Mexico, where he lived for fifty years. He compiled the *Historia general de las cosas de Nueva España*, a twelve-volume chronicle exploring the history, cosmology, religion, rituals, customs, social structure, and economy of the indigenous Mexica, now commonly referred to as the Aztecs. This is the text from which Bataille receives most of his knowledge about Aztec sacrificial rituals and society generally. The original text, of which the so-called Florentine Codex is the most famous extant manuscript, was written simultaneously in Spanish and Nahuatl on opposing folios. During its composition, Sahagún pioneered modern methods of gathering and independently verifying his information, earning him the popular moniker of "the first anthropologist." The *Historia* and its author are particularly notable for their generally sympathetic treatment of the Aztecs; as an evangelist, Sahagún propagated the then-uncommon view of the native peoples' full humanity and capacity, and the *Historia* tells of the conquest of Tenochtitlan (now Mexico City) from the point of view of the city's defenders. In 1536 Sahagún founded the Colegio Imperial de Santa Cruz de Tlatelolco (now the Colegio de Santa Cruz), the first European institution of higher education in the Americas.

11. Trs. note: The passage that follows in square brackets is included in *The Accursed Share* (hereafter *AS*), translated by Robert Hurley, which we reproduce here (*AS*, vol. I, pp. 46–49; *OC*, vol. VII, pp. 52–54).

12. Gallimard eds. note: Here we follow Ms 1 [13, G: 147–150]. Ms 1 [13, G: 136–142] offers the following for pages 189–192 of *OC*, vol. VII and pp. 8–12 of this edition:

The Poverty of the Human Position

If death were not its crowning achievement, then human life would run in a direction completely contrary to that of every world. Nothing is more contrary to the effulgence of stars, to the multitudinous festivals of the galaxies, than the life of a human being. Its sole aim has been using up the terrestrial globe. It is similar to a feudal lord who makes himself independent if the state's central power stops taking any action. But the greed of man goes further than that of the local lord. The latter does not let the king's agent control his affairs. Man forgets the presence of the universe that created him—the way a parasite ignores its host. Man even seeks to close the world around him down even further by taking as his first principle the idea that the ground is stable. He tends to reduce everything to his own level of weakness.

Worst of all is when he makes his greed into a moral law. The violence and greed of the most powerful are the cause of many evils. But these evils are nothing in comparison to the sickness and ruin that arise when morality is aligned with greed. Greed that satisfies itself is not moral. But the greed of those who suffer and cannot satisfy themselves creates obligations for all men. These obligations cannot be ignored, but when they form the principle directing our actions, the result is severe misfortune. Men are already stuck in the realm of the ground and all things solid: this realm is pallid and sad, manifestly *fallen*, cut off from the "games of heaven." Their lives become even poorer when they kowtow to the principle of *utility*. Greed, the need to acquire, becomes their *end*, the *end* of all their vast activity. Miseries become the only object of their thoughts, miseries that they must try to soften. Depression and gray days stretch on: they are given the power to destroy.

Were life an effect of the cold, and were I, as a living particle, nothing but thirst, I would have to curse myself. The conditions of my infinite sadness seem given. But unreflecting man is not so sad. He sometimes thinks himself cursed, but from a benign malediction, one that his zest for life will escape from one way or another. The principle of utility was derived by aged men, harried by reflection. Reflective reason is perhaps the strangest thing in this world that it reflects: it does everything it can to try and deny that world; it logically lays out the earth's error. It is fortunate that it is able to reflect on itself and be dissatisfied with what it finds. Developed to the extreme, and without logic, reflection perhaps has the means to rediscover the truth of primitive man, who neither curses himself nor becomes sad. It is this redemption that I undertake.*

[*Crossed out: Glory and Sacrifice*

I believe I have elaborated the conditions of existence more accurately than usual: I have situated them within the play of the universe. Man fulfils the movement of the celestial body that bears him. This movement sets free particles that take form and grow—particles that struggle with one another to decide which will gather more force, which will expand to gain power. This freeing of particles is without question a sign of decline; it derives profits from a planet being exhausted: nevertheless, it is grand and glorious. By definition, those who live according to the rules of this game desire it. Misery comes from rationality seeking to derive this movement from its irrational route; in the face of such rationality, only nothingness itself would be saved.]

Primitiveness Unites Man to the Glory of the Universe

Primitive fantasies offered an image of the world that was closer to modern ways of seeing than the representation provided by "common sense." Simpler men regarded the heavens with eyes filled with sacrificial madness. They divined the festival of the universe, and since thought was still linked to actions in their mind, their turmoil followed the universe's movement.

The man who reduces existence to utility forfeits and ignores the "glory" of the heavens. But he cannot recognize such a grand "glory" except by conducting himself in a glorious fashion. The Aztecs tied man to the glory of the universe by making the Sun's brilliance the result of an act performed by man: they thought that sacrificing a god in human form had given birth to the star that illuminates us. In this way, the Aztecs saw what we might be able to see: they made an act at the scale of light something exemplary for other men; what they rightly saw was the unity of sacrifice and shining light, of the gift of the self and glory.

Solar Brilliance and the Sacrifice of Nanauatzin

The friar Bernardino de Sahagún [. . .] "I am the one who will illuminate it." The gods // Then the moon [. . .]

[This would return the manuscript approximately to *The Limit of the Useful* (*OC*, vol. VII, p. 192, p. 13 in this edition.)]

*Gallimard eds. note: *In the margin:* define this possibility of redemption

modern man is without doubt more alien to the universe than any creature that has ever lived. He comes to live in it in such a way that he thinks his own peculiar and meaningless problems are the only things in existence. More and more, he tends to devalue those parts of himself that are most connected to the world of light and splendor: the desire he once had for glory. "Common sense" measures everything according to man's image. Modern man conducts himself on the whole like a commoner in a palace, one who would hang up his hat on the head of a goddess [cf. note 9 above]. Still, there is perhaps a kind of comedy in this gesture, in which we see [*the end of the sentence is illegible*]

13. Gallimard eds. note: Here we take back up Ms 2, folders (25)–33, resumed in *The Accursed Share.*

14. Trs. note: This passage is taken from *AS*, vol. I, pp. 49–52; *OC*, vol. VII, pp. 55–58.

15. Trs. note: This passage is taken from *AS*, vol. I, pp. 52–53; *OC*, vol. VII, pp. 58–59.

16. Trs. note: This passage is taken from *AS*, vol. I, pp. 53–54; *OC*, vol. VII, p. 59.

17. Gallimard eds. note: Ms. 1 [Box 13, G: 152–159] gives here:

Death in War in Mexico

The horrific execution of troops of slaves and enemies has little to do with the mythical sacrifices that endowed those performing them with a solar nature. These fear-induced butcheries went against the *gift* that a small god had made *of himself* to become the sun in all its glory. It must be said, however, that the butchers were scarcely less prodigious with their lives than with those of others. Rarely have people lived more completely in death's embrace; rarely too has courage ever rendered death more accessible. The horrors of the priests were paid for with the blood of soldiers. On the battlefield, people directly suffered the misfortune that was directed toward others in the temples. The Aztecs who fell in battle gave death a meaning that accounted for their sacrificial excesses. But they faced it like the *buboso*, not like the priest. The prayers that requested the gods' blessing for the soldiers did not ask for their lives to be spared: ["In truth," they said to the gods, "you are not wrong to want them to die in battle, for you did not send them into this world for any other purpose than to serve as food for the sun and the earth, with their blood and their flesh" (Sahagún, book VI, ch. 3).] These priests did not demand anything but a happy death. They said: ["Make them bold and courageous; remove all weakness from their hearts so that they may not only receive death joyfully, but desire it and find charm and sweetness therein; so that they do not fear arrows or swords but rather consider them a pleasant thing, as if they were flowers and exquisite dishes of food." (Sahagún, book VII, ch. 20)]

With narrow-mindedness, we avert our eyes from a world that appears so inhuman. (In the same way, we avert them from the sun, unable to bear its radiant excess.) But if the mad cruelty of their religion means that the Aztecs cannot have any value as an example, it increases its value as a demonstration: an excess renders the effect of a force more visible. If it is true that many of our conceptions are tainted with error—linked as they are to the deceptive immobility of the earth—we must turn our habitual ways of thinking around to rediscover the path of free existence—the path that is all movement and light. By *inverting itself*, the human mind can escape its world of illusions. Scientific analysis does not suffice for this: science creates abstractions, and each abstraction is placed within the sensible world that surrounds us. To oppose that which misleads us, we need another kind of sensibility, not one that relies on schematic statements, as in celestial mechanics. If I want to escape being bewitched by this static reality, I must be moved by *strong feelings*. A world of acts and thoughts dependent on violent feelings makes more sense. If I attentively and honestly examine what a tradition of writing allows me to know about the Aztecs, I quickly perceive that at stake within it are the worst kind of anguish and a nostalgia: the desire to live *at the height of death* and *outside the self*. [*On the verso*: However, the inclination to arouse strong feelings entails a risk. I myself want to mark how small the distance is that separates the use that I have made of Mexican customs from mere vulgar provocation. Here is what we could deduce from it: in my eyes, the Mexico of sacrifices is like a beacon to which I would like to direct others. If that were the case, then I would only be lying to myself and others. I'm committed to seeking glory but, on this path, what must first be shown is inevitable anguish. Anguish alone keeps us from presumptuousness.]

The Anguish and Rigor Necessary for One Wishing to Find Glory

I don't want anyone to confuse my attempt with a malign provocation. If others were to say that one must take the Aztecs as an example, I would show them the moral uncertainty in which they would embroil themselves. He who wants glory must first face inevitable anguish. Anguish alone keeps us from presumptuousness. The danger of "strong feelings," which we speak of before experiencing them: we think that we can provoke them through violent words but the violence of those words does not carry any force. I do not believe I have tumbled into this predicament by speaking about what the Mexicans did. Because I spoke of what really *existed* (of what was forced on our fellow men). It emerges from a greater savagery of strong feelings, but its *reality* introduces nothing but an anguished and humble search. To change the sensible notion that we have of ourselves and the universe, I believe slow rigor is also necessary. I have suffered too much from how people espousing the platitude of "reasonable man" have tried to close life down. In my ignorance, I am searching for the similarity between the glorious reactions of more primitive men and the ones that I sense deep within myself. My search is led by a great anguish: and there is nothing easy about it. If reason entails a weight, I want to relieve it and not escape out from under it.

CHAPTER II

1. Trs. note: *Puissance*. Usually, Bataille uses this word to designate the ability or potential ability to produce a tangible effect. It is often used specifically in relation to political, social, or personal power. *Puissance* was traditionally used to describe the power of lords and kings. This usage is marginally more restricted in meaning than his more general term *force*, which can mean power, energy, drive, strength, vitality, impulse, or collectivity of beings (as in "armed force" or "workforce"), depending on context. As Bataille's ontology proposes a continuum between the *force* animating the universe and that animating human beings, societies, ecosystems, molecules, and more, the reader might be well served in reading any of these terms as, at the very least, intimately related to the rest.

2. Gallimard eds. note: Lacking MS 2 f 39, we adhere to MS 1 [Box 13, G: 164] and to *The Accursed Share*.

3. Trs. note: This passage is taken from *AS*, vol. I, pp. 63–64; *OC*, vol. VII, pp. 66–67.

4. Trs. note: Here Bataille may well be thumbing his nose at some of the agents of Native American conversion, specifically the Jesuits, whose motto is *Ad majorem Dei gloriam*. Here we are given the diabolical inversion, "to the greater glory of his people" in place of "to the greater glory of God."

5. Gallimard eds. note: In Ff [Box 13, G: 165], in note*:* In the ball court game in which, according to Sahagún, one did not use either the hand or the foot but the buttocks, or in a kind of hopscotch.

Trs. note: The game being referred to here is seemingly the Mesoamerican precursor to the game now known as "Ulama," in which one attempts to hit the ball using the hips.

6. Trs. note: . . . *de tout mettre en comptes*. When the word "account" arises in this translation, it is not typically used in the sense of telling a story, in the sense that one might say one's version of events is an "account." Rather, Bataille uses *comptes* as an enumeration of a given numerical quantity, specifically of receipts and expenses. One might think of it in shorthand as a bank account. For Bataille, the paradigm of utility tends to make accountants of us all, shackling thought to the logic of double-entry bookkeeping, whereas for him, a much older and more all-encompassing tendency toward unaccounted and unaccountable expenditure obtains.

7. Trs. note: This passage is taken from *AS*, vol. I, pp. 64–65; *OC*, vol. VII, pp. 67–68.

8. Gallimard eds. note: Ms 1 [Box 13, G: pp. 160–164 and 166–168] gives the following for *OC*, vol. VII, pp. 197–199, pp. 25–29 of this edition [following on from ch. 1, n. 17 of this edition: "If reason entails a weight, I want to relieve it and not escape out from under it."]:

Necessary Inversion of Judgments

If one does not wish to adhere to narrow scholarly principles and wants instead to show how *acts of glory* operate in the formation of societies, then it is a good idea to begin with a single people and not with people in all places at all times. One should not limit oneself to discussing disparate examples; rather, one should follow a single isolated action and elaborate the effects that it has on a single group. The diversity of *glorious acts* common to the Mexicans before Cortés allows me to show that there is one single force that governs communal life. I will then be free to return to isolated examples, once I have shown how the will to glory is the lifeblood of the people. War, festivals, and sacrifices consist in bringing men together. As such assemblies are sources of power, their realization is the crowning achievement of all activity. It was not in vain that the Mexicans handed over the power to fertilize their fields to acts of sacrifice and dance. The cycles of communal activity were organized around such acts. Men did not *clearly* distinguish their own lives from that of nature. They thought that human action and the play of the universe were not strangers to each other: in this they erred less than us. Nothing is exactly connected in the way it was thought to be, but our lives achieve nothing in isolation from the life of the universe. Even our economic activity aligns with the splendor of the heavens: it is in the context of such an alignment that agricultural rites develop, though one must *invert* their meaning to understand them. Men cannot make nature obey them, but they can obey nature.

The Generosity of the Sovereign

In their festivals and wars, the Mexicans tied themselves to the universe; they tied the soul and turmoil of all the people to the universe. Agriculture and commerce were made fruitful by the glorious actions of men. The purpose of this activity was not simply to keep a miserable life going, but to keep glory alive in the person of the sovereign. The sovereign is the living expression of a people and that is why one must ascribe more meaning to what his crowd of subjects expected from him than to anything else. The will of the people was that he be prodigal. "The kings," says Sahagún, "looked for opportunities // [cf. *AS*, vol. I, pp. 63–64; *OC*, vol. VII, pp. 66–67].

[*Crossed out*: An economist or a banker does not *divine* gold.] In the words of Nietzsche, neither of them would be able to reflect for a single moment: they will die with their hollow heads chained to serious calculations. "Why is it," Zarathustra asked, "that gold is of the highest value? Because it is rare and useless, and because it glows softly; it always makes a gift of itself." A little further on: "The look of the gift giver shines like gold" (Part I, "*Of the Gift-Giving Virtue*"). For those who expected splendor from kings, those words would have taken on their full meaning; for those whose only god is gold, those words are dead, incomprehensible!

The Gift as a Form of Exchange

Generosity, in ancient Mexico, was one of the attributes of the sovereign. But the sovereign was merely the richest individual among many who were expected to satisfy the expectations of the community. The rich, the nobles, the merchants were all still required to satisfy those same expectations, each according to his ability. Festivals demanded a wasting of wealth, and all the powerful individuals had to accumulate that wealth to pay for those festivals. The slave victims were offered to the gods by dignitaries or merchants, who were also obliged (according to custom and on account of their concern for glory) to offer sumptuous feasts. The richest merchants obeyed rules that were far removed from any commercial mindset. As far as it seems, they practiced exchange in the form of gifts. They received riches as a gift from the sovereign of Mexico: they offered these riches to the lords of a particular province. "In receiving //

[This would return the manuscript approximately to *The Accursed Share* (*AS*, vol. I, p. 65; *OC*, vol. VII, p. 68) or *The Limit of the Useful* (*OC*, vol. VII, p. 199; p. 29 of this edition.)]

9. Trs. note: This passage is taken from *AS*, vol. I, pp. 65–66; *OC*, vol. VII, pp. 68–69.

10. Trs. note: *Consumation.* Among the most fraught of Bataille's many purposefully undecidable terms, *consumation* bears connotations of consumption and sexual consummation while also implying a final goal or perfected form (as in, for example, "the consummate professional"). It notably also connotes consumption by fire, as in ritual immolation, as well as total destruction or pure loss more generally—likely the reason Bataille chose this word as the title of his first volume of *The Accursed Share*, the only one he finished and the only one published in his lifetime. It also stands as a watchword for the kind of linguistic excess that Jacques Derrida, among others, has noted in Bataille's very approach to the discursive construction of sense and meaning, as for Bataille even language itself is a system productive of its own excess. In Bataille, "meaning itself," Derrida writes, "is destroyed and consumed [*consumé*]" ("From Restricted to General Economy: A Hegelianism Without Reserve," in *Writing and Difference* [Chicago: University of Chicago Press, 1978], 261).

11. Gallimard eds. note: Lacking Ms 2, folder 51, we complete this passage with Ff [Box 13, G: 173], then with Ms 1.

12. Trs. note: A central concept for this chapter and throughout the book (part of the subheading for this section), the term *conduites* connotes

several things not entirely conveyed by the English word "acts." *Conduites* can refer to habitual ways of acting ("conduct") as well as singular actions. Etymologically, the word comes from the Latin *conducere* ("to lead, bring together, or contribute"). It thus also contains a sense of passage, communication, and movement. This sense in particular is significant in light of Bataille's contention that expenditure catalyzes communication: itself a movement from self-enclosure to the openness of communal experience characterized as an opening, laceration, or loss of subjectivity.

13. Gallimard eds. note: Ms 1 [Box 13, G: 169–170].

14. Gallimard eds. note: Nothing remains of this §II (9 pages according to the tables of contents) but the first page in Ms 1 [Box 13, G: 171] and the last in Ms 2. We restore the missing titles in brackets, according to table of contents B.

15. Gallimard eds. note: Cf. *OC*, vol. III, pp. 155–156, "Rationalism" (fragment linked with "The Notion of Expenditure"):

> Rationalism [. . .] holds that the consumption of wealth by men is equivalent to a motor's consumption of fuel: it is just a necessary part of productive activity. This principle is expressed with more than average childishness in an account published in a Russian newspaper that sets two workers off against each other. In the account, a miller responds to a heavy industry worker who has stated that his activity is of the utmost importance. The miller—in the full fervor of the five-year plan—does not dispute that importance but rejects the idea that his enterprise should be thought of as inferior. He takes pride, therefore, in using evidence to show that, without millers and without flour, the heavy industry worker would be incapable of work . . . Consumption in this naïve representation is nothing but the fundamental condition of production [. . .]

Gallimard eds. note (continued): Elsewhere, we find [Box 13, F: 1] this clipping from a 1933 newspaper that we cannot identify (Of "some characteristic extracts," we have kept only the response of the miller):

Should Panfilov quit light industry to go and work in heavy industry? The young worker Panfilov, working in a textile factory, has left this work to become a worker with the "socialist giants." Was this a good idea? The newspaper *Komsomolskaia Pravda* has opened a debate on this subject, and we publish here some characteristic extracts from it.

[. . .]

It is You Who Stands Accused, Panfilov.

—I am the chief mechanic at the "Belmuk" steam mill in the town of Polotsk. Our enterprise is rather small: there are only 48 people working there. No writer has published any reports about the life of our mill, and it is difficult to find even a little note that mentions us in a newspaper. Nevertheless, comrade Panfilov, I consider myself to be a hero of labor. I am a hero because the successful construction of the metallurgical factory in Magnitogorsk, and of the electrical plant in the Dnieper, as well as all the cars that come out of the Amo factory rely on my work. So, think on this, comrade Panfilov: what would have happened if I had followed your example by leaving the mill and going to work for an industrial giant? My departure might have spoiled the plan for grinding wheat. Yet it is from our flour that the bread for you and the workers at the Amo is made.

I am even more surprised that you hold others responsible for every fault. What about you? Tell me, my friend, what have you done, you young communist, to make sure that the team at your factory works well? Who gave you the right to play the role of a public prosecutor? It is you who stands accused.

V.I. Balode

16. Trs. note: This passage is taken from *AS*, vol. I, pp. 67–68; *OC*, vol. VII, pp. 70–71.

17. Gallimard eds. note: A reminder that from here until *OC*, vol. VII, p. 212, p. 49 of this edition, Ms 2 is incorporated into Ms 4 (see the

description of Ms 2, *OC*, vol. VII, p. 506, pp. 167–168 of this edition). We place the text of Ms 4 in square brackets, corresponding to the missing pages of Ms 2.

18. Gallimard eds. note: The title is restored following table of contents B. Ms 4 gives the following:

[*Crossed out:* The economy of the festival and the Church] I. *Capitalist Society*

19. Trs. note: The reference appears to be to Nietzsche's so-called "slave revolt in morality," outlined in the First Essay of *On the Genealogy of Morals*. Nietzsche here outlines how the slave class's reactive morality or *ressentiment* generates a moral system that vaunts values such as meekness and poverty while demonizing contrary qualities like pride and prodigality, eventually overturning the social order in such a way as former slaves take the place of the masters and vice versa. The influence of Kojève's reading of Hegel, mentioned in the Introduction, is also apparent.

20. Gallimard eds. note: Lacking Ms. 2, folder 76, we restore the title and subtitle from table of contents B.

21. Gallimard eds. note: Lacking Ms 2, folder 81, we restore the subtitle from table of contents B. Ms 4 crosses out the end of this sentence and gives:

The Reformation and the end of the festival economy

Nothing was more contrary to [. . .]

22. Trs. note: The reference is to the critique of ostentatious giving in the Sermon on the Mount, Matthew 6:3–4: "But when thou doest alms, let not thy left hand know what thy right hand doeth. That thine alms may be in secret: and thy Father which seeth in secret himself shall reward thee openly."

23. Trs. note: This line echoes the second verse of William Blake's poem "And did those feet in ancient time" (1808). In it, the speaker muses on the abandonment of divinity from his rapidly industrializing environs: "And did the Countenance Divine / Shine forth upon our

clouded hills? / And was Jerusalem builded here / Among these dark Satanic mills?"

24. Gallimard eds. note: Ms 4 replaces the title and subtitle with: *The Development of the Capitalist Economy.*

25. Trs. note: Interest in the sense of "useful aims" but also monetary interest: the methodical extraction of surplus value from production and then the reinvestment of that surplus value in production.

26. Trs. note: When the Puritans came to power in England in 1647, they outlawed Christmas, Easter, and Whitsuntide, while also suppressing other supposedly pagan-inflected or otherwise un-Christian popular diversions like gambling and non-devotional theater. The Puritan colonies of New England followed suit. Christmas in particular was then associated with carnival-like behavior involving heavy drinking, gluttony, sexual promiscuity, role inversion, rowdiness, and disrespect for authority. Revelers were even known to storm the homes of the wealthy, demanding alms.

27. Gallimard eds. note: Subtitle crossed out in Ms 4.

28. Gallimard eds. note: Subtitle crossed out in Ms 4.

29. Trs. note: This passage is taken from *AS*, vol. I, pp. 121; *OC*, vol. VII, pp. 126. The quotation from Franklin is taken from *Advice to a Young Tradesman* (1748), which Weber refers to in *The Protestant Ethic and the Spirit of Capitalism*, 14–15.

30. Gallimard eds. note: Ms 1 [Box 13, G: 187]:

// of pounds. [*Crossed out*: Sheared of Christian formulas, this profession of faith is nothing less than an aggressive moral stiffness. Whatever the baseness desired, the code of economy obliges one—or pretends to oblige one—like a code of honor: whoever lacks it is criminal!]

Never has the impudence of the bourgeoisie been revealed in a more diabolical fashion, showing a complete aversion to the spirit of festivals and sacrifices. At least the Puritans lived to glorify God. If they jealously consecrated their earthly existence to work, it is because they judged that existence vain and even accursed. The moneyed man, to whom their austerity opened the path [. . .]

31. Gallimard eds. note: Subtitle crossed out in Ms 4.

32. Gallimard eds. note: Ms 1 [Box 13, G: 194–196]:

[. . .] all reality is overwhelming and the best take refuge in flight. Americans sometimes stop themselves, having the feeling of being strangers in the real world. The rapid life that fetters them is an abstract, bloodless pantomime, all the more empty as it seems vigorous and sure of itself.

Americans have never known hierarchies or traditional values of any kind. By contrast, Europeans, throughout their history, have endlessly encountered these hierarchies and these values—some have struggled to destroy them, others have struggled to safeguard the power residing in them. This rupture paralyzed economic growth—for many the rotten part of Europe, [making it] unstable and unwelcoming for a portion of the continent. The striking vitality of America is the proof that that there is no contradiction in it, no brakes to counter industry on a huge scale; its very vitality has brought it rapidly into a moral and material impasse. With regard to America, Europe seems indecisive: it has delayed, gone astray several times, approached mortal danger, a catastrophic end, but it has remained relatively close to profound resources. Our convulsions appall timorous spirits: they do not see that we are less advanced in terms of what is not possible.

33. Gallimard eds. note: Ms 1 [Box 13, G: 199–200] gives as follows:

Extreme wealth is born from poverty, from the humiliating, degrading disorder that follows a Wall Street crash—economic science [*crossed out*: has wanted] would be held accountable for this. But it couldn't deduce facts, general laws, or details: it wasn't in a fit state to develop solutions; it added to practical impotence the vanity of theoretical advice. I will not try to do what economic science could not. Production is entangled in a great many operations whose sequence science can only follow (or pretend to follow). I have nothing I want to say about these operations and their details. I seek nothing but the *total* conditions linked to them. I seek nothing but their moral ins and outs, lost in the religious heights of the heavens. A science //

CHAPTER III

1. Gallimard eds. note: Chapter III is taken from Ms 3.

2. Trs. note: That is, the devotional hours of religion. This, along with the reference to "moral nostalgia," refers to the kind of unproductive use of time associated with religious devotion that still persisted in early capitalist enterprise. Before the age of what Bataille calls "mature capitalism," time devoted to production was still tempered by the time dedicated to worship.

3. Trs. note: *La mise en project,* literally: "putting-into-project." This becomes a central phrase in Bataille's argument here (it is contained in the title of this section), and it will evolve into a major idea in his thought as a whole. Its meanings are very difficult to render in English. As the etymology of *pro-* ("forward") *-iacere* ("throw") implies, for Bataille "project" refers to any material activity or conceptual structure that subordinates the present to the future. Investment is therefore the "putting-into-project," the "throwing-forward" of money; discursive reasoning is also a kind of project, as it subordinates the immediacy of experience to the mediacy of logical and linguistic sequence. This partially explains what Bataille calls his "opposition to the idea of project," proposed as one of the main theses of *Inner Experience,* on which Bataille was working at the same time as *The Limit of the Useful* (cf. *Inner Experience,* translated by Stuart Kendall [Albany: SUNY Press, 2014], 13). However, even in that work, he recognizes the necessity of "projecting" and the "project" which, while smothering experience, render it intelligible, and thus retroactively accessible via the immanent critique of project itself. This recursive logic (or critique of logic—each amounts to the same thing in this instance) is evident in *Inner Experience,* where he writes:

> Nonetheless inner experience is project, no matter what.
>
> It is project, man being entirely project through language that, in essence, with the exception of its poetic perversion, is project. But the project is no longer in this case that, positive, of

> salvation, but that, negative, of abolishing the power of words, therefore of project. (29)

4. Trs. note: *Jouer* and *jeu* (contained in the title of this section) are, appropriately, some of Bataille's more fickle terms. Bearing connotations of playing, interplay, games, gambles, wagers, jokes, and even tricks, they should first and foremost be understood as the counterpoints to *projet*, outlined in n. 3 above, as well as in the introduction. Where the project subordinates present deprivation to future gain based on rational reasoning (as in capital investment), the wager, subject to the unknowable machinations of chance, is resolved in the instant, and can lead as easily to loss as to gain. Depending on the context, in this section we translate *jouer* and *jeu* by a range of terms referring to gambling, playing, and wagering, though readers should bear all possibilities in mind when they encounter any of these terms. Another frequently used term in this section is *mettre en jeu*, which means to put at stake in the sense of gambling or wagering (though it can also mean "to put into play" and should be considered a kind of obverse to *mettre en projet*, outlined in n. 3 above). Also, it should be noted that *mettre en jeu* is the phrase used by Alexandre Kojève (and Bataille) to describe how the lord and bondsman face each other in Hegel's philosophical parable of the origins of human consciousness in *The Phenomenology of Spirit*. For Bataille and Kojève, the lord is the one who stakes (*met en jeu*) his life for pure prestige in order to be recognized as a subject, while the bondsman subordinates himself to remain alive, thereby making himself an object. Thus, for Bataille a gamble for glory is at the root of sovereign human consciousness itself, while project is at the root of human servility. Bataille provides an outline of his various understandings of *la mise en jeu* in his notes to *The Limit of the Useful* (*OC*, vol. VII, 579, p. 277 in this edition). Further texts on *jeu* include the "Series of Chances" subsection of "The Sorcerer's Apprentice," in *Visions of Excess*, 229–230, and "Le Jeu," in *OC*, vol. XII, 547.

5. Trs. note: As the quote from n. 3 above shows, Bataille's conception of the capacity for poetry to subvert the project would evolve. For Bataille, poetry must aim to surpass its own project-oriented nature. Appropriately, Bataille's own volume of poetry, published in 1947, would

be titled *Haine de la poesie* [*Hatred of Poetry*]. In a draft of a piece on Arthur Rimbaud that is associated with this text, Bataille wrote, "The movement of poetry departs from the known and leads to the unknown. It touches madness at its zenith. . . . Poetry is in every manner negation of itself: it denies itself in conserving itself and denies itself in surpassing itself" (*OC*, vol. III, n. 533).

6. Trs. note: *Aventurier*. We have interpreted this seemingly incongruous word as entrepreneur, in keeping with the idea of "one who ventures." Indeed, we might today translate it using the term "venture capitalist," which is etymologically linked to the term "adventurer." The *speculateur* that Bataille is describing in this section seems to fit with the modern notion of a venture capitalist, and the history of venture capitalism is itself often traced to mid-twentieth-century Paris, around the time when Bataille was writing. For Bataille, *aventurier* is also probably meant insultingly, as in the now-outmoded sense of calling a rogue or opportunist an "adventurer."

7. Gallimard eds. note: See *OC*, vol. VI, "Collège socratique," p. 280.

8. Trs. note: That is, concerning the necessity for expenditure.

9. Gallimard eds. note: Ms 3 pauses here. We restore the following subtitles and titles from table of contents B.

10. Gallimard eds. note: In the absence of all other manuscripts, we give here the fragments taken from Ff: Ff [Box 14, C: 42–44], pages paginated 144–146.

11. Gallimard eds. note: In the absence of all other manuscripts, we give here the fragments taken from Ff: Ff [Box 14, C: 45 and Box 13, C: 225–238], pages paginated 144–148.

CHAPTER IV

1. Gallimard eds. note: Chapters IV and VII are taken from Ms. 1.

2. Trs. note: *Le don de soi*. Several overlapping allusions are at play here: first, the theory of the gift as presented in Marcel Mauss's *The Gift: Forms and Functions of Exchange in Archaic Societies,* mentioned in the introduction (p. xxxii). Mauss's work deeply informed Bataille's

conception of human history and pre-history. Second, Friedrich Nietzsche's "On the Gift-Giving Virtue," from Part I of *Thus Spoke Zarathustra* (in *The Portable Nietzsche*, edited and translated by Walter Kaufmann [London: Penguin, 1954]), which reads in part as follows:

> Tell me: how did gold attain the highest value? Because it is uncommon and useless and gleaning and gentle in its splendor; it always gives itself. Only as the image of the highest virtue did gold attain the highest value. . . . Uncommon is the highest virtue and useless; it is gleaming and gentle in its splendor: a gift-giving virtue is the highest virtue.
>
> . . . This is your thirst: to become sacrifices and gifts yourselves . . . Insatiably your soul strives for treasures and gems, because your virtue is insatiable in wanting to give. (186–187)

Finally, the profound association between gift-giving and war recalls John 15:13, a verse particularly in currency during the years of World War I: "Greater love hath no man than this, that a man lay down his life for his friends." In French, the verse reads: "*Il n'y a pas de plus grand amour que de donner sa vie pour ses amis.*"

3. Gallimard eds. note: This paragraph and the following one (The law of concomitance . . . , pp. 239–241) borrow from the fragment of *The Manual of the Anti-Christian*: "Wars are for the moment the most powerful stimulants of the imagination" [Envelope 82, dated 1939]—cf. *OC*, vol. II, pp. 392–399 and 457–458.

CHAPTER VI

1. Gallimard eds. note: Jünger: cf. *OC*, vol. V, *Le Coupable*, p. 247.

Trs. note: Ernst Jünger (1895–1998) was a German author and soldier whose books brutally depict the reality of life in the trenches of World War I. *Storm of Steel* (1920), his most famous work, was reissued (and repeatedly revised) many times throughout his life. He received at least fourteen wounds in the field and ended the war as a highly decorated soldier for the German Imperial Army, receiving the order *Pour le Mérite* in 1918. After briefly fighting for the French Foreign Legion, he returned to Germany and avoided prosecution for defection largely as a result of his status and connections. Though an avowed conservative and critic of democracy, he consistently denied the overtures paid him by the Nazis by openly rebuking many of the rising party's philosophies and policies, disallowing Nazi publications of his works, and refusing positions offered him in the Reichstag. Even so, he served as an officer in World War II, being assigned to an administrative position in Paris, which he used to hobnob with artists and intellectuals. His honest treatment of the brutality of war and idiosyncratic view of combat as a catalyst of mystical, transcendent experience has earned him a complicated legacy, especially in France, where his books were particularly popular. Notable fans have included Bertolt Brecht and François Mitterrand, while Jean-Paul Sartre laconically answered a query about Jünger with the sentence, "I hate him."

2. Trs. note: *Holocaust* is here used in the classical sense of a burnt offering. These passages were taken, as Bataille notes below, from the book *War as an Inner Experience* (translated into French as *La Guerre, notre mère* [*War, Our Mother*]), which was published in 1922 and thus two decades before the term *holocaust* became prominent as the popular name for the genocide of European Jewry at the hands of the Nazis. (Additionally, it is unlikely that the contemporary usage was in Bataille's orbit at the time he wrote this chapter.) *War as an Inner Experience* is Jünger's most morbid work—Michael Hofmann, the translator of Penguin's most recent edition of *Storm of Steel* (2003), calls it an "unpleasant treatise . . . of which I could not bring myself to read more than the excerpts I read years ago in a book on German history" (xv).

CHAPTER VII

1. Gallimard eds. note: Throughout, chapter VII returns to passages on *communication* in *Inner Experience*, dated April–May 1940 (cf. *OC*, vol. V, pp. 109–115 and corresponding notes), as well as *The Anti-Christian Manual*, cf. *OC*, vol. II (pp. 390–391 and corresponding notes).

2. Trs. note: Bataille appears to refer both to the supposed Canaanite god and to the form of sacrifice associated with him. Medieval sources portrayed Moloch as a bull-headed, humanoid idol with arms outstretched, within or before which a child would be burned as a sacrifice. This ritual is associated with Tophet (e.g., in 2 Kings 23:10), a place in the valley of Gehenna where worshipers in ancient Judah gathered to perform child sacrifice. Leviticus forbids sacrifice to Moloch five times; however, mention of Tophet by the prophets Jeremiah, Ezekiel, and Isaiah indicates that the practice persisted.

3. Trs. note: Sir James George Frazer (1854–1941) was a Scottish anthropologist and folklorist most famous for his work *The Golden Bough: A Study in Comparative Religion* (1890). *The Golden Bough* was directed toward a general audience and studied shared aspects of various religious beliefs such as sacrifice and fertility rites. Frazer notably and, at the time, scandalously treated the death of Jesus Christ as a mere repetition of more ancient myths; subsequent editions would move this section to a speculative appendix or cut out discussion of Christianity altogether. The work proved immensely popular, and though many of Frazer's analyses were quickly superseded and often denounced with extreme prejudice in subsequent anthropological studies, the book remained a deep influence on the direction of the discipline and resonated in particular among many twentieth-century writers, such as D. H. Lawrence, James Joyce, and T. S. Eliot.

4. Trs. note: Presumably Bataille here means the explanation provided by the "French sociologists."

5. Trs. note: Originally published in 1936, "The Labyrinth" (in *Visions of Excess*, pp. 171–177) serves as an extended meditation on Bataille's vision of being as "composed."

6. Gallimard eds. note: This date of 10 May 1940 reflects that of *Guilty* (*OC* vol. V, p. 289 and 520–521; [cf. *Guilty*, translated by Stuart Kendall (Albany: SUNY Press, 2011), 45, 191]): 20 May 1940.

> During the night of the 9th to the 10th of May, I knew nothing, I sensed nothing: I was waking up over and over and, as I never have, I was moaning, murmuring on the pillow, miserably:

> Mercy! [I was moaning near the one next to whom I was laying: she was hugging me softly to calm me down. An alarm woke us, we were mingled for a long time. When I] descended into the sun-soaked garden, I saw on the other side of the fence the old man who they call the "Commandant" sporting the blue smock of a gardener: with his brassy, racy peasant's accent, affectedly, but simply, he told me what they announced on the radio: the Germans in Belgium and in Holland.

7. Trs. note: *rejaillissement*: gush, spurting forth, overflow. The root verb, *jaillir*, is a euphemism for ejaculation.

8. Trs. note: Presumably Henri Bergson (1859–1941) who wrote three essays on laughter that comprise the book, *Laughter* (1900). Bataille met Bergson in 1920 while the former, then a young medievalist, was in London working on his thesis. Bataille read *Laughter* in anticipation of the meeting, which he claims in *Inner Experience* to have found "irritating," and dismissed its author as a "careful little man philosopher!"

9. Gallimard eds. note: The reference is missing in the manuscript. See *OC*, vol. II, p. 287 (presented on January 17, 1938, to the Society of Collective Psychology):

> Valentine, in a recent article in the *Journal of Psychology*, cites in this way a young woman who is generally very kind and good-hearted who, each time that she heard someone speak of a dead person could not keep herself from laughing.

(Cf. also *OC*, vol. II, pp. 312, 314–315 . . . , Conference of January 22, 1938, at the College of Sociology.)

10. Trs. note: *The Gold Rush* (1925) was written, produced, and directed by Charlie Chaplin, whose Little Tramp was also the film's main character. Chaplin himself says the film explored the proximity of tragedy and comedy, horror and laughter, and that he drew inspiration from the stories of the 1896 Klondike Gold Rush and the Donner Party catastrophe.

11. Gallimard eds. note: My laughter under an umbrella: cf. *OC*, vol. V, *Inner Experience*, pp. 46–47.

Trs. note: Stuart Kendall's translation of *Inner Experience* has the following:

> Glimpses where I perceive the path traveled.—Fifteen years ago (perhaps a little more), I returned from I don't know where, late at night. The Rue de Rennes was deserted. Coming from Saint-Germain, I crossed the Rue du Four (the post office side). I held in my hand an open umbrella and I believe it wasn't raining. (But I hadn't been drinking: I say it, I'm sure.) I had this umbrella open without needing it (if not for what I will speak about later). I was very young then, chaotic and full of empty drunkenness: a round of indecent, dizzying ideas, but already full of anxieties, rigor, and crucifying, running their course . . . In this shipwreck of reason, anguish, solitary degradation, baseness, worthlessness came due: a little later the festivity started again. What is certain is that this ease, simultaneously a collision with the "impossible," burst in my head. A space constellated with laughter opened its dark abyss before me. Crossing the Rue du Four, I became in this unknown "nothingness," suddenly . . . I negated these gray walls that enclosed me. I rushed into a kind of rapture. I laughed divinely: the umbrella came down on my head covering me (I covered myself expressly with this black shroud). I laughed as perhaps no one had ever laughed, the final depth of each thing opened, laid bare, as if I were dead.
>
> I don't know if I stopped, in the middle of the street, masking my delirium under an umbrella. Perhaps I jumped (no doubt it's illusory): I was convulsively illuminated, I laughed, I imagine, while running. (40)

12. Gallimard eds. note: The manuscript breaks off in the middle of the page. Here we provide some notes [Box 12, E: 64–67] extracted from section 2 of the "Dossier of Bataille's Notes and Outlines for *The Limit of the Useful*" (*OC*, vol. VII, p. 538; p. 205 of this edition):

[*In the margin*: Street singer—popular songs: principles: world of reason, easy and null communication, world of the gift, difficult and full communication, quasi-impossibility of speech, one must sing]

In laughter communication replaces anguish which is eased, sacrifice is also communication, but it is the communication of anguish.

(During the whole development, it would not only be necessary to develop the comparison with laughter on each point, but to maintain by some means the proximity of a mad laugh)

Instead of easing anguish, sacrifice makes it heavier, makes it linger; the victim is not thrown back into an unserious world but into a divine world, undoubtedly into a beyond, but superior to man, no longer inferior to him, it is in these conditions that anguish is brought forth, by not eased. Anguish is communicated to all the others.

[*In the margin*: this will introduce at the end the gods having men for playthings—but the gods are not mythic creations, we could be gods—showing at the end the identity of superior and inferior worlds]

Through his anguish, man enters the superior world, in the same way that through the unchained convulsion of his laughter he entered a world that was inferior to him, but if he enters in giving himself entirely, this time he will actually meet his death. The question of death is posed in its humble truth even though it had disappeared in a mad laugh, which only passed into the beyond due to the real world's lack of seriousness.

The sacrificial victim or the spectator, in their anguish, perceive death as inevitable—as the inexorable requirement of the superior world—and desirable at the same time. But their anguish is formed precisely from desire, desire augments anguish.

Desire wishes for death to occur but only to others—to god, the human victim, the animal, or simply the symbol of god.

[*In the margin*: superhumanity accessible only by way of a rite?—glory and gift reintroduced as motive force—reread all to link this up, also reread Caillois]

1. Automatic character of everything that I've described. Near total absence of idiosyncrasy

So what happened, by contrast, would arise out of the human domain, properly speaking.

2. Even the simple difference I've introduced—I describe mad laughter as if it were serious—supposes that we pass over to another existence—no longer human but divine. Naturally a man can think in numerous ways, but a new reflex would introduce a veritable divinity.

3. It is nevertheless what I try to introduce and it is for that that my attitude is comparable to that of one who commits a sacrifice, not of a simple intellectual. Because I seek to introduce it not in the mode of thought but of action. And I probably can do no more than remain at the door, on the threshold, not yet beyond it.

4. There is moreover an essential difficulty—there can be no question of taking mad laughter seriously, because taken seriously we kill it in some fashion. Laughter is linked to the lightness of things, if one weighs it down, it is no longer laughter. It must be left suspended, then. It is in this state of mental suspension at the limit of extreme relief from laughter and seriousness that we can tackle the enigma of sacrifice.

(appendix)

How in responding to the enigma of sacrifice and in giving it as I have, I was taken by a pride that suffocated me.

But at the same time the consciousness that I was presiding over—inevitable, sacred terror, teeth clenched close to crying, the profound humility of the officiant.

(Caillois and the theory of the festival. Pointlessness of critiques below.)

(the exchange side in the Manual)

PRELIMINARY ESSAYS FOR *THE ACCURSED SHARE*

ECONOMY AT THE SCALE OF THE UNIVERSE

1. Trs. note: *Outillage*. The tools necessary for work. Bataille is explicitly contradicting a kind of vulgar, utilitarian history of economic development here. Etymologically, the "outillage" are those things that are necessary and useful tools for work. The word, like the adjective *util* (useful), derives from old French *ustilz*, meaning "an object made for work."

Incidentally, in old French *ustilz* also carried the sense of "male member," or "penis," an etymological curiosity perhaps not entirely lost on Bataille.

2. Trs. note: *se perd sans compter, sans contrepartie.* It is difficult to capture the sense of *spending*, the sense of *wasting*, and the oblique reference to religious ecstasy contained within this important phrase. Bataille employs the reflexive verb, "se perdre," meaning both "to waste itself"—as one might waste one's resources—as well as "to lose itself"—as one might lose oneself in prayer, meditation, or sacrifice (Bataille speaks of Saint Teresa of Avila "losing herself" in her raptures). There is also, though, the sense of "spending itself" frivolously, without taking account of how much is being spent (*sans compter*). Bataille's primary point is that the sun asks for nothing in return (no "*contrepartie*") for the liberal, frivolous, even sacrificial waste that it makes of its own energy resources. The sun does nothing but give. Throughout, we have tended to translate "se perdre" as some variation on "to spend itself," but the connotations of waste and loss, as well as religious abandon, should be borne in mind by the reader.

3. Trs. note: *Maudit*. "Accursed, wretched, diabolical." This term would go on to form part of Bataille's title in his most famous published version of his theory of general economy, *La Part maudite*. "The accursed share" is precisely this aspect of production/consumption that takes the form of pure expenditure; it is the "share" that cannot be accounted for within the framework of a utilitarian economics or energetics. If reproduction is the goal of life, then the vast waste of life that occurs in sexual intercourse cannot but be thought of as an "accursed" waste of resources.

4. Trs. note: *Consume. Consommer*, the verb used in the first paragraph of this essay, is largely a cognate with the English verb "to consume," and covers the same semantic ground. However, the verb used here, *consumer*, means simultaneously to consume (as one consumes energy or food), to destroy progressively or completely ("as if by fire," according to Larousse), and to totally expend one's resources. Additionally, in its noun form, *consumation* dovetails not only with the English "consumption," but also with "consummation," in the sense of "a summing up," "an ending," or "bringing to term." In French as in English the term has been employed in a sexual sense since the sixteenth century, a connotation

obviously at play in Bataille's use of the word. One might additionally recognize the term's clear relevance to Bataille's notion of *la dépense* (expenditure), which is also freighted with the combined significations of consumption, destruction, dissipation, termination, and sexual excess. In fact, the societies Bataille would associate with the "notion of expenditure" in his renowned essay of the same name—specifically the indigenous peoples of Mesoamerica and of the North American pacific northwest—would come to be rendered as "societies of consumption [*consumation*]" in *The Accursed Share*. In a general sense, the semantic confusion implicit in the use of *consumer* may be seen as both a reflection and enactment of Bataille's broader militancy against the "mathematical frock-coat" of idealism and rationalism—the one-to-one correspondence between thought and experience, between language and reality—here rendered as a purposeful derangement of any clear relationship between signifier and signified. Bataille writes in *On Nietzsche* that a language consummate with life would necessarily take shape as an "empty consumption [*consumation*]": "Lacking relation to any reward," he writes, "this consumption [*consumation*] is not even intelligible." That is, it cannot be pinned down to any one meaning, any single sense—such a *consumation* is itself the accursed share, semiotically rendered. For this reason Derrida writes that in Bataille's language, "sense itself is absolutely destroyed and consumed [*consumé*]."

5. Trs. note: Bataille's distinction between "active" and "passive" solutions to the inevitability of expenditure is markedly unclear in this passage and, indeed, throughout the essay. Here it seems that Bataille conceives of the carnivorous animal (the predator) as being far more "active" in its expenditure of energy than the rather more "passive" herbivore. However, later Bataille will also refer to "the plague of unemployment" as a "passive" solution to excesses of energy. Perhaps because of their generality, Bataille would drop the use of "active" and "passive" in distinguishing modes of expenditure in *The Accursed Share*, opting for the more descriptive distinction of the "glorious" and the "catastrophic." There he writes, "if the system can no longer grow, or if the excess cannot be completely absorbed in its growth, it must necessarily be lost without profit; it must be spent, willingly ['actively'] or not ['passively'], gloriously or catastrophically" (*AS*, vol. I, 21). "Incomprehension does not

change the final outcome in the slightest," he continues, "Our ignorance only has this incontestable effect: it causes us to *undergo* ['passively'] what we could *bring about* in our own way ['actively'], if we understood. It deprives us of the choice of an exudation that might suit us. Above all, it consigns men and their works to catastrophic destructions" (23–24). We can thus recognize the general contours of Bataille's thinking on modalities of expenditure as it developed between this essay and *The Accursed Share*: the "active" carnivore, whose excess energy derives from and returns to the killing of helpless prey, retroactively comes to represent the "glorious" solution to the problem of expenditure. On the other hand, the "passive" herbivore is resigned to undergo, via its own "catastrophic" death in the jaws of the predator, the destructive exigencies of an energetic movement that both precedes and exceeds it. Though each offers a "solution" diametrically opposed to the other, both are united by the inevitability of expenditure. In a macroeconomic sense, then, we may trace Bataille's thinking on how the "plague of unemployment" is a "passive solution" to the problem of expenditure in the following way: If *a*) the capitalist mode of production necessarily cannot incorporate its own productive excess (the growing proletarian class) back into the process of production and *b*) capitalism in both ethic and practice abrogates the "sumptuous expenditures" characteristic of pre-capitalist "societies of consumption [*consumation*]," then a certain, growing segment of the proletariat must needs remain, as Marx says, in reserve, "passively," "catastrophically" squandering its productive capacities through mere idleness rather than through the "active," "glorious" practices of the festival, potlatch, feast, orgy, sacrifice, etc.

6. Trs. note: The reference seems to be to an example from Keynes's last and most famous work, *The General Theory of Employment, Interest and Money* (1936). Keynes famously made a distinction between classical political economy and general economy, and invoked a move from micro- to macro-economics, thereby instigating a theoretical shift similar to Bataille's. Bataille, of course, felt that Keynes's general economy was far from general enough. The bottle example comes from Book 3, chapter 10, section 6: "If the Treasury were to fill old bottles with banknotes, bury them at suitable depths in disused coalmines which are then filled up to the surface with town rubbish, and leave it to private enterprise

on well-tried principles of laissez-faire to dig the notes up again (the right to do so being obtained, of course, by tendering for leases of the note-bearing territory), there need be no more unemployment and, with the help of the repercussions, the real income of the community, and its capital wealth also, would probably become a good deal greater than it actually is. It would, indeed, be more sensible to build houses and the like; but if there are political and practical difficulties in the way of this, the above would be better than nothing."

7. Trs. note: Bataille is referring to coal mining, which releases the stockpiled energy of dead and compacted biological matter.

8. Trs. note: Bataille seems to be playing here on the old adage that one must "rob from Peter to give to Paul," a phrase that most likely referred to competing taxes owed to the Head of St. Peter's Basilica (i.e., the Pope) and the Head of St. Paul's Cathedral (i.e., the English monarch). Caught between these two taxes, English citizens would divert their taxes from the leader of the Catholic church to the crown. Bataille's point seems to be that both Peter and Paul are elite, governing minorities, and so it is strange to envisage inequality as a redistribution of tax funds from one authority to another.

THE ACCURSED SHARE, OR THE LIMIT OF THE USEFUL: TABLES OF CONTENTS AND SUMMARY OF MANUSCRIPTS

1. Gallimard eds. note: December 29, 1945, in a letter to Éditions Gallimard, Bataille writes: "Over the next months I intend to give you . . . *The Accursed Share*, which I have worked on over the past fifteen years: it is the work that I spoke to you about during one of our interviews, which touches on a subject of public interest, and which will be easy, often even amusing to read from beginning to end. The work is already well advanced, and I think I will see the end of it around March."

2. Gallimard eds. note: *The Torment* was written between November 1, 1941 and March 7, 1942.

3. Trs. note: The *OC* contains an abridged version of this passage from the preface to *Inner Experience*. We have included the entire passage.

DOSSIER OF BATAILLE'S NOTES AND OUTLINES FOR *THE LIMIT OF THE USEFUL*

NOTES AND APHORISMS

1. Trs. note: *Soleil-œil-sanglot*. This surreal trifecta recalls the kind of linguistic deformation or automutilation that is a favored technique of Bataille's, particularly in his fiction and poetry. In his rightly celebrated article, "The Metaphor of the Eye," Roland Barthes explores the *Story of the Eye*'s central image: the eye (*œil*), which in the narrative's "metaphorical composition" mutates in relation to such images as the egg (*oeuf*), milk (*lait*), and the sun (*soleil*). The eye is thus, according to Barthes, "varied through a certain number of substitute objects standing in a strict relationship to it . . . The Eye's substitutes are *declined* in every sense of the term: recited like flexional forms of the one word; revealed like states of the one identity; offered like propositions none of which can hold more meaning than another; filled out like successive moments in the one story. On its metaphorical journey the Eye thus both varies and endures; its essential form subsists through the movement of a nomenclature like that of a physical space, because here each inflexion is a new noun, speaking a new usage."

2. Trs. note: The works of Georg Wilhelm Friedrich Hegel (1770–1831), as the reader has surely gleaned by now, make up much of the background of Bataille's thought—a fact that he finally makes explicit in this paragraph. In his perennially perspicacious article on Bataille, "From Restricted to General Economy: A Hegelianism Without Reserve," Jacques Derrida writes that "[taken] one by one and immobilized outside their syntax, all of Bataille's concepts are Hegelian" (in *Writing and Difference*, trans. Allan Bass [London: Routledge, 1985], 253). In fact, second only to Nietzsche, Hegel—particularly as filtered through the reading of Kojève—is Bataille's most significant philosophical influence. This relationship is extensively explored in Christopher M. Gemerchak, *The Sunday of the Negative: Reading Bataille Reading Hegel* (Albany: SUNY Press, 2003). Bataille himself writes the following in *Sovereignty*, in *The Accursed Share Vols. II and III* (New York: Zone, 1991 [1976]), 369–370:

> The difference between my dialectical thought and that of Hegel is difficult to formulate, since contradiction can constantly resume the development of both. There is nothing that I do not follow in the overall movement that Hegel's thought represents in my eyes. But the autonomy of Hegel's "absolute knowledge" is that of discourse unfolding in time. Hegel situates subjectivity not in the object's disintegration (always begun anew) but in the identity that the subject and the object attain in discourse. But in the end, "absolute knowledge," the discourse in which the subject and the object become identical, itself dissolves into the NOTHING of unknowing, and the vanishing thought of unknowing is in the moment. On the one hand, there is an identity of absolute knowledge and this evanescent thought; on the other, this identity is reencountered *in life*. "Absolute knowledge" closes, whereas the movement I speak of opens up. Starting from "absolute knowledge," Hegel could not prevent discourse from dissolving, but it dissolved *into sleep*. The vanishing thought of which I speak is the awakening and not the sleep of thought: it is reencountered in an equality—in the *communication*—with all the *sovereign moments* of all men, insofar as the latter do not want to take them for things.

3. Gallimard eds. note: All of this fragment returns in *OC*, vol. V, pp. 540–541, note dated July 14, 1941 in *Guilty*.

4. Gallimard eds. note: Cf. the passage from *Inner Experience* cited at the beginning of these notes, *OC*, vol. VII, p. 502., pp. 160–161 of this edition.

5. Trs. note: *Communielle*. While "communal" most capaciously represents Bataille's meaning, this specific adjective also refers to holy communion, and thus approaches the narrower rendering of "eucharistic."

6. Gallimard eds. note: In the margin (cf. *OC*, vol. VI, *Sur Nietzsche*, p. 82): artificiality—cf. feeling of nature—laughter before the Siena cathedral.

7. Gallimard eds. note: This whole passage (beginning with "Difference with the phenomenologists") is recopied from the manuscript of *Madame*

Edwarda (September–October 1941)—cf. *OC*, vol. V, notes from *Guilty*, pp. 541–542.

8. Trs. note: *Voici l'homme*. No doubt an echo of the words of Pontius Pilate (and the title of Nietzsche's final book): *Ecce homo*.

9. Trs. note: *Fatalité*. Bataille usually uses *destin* or *sort* in this sense; the use of *fatalité* here implies a specific relation with death.

10. Trs. note: *Connaissance est reconnaissance*. A difficult turn of phrase to render in English.

11. Trs. note: This deeply speculative paragraph seems to lead from Plato—where all knowledge is immanent to the self, and "knowing is recognizing"—to Hegel, for whom knowledge of subject and object is founded on the mortal struggle of the Lord and Bondsman. Bataille establishes this philosophical foundation in order to move past it in the following paragraph. As Bataille indicates in *Sovereignty*, Hegel's philosophy terminates in a complete adequation of the subject and object of knowledge, wherein "the philosopher . . . could not will anything that was not the dominant reality, and the latter could not bring about anything that did not correspond to the philosopher's thought." By contrast, as he shows here, Bataille continues the movement of negativity via a "*loss of self*," where the "subject drowns himself in the object" to the end of effecting an intimate, kenotic experience of what he will come to call non-knowledge: an expenditure (*dépense*) that is an unthinking (*de-penser*).

12. Trs. note: Bataille's religious background shines through once more in this formulation. In contrast to the doctrine whereby salvation is supposed to be a result of the performance of earthly good works (following James 2:17–26, where the author claims that "faith without works is dead"), the doctrine of faith holds that salvation can be achieved regardless of works and depends rather on receiving God's grace through faith alone. (Cf. Ephesians 2:8: "For by grace are ye saved through faith; and that not of yourselves: it is the gift of god.") Bataille here contrasts knowledge as "method"—knowledge that one labors to achieve, that is extended through time via discursive reason—with knowledge that assumes a state of grace, which is immediate and non-discursive: a gift, not a product.

13. Trs. note: Presumably Bataille is here referring to the silver-plated copper sheet on which Daguerreotypes were inscribed. The earliest form of photograph, Daguerreotypes were made by polishing such a silver-plated copper sheet to a mirror finish, treating it with iodine or, later, halogen fumes to make it sensitive to light, then exposing it through a camera for a sufficient amount of time to produce a latent image.

PLANS AND NOTES, 1939–1941

1. Gallimard eds. note: With regard to these two notes: we cannot identify the *text from August 1938 on expenditure*, but there is, among Bataille's papers, a *chapter IV: Joy before death*, which seems to follow *chapter III: Sacrifice* (overprinted: *Love's sacrifice*)—cf. *OC*, vol. II, *Sociological Essays*, pp. 238–247 and *Notes*, pp. 441–442.)

2. Trs. note: Cf. Bataille, "The Labyrinth," in *Visions of Excess*, pp. 171–171.

3. Trs. note: A Hegelian term usually translated as "incarnation." Literally "man-becoming," the German term carries a more pronounced suggestion of historical movement than its English counterpart. For Hegel, *Menschwerdung* refers to the process by which alienation is overcome and the object is incorporated into the subject.

4. Gallimard eds. note: All of this note relates to the book by Pierre Janet, *From Anguish to Ecstasy: Studies on Beliefs and Feelings* (Paris: Alcan, 1926). Cf. *OC*, vol. V, notes for *Inner Experience*, p. 429: "Pierre Janet . . . had the chance to heal an 'ecstatic' in a hospital ward. He writes of it in his works under the familiar name of Madeleine . . ."—and p. 430 (August 2, 1942): "I am coming to explain myself concerning my manner of writing. The 'introduction' had three pages: I let it go, I wrote the preface, which had no explicit intention. With great difficulty I finished by touching on 'dogmatic servitude.' Then I put myself to the task of reading Janet, imagining it necessary to use the subtlety thereof to go further. Without writing it down, I elaborated a development on it which began . . ."

5. Trs. note: Pierre Janet (1859–1947) was a French psychologist and philosopher who profoundly influenced the modern study of psychology.

Many of his ideas preceded those of Sigmund Freud, who acknowledged Janet's influence. Janet was fascinated by dissociation and the effects of trauma on the mind. He also studied the psychology of supposedly mystic states of delirium, which took center stage in his work, *De L'Angoisse à l'extase* (1926).

6. Trs. note: Salomon Reinach, *Orpheus: Histoire generale des religions* (Paris: Alcide Picard, 1925).

7. Trs. note: René Dussaud, *Introduction à l'histoire des religions* (Paris: Leroux Ernest, 1914).

8. Trs. note: Cf. Leviticus 16.

9. Trs. note: Alfred Loisy, *Essai historique sur le sacrifice* (Paris: Nourry, 1920).

10. Trs. note: Though Bataille references Question 75 of the Second Part of Thomas Aquinas' *Summa Theologica*, the quoted passage comes from Article 2 of Question 85, "On Sacrifice."

11. Trs. note: Cf. "On the Gift-Giving Virtue" in Nietzsche's *Thus Spoke Zarathustra.*

12. Trs. note: This paragraph recalls "The Jesuve" and "The Pineal Eye," cf. *Visions of Excess*, pp. 73–78 and 79–90.

13. Trs. note: Carnot's theorem was developed in 1824 by Nicolas Léonard Sadi Carnot. It is a consequence of the second law of thermodynamics and stipulates the maximum amount of efficiency that a heat engine can reach. The relevance to Bataille's dream-driven analysis here seems to be that Carnot's theorem predicts that all heat engines operating within the same heat reservoirs will be equally efficient. In Bataille's terms, therefore, the quantitative laws of thermodynamics translate different sources of heat into equivalences. Though it is not clearly elaborated here, the racetrack seems to embody, for Bataille, a space in which, by contrast, equivalences are transformed into differences. This may be because staking a wager on a horse race entails the risk of loss as much as the opportunity for gain, an idea that Bataille elaborates elsewhere in the text.

14. Trs. note: Presumably the Bois de Boulogne. The Auteuil racetrack takes up its southwestern corner.

15. Trs. note: The dialectical complement of *Menschwerdung*, *Gottwerdung* (literally "god-becoming") is usually translated in Hegel as apotheosis or deification.

16. Trs. note: Cf. pp. 12, 223, 319, n. 8, and 323, n. 12.: "Modern man conducts himself on the whole like a commoner in a palace, one who would hang up his hat on the head of a goddess."

17. Trs. note: An aboriginal ceremony practiced in central and northern Australia, the purpose of which is to multiply the number of totemic plants or animals

18. Trs. note: Presumably a reference to D. H. Lawrence's *The Plumed Serpent* (New York: Knopf, 1926). In this fraught and divisive novel—which Lawrence himself considered his best—the Morning Star, representing the Aztec god Quetzalcoatl, is a recurrent motif.

PLANS AND NOTES, 1941–1943

1. Trs. note: *la mise en jeu et la mise en action*. Given our general rendering of "mise en jeu" (discussed on p. 336, n. 4, above), this clear parallel is difficult to register.

2. Gallimard eds. note: Cf. *OC*, vol. VII, p. 554, p. 232 of this edition, "final outline" [Box 13, C: 106–107] and below [Box 13, C: 110–114] *OC*, vol. VII, p. 558, p. 238 of this edition.

3. Trs. note: *The Spirit of Nature*.

4. Gallimard eds. note: Cf. *OC* v. II, "La Royauté de l'Europe classique" (1939?), p. 223: "'That one there' is king; it could not have been anyone else [. . .] The appointment literally fell from heaven. The one marked with the seal is comparable to a meteorite fallen in the middle of a field and surrounded by other stones that look just like it. Nothing can change the fact that the meteor, and only the meteor, fell from the heavens [. . .]"

5. Gallimard eds. note: These chapters III, IV, V, and VI correspond to the "final plan" [Box 13, C: 106–107] given in *OC*, vol. VII, p. 544, p. 232 of this edition, as well as the summaries that follow hereafter [Box 13, C: 110–114].

6. Trs. note: Lord and bondsman, commonly translated as master and slave in Bataille's time. See p. 336, n. 4 on the vicissitudes of Bataille's concept of *mettre en jeu* above.

7. Trs. note: *Abbé commendataire*. An abbot who held an abbey *in commendam* and had the right to draw personal revenue from it without contributing to its maintenance. While ostensibly obliged to feed the wealth back into the community, often this did not happen in practice. In the Ancien Régime in France, commendatory laws played an important role in ensuring the ongoing wealth of the First Estate (the clergy), whose power was significantly reduced after the French Revolution.

8. Gallimard eds. note: These pages of Notebook 5 are inserted between the notes for *The Laughter of Nietzsche* (cf. *OC*, vol. VI, pp. 476–484) and a rough draft of *Oresteia* dated November 1942 (cf. *OC*, vol. III, pp. 524–526).

9. Trs. note: Presumably Roger Caillois.

10. Trs. note: In the original text, pp and pc appear to be mistakenly inverted here.

11. Trs. note: Presumably Bataille means second largest and/or most lucrative.

12. Trs. note: "in. exp." is likely "inner experience." The "autodigestion of spirit" likely refers to *The Phenomenology of Spirit*—on the theme of autodigestion in that text, cf. Rebecca Comay, "Hegel's Last Words: Mourning and Melancholia at the End of the Phenomenology," in *The Ends of History: Questioning the Stakes of Historical Reason* (Taylor and Francis: 2012).

13. Gallimard eds. note: The previous pages are given in *OC*, vol. III, notes for *L'Impossible* (*Être Oreste*), pp. 536–540.

14. Gallimard eds. note: In the margin—cf. *OC*, vol. VII, pp. 229–230, pp. 70–73 of this edition: the tie—pages written in February '42.

NOTES FROM 1944

1. Gallimard eds. note: Cf. *OC*, vol. VI, p. 399.

2. Trs. note: Nostalgia for a lost immanence with nature, which Bataille appears to be working out throughout this section, would form the basis of *Erotisme* (1957) and the posthumously published *Théorie de la religion* (1973).

3. Gallimard eds. note: Cf. *OC*, vol. VI, *Sur Nietzsche*, p. 60 ("conference on good and evil" given March 5, 1944 at Marcel Moré's).

PLANS AND NOTES, 1945

1. Gallimard eds. note: These notes should be linked with those on "effusion" recorded in the 1945 manuscript of *Method of Meditation*—cf. *OC*, vol. V, pp. 475–482.

2. Trs. note: A form of collective farm in the Soviet Union.

3. Trs. note: *déchue*. This is another example of Bataille's variegated use of *déchéance*, which in the first chapter he uses to describe a dramatic, even biblical fall from grace and in the final chapter he uses to describe a literal, comedic fall. Here we may understand *déchue* as "deteriorated" while also bearing the connotation of deposition: as when a sovereign falls from a position of power.

4. Trs. note: Bataille tellingly writes "*happy ending*" in English.

BIBLIOGRAPHY

Ambrosino, Georges, and Georges Bataille. *L'Expérience à l'épreuve: Correspondance et inédits (1943–1960)*. Edited by Claudine Frank. Meurcourt: Éditions les Cahiers, 2018.

Barthes, Roland. "La Métaphore de l'œil." *Critique* 195–196 (August–September 1963): 770–777.

Bataille, Georges. *The Accursed Share*. Vol. I, *Consumption*. New York: Zone Books, 1988 [1949].

Bataille, Georges. *The Accursed Share*. Vols. II and III, *Sovereignty* and *The History of Eroticism*. New York: Zone Books, 1991 [1976].

Bataille, Georges. "Celestial Bodies." Translated by Anette Michelson. *October* 36 (Spring 1986): 75–78.

Bataille, Georges. *Guilty*. Translated by Stuart Kendall. Albany: SUNY Press, 2011 [1944].

Bataille, Georges. *Inner Experience*. Translated by Stuart Kendall. Albany: SUNY Press, 2014 [1943].

Bataille, Georges. *Lascaux, or The Birth of Art: Prehistoric Painting*. Translated by Austryn Wainhouse. Geneva: Skira, 1955.

Bataille, Georges. *La Limite de l'utile*. Fécamp: Éditions Lignes, 2016.

Bataille, Georges. *L'Érotisme*. Paris: Les éditions de Minuit, 1957.

Bataille, Georges. *Œuvres complètes*. 12 vols. Paris: Gallimard, 1970–1988.

Bataille, Georges. *On Nietzsche*. Translated by Stuart Kendall. Albany: SUNY Press, 2015 [1945].

Bataille, Georges. *Theory of Religion*. Translated by Robert Hurley. New York: Zone Books, 1992 [1976].

Bataille, Georges. *Visions of Excess: Selected Writings, 1927–1939*. Edited by Allan Stoekl. Translated by Allan Stoekl, Carl R. Lovitt, and Donald M. Leslie Jr. Minneapolis: University of Minnesota, 1985.

Bergson, Henri. *Le Rire. Essai sur le signifiance du comique*. Paris: Alcan, 1924.

Comay, Rebecca. "Hegel's Last Words: Mourning and Melancholia at the End of the Phenomenology." In *The Ends of History: Questioning the Stakes of Historical Reason*, edited by Amy Swiffen and Joshua Nichols, 141–160. New York: Taylor and Francis, 2012.

Derrida, Jacques. "From Restricted to General Economy: A Hegelianism without Reserve." In *Writing and Difference*, translated by Allan Bass, 251–277. Chicago: Chicago University Press, 1978.

Dussaud, René. *Introduction à l'histoire des religions*. Paris: Leroux Ernest, 1914.

Eddington, Arthur Stanley. *The Rotation of the Galaxy*. Oxford: Clarendon Press, 1930.

Franklin, Benjamin. "Advice to a Young Tradesman, Written by an Old One (21 July 1748)." In *Franklin: The Autobiography and Other Writings on Politics, Economics, and Virtue*. Edited by Alan Houston Cambridge: Cambridge University Press, 2012.

Frazer, James George. *The Golden Bough: A Study in Comparative Religion*. Vols. I and II. New York: Macmillan, 1894.

Gemerchak, Christopher M. *The Sunday of the Negative: Reading Bataille Reading Hegel*. New York: SUNY Press, 2003.

Hegel, Georg Wilhelm Friedrich. *Hegel's Phenomenology of Spirit*. Translated by A. V. Miller. Oxford: Oxford University Press, 1977 [1807].

Hollier, Denis, ed. *The College of Sociology (1937–1939)*. Minneapolis: University of Minnesota: 1988.

Janet, Pierre. *De l'Angoisse à l'extase: Études sur les croyances et les sentiments*. Paris: Alcan, 1926.

Jünger, Ernst. *Storm of Steel*. Translated by Michael Hofmann. New York: Penguin, 2016 [1920].

Jünger, Ernst. *War as an Inner Experience*. Translated by Kasey James Elliott. Middletown: Anarch Books, 2016 [1922].

Kendall, Stuart. *Georges Bataille*. London: Reaktion Books, 2007.

Keynes, John Maynard. *The General Theory of Employment, Interest and Money*. London: Palgrave Macmillan, 1936.

Kojève, Alexandre. *Introduction to the Reading of Hegel: Lectures on the Phenomenology of Spirit*. Edited by Raymond Queneau and Allan Bloom. Translated by James H. Nichols, Jr. New York: Basic Books, 1968 [1947].

Lawrence, D. H. *The Plumed Serpent*. New York: Knopf, 1926.

Limousin, Christian. "Vue d'ensemble." In *La Part maudite de Georges Bataille: la dépense et l'excès*, 21–42. Paris: Classiques Garnier: 2015.

Loisy, Alfred. *Essai historique sur le sacrifice*. Paris: Émile Nourry, 1920.

Mauss, Marcel. *The Gift: Forms and Functions of Exchange in Archaic Societies*. Translated by W. D. Halls. New York: Routledge, 2005 [1925].

Mong-Hy, Cédric. *Bataille Cosmique: Georges Bataille: Du système de la nature à la nature de la culture*. Paris: Nouvelles Éditions Lignes, 2012.

Nietzsche, Friedrich. *La Volonté de puissance*. Edited by Friedrich Wurzbach. Translated by Geneviève Bianquis. Paris: NRF Gallimard, 1937.

Nietzsche, Friedrich. *On the Genealogy of Morals and Ecce Homo*. Translated by Walter Kaufmann. New York: Random House, 1967 [1887].

Nietzsche, Friedrich. *Thus Spoke Zarathustra.* In *The Portable Nietzsche.* Edited and translated by Walter Kaufmann. New York: Penguin, 1954.

Patron, Sylvie. "La Part critique." In *Les Temps modernes,* 181–8. Paris: Gallimard, 1998.

Reinach, Salomon. *Orpheus: Histoire générale des religions.* Paris: Alcide Picard, 1925.

Surya, Michel. *Georges Bataille: An Intellectual Biography.* Translated by Krzysztof Fijalkowski and Michael Richardson. New York: Verso, 2002 [1992].

Vernadsky, Vladimir. *The Biosphere.* Translated by M. A. S. McMenamin and D. B. Langmuir. New York: Copernicus, 1998 [1926].

Weber, Max. *The Protestant Ethic and the Spirit of Capitalism and Other Writings.* New York: Penguin, 2002 [1905].